THE 1 CORINTHIANS 13 PARENT

Raising Big Kids with SUPERNATURAL Love

THE 1 CORINTHIANS 13 PARENT

RAISING BIG KIDS WITH SUPERNATURAL LOVE

LORI WILDENBERG

BECKY DANIELSON M.ED.

Bold Vision Books
PO Box 2011
Friendswood, Texas 77549

Copyright ©2014, Lori Wildenberg and Becky Danielson

ISBN 978-0-9912842-7-6

Library of Congress Control Number: LCCN

Published in association with Books & Such Literary Management, 52 Mission Circle, Suite 122, PMB 170, Santa Rosa, CA 95409-5370 www.booksandsuch.com

Printed in the United States of America.

Cover and Interior Design by kae Creative Solutions

Editing, Karen Porter, Katie McDivitt

Cover photograph by Monkey Business Images

Bold Vision Books
PO Box 2011
Friendswood, Texas 77549

Praise for Raising Big Kids with SUPERNATURAL Love

You'll want to read *Raising Big Kids with Supernatural Love* with a pen and highlighter handy. If you're like me, you'll highlight ideas, Scripture, and illustrations that help you understand your children. You'll put people's names in the margin to remind you to share the ideas with them. You'll write your children's names there to remind you to use the ideas with them. I bet you turn over the corners of pages, too. This is a book you'll continually turn back to as children grow and experience new challenges. It's rich! The way the authors breakdown the truths of 1 Corinthians 13 will forever influence the way you love. I've never seen something this detailed about something so valuable – love! The insights are relevant, timely, practical, and biblically-accurate. Your children will be glad you read this book.

Kathy Koch, Ph.D., Founder and President Celebrate Kids, Inc.
Author of *Finding Authentic Hope and Wholeness*
and *How Am I Smart?*
and coauthor, with Jill Savage, of *No More Perfect Kids.*

This book isn't just a gold mine of great parenting helps, this is Fort Knox. Do not loan this book to your friends…you'll never get it back.

Tim Shoemaker, speaker and author many books including,
Super Husband Super Dad: You Can Be the Hero Your Family Needs

"There are just too many positive books about parenting teenagers," said no Mom or Dad ever! How thankful I am for authors Lori Wildenberg and Becky Danielson as they offer sane, sensible, and insightful perspectives, hard-earned wisdom, and practical how-to's for loving and parenting your teen. These strengths, coupled with sound biblical principal, are sure to shore up the wobbliest of parents confidence for these important years.

Julie Barnhill is the mother of three former teenagers and speaker, entertainer, and author of eleven books including the ever popular,
She's Gonna Blow! Real Help for Moms Dealing with Anger.

Lori and Becky show a unique depth of understanding regarding the very real issues and challenges of raising teens. With love, grace, and compassion, they offer parents practical guidance on how to be their teen's godly coach and consultant—a very different role than the one they filled when their children were younger. Each chapter provides parents with the biblical tools and principles necessary to foster healthy closeness and communication with their teen. They will turn the last page armed with the courage to allow their teen to grow in character through hardships, disappointments and the consequences of their own sometimes unwise choices. Every parent of a teen will benefit from the honest, transparent, and equipping approach Lori and Becky offer.

Melinda Means, co-author of *Mothering From Scratch: Finding the Best Parenting Style for You and Your Family*

Authors, Lori Wildenberg and Becky Danielson, give every parent the tools to do the impossible; *Raising Big Kids with Supernatural Love*. Lori and Becky put their arms around every mom and dad who may be thinking, this isn't what I signed up for, and gently guide them back to that holy place where the parent-child relationship makes sense—God's supernatural love.

Joanne Kraft, author of *Just Too Busy* and *The Mean Mom's Guide to Raising Great Kids*

If you are the mother of a tween or teenager and you're looking for help, look no further. This book is a must read. Lori Wildenberg and Becky Danielson are real moms with real experience and expertise. These two parenting professionals skip the platitudes and instead offer real help in navigating the tumultuous adolescent years. You will be encouraged by reading the true stories of other families, empowered by the scripture provided, and equipped with the strategies and info you need to stay connected. Hang out with two moms who understand. You and your family will be blessed!

Claudia & David Arp, authors of *Suddenly They're 13 - or the Art of Hugging a Cactus* and the *10 Great Dates* series

In a time when parents have a tendency to feel inadequate and believe they are just hanging on, both books in The 1 Corinthians 13 Parent Series are a breath of fresh air. The 1 Corinthians 13 Parent books give us powerful principles, real-life examples, and a clear path to success. Not just books to read, but to study and let them take you on a journey that will make you a better parent and a better person. Every church should use these resources for small group study for parents of children of all ages.

Dr. Chuck Stecker, President of A Chosen Generation, author, speaker and ministry leader

Experts on family report that the number one reason children become prodigals is because they're searching for love and acceptance. Parents love their children, but it takes the supernatural love described in 1 Corinthians 13 to help tweens and teens navigate today's culture and experience a love that only Jesus can provide through parents who seek His wisdom and His ways. Lori and Becky put that kind of unconditional love into practical, biblical, and tested counsel for parents. In *Raising Big Kids with Supernatural Love,* Becky and Lori mentor every parent in how to navigate the slippery slopes of parenting tweens/teens. The parenting tips and discussion questions at the end of each chapter are perfect tools for parents of tweens/teens small groups—because we're always better together.

> Janet Thompson, speaker and author of 17 books including *Woman to Woman Mentoring* and *Praying for Your Prodigal Daughter*

Worried about your tweens or teens self-worth? Want to build family unity? Wonder what to do when your kid's conduct doesn't quite match your hopes or expectations? Today's world holds many challenges for kids and parents. In Raising Big Kids with Supernatural Love, Lori Wildenberg and Becky Danielson supply powerful strategies and keen insights to help you foster a relationship with your children that will last a lifetime.

> Julie Gorman Founder of For Your Inspiration (FYI) and author of *What I Wish My Mother Had Told Me About Men*

Lori and Becky are moms who get it. Really get it. They help us understand how everything that is important is based on honest loving relationship. Humility not platitudes. Practical life principles that will build a relationship to last a lifetime with your kids EVEN when, especially when, they are acting like...well a teenager!

> Tammy H. Maltby Speaker and author of *The God Who Sees You* and *Confessions of a Good Christian Girl: the Secrets Women Keep and the Grace That Saves Them.*

Raising Big Kids with Supernatural Love should be every parents handbook for parenting their teen. Filled with practical and insightful wisdom, Lori and Becky, parenting experts, offer not just advice, but experience lived out. As the mother of four almost grown adult children, I found myself nodding along in agreement. I pray every parent who wants to raise successful adults, not only reads this book, but applies the knowledge.

> Michelle Borquez, Executive Director of God Crazy Ministries, author, speaker, wife, and mother of four young adults.

Raising kids tops the list of the world's toughest jobs. But raising teenagers is tougher still! In their book, *Raising Big Kids with Supernatural Love*, Lori Wildenberg and Becky Danielson give parents of teens the tools they need. Biblically-based and practical, this book is packed with real life examples to help readers see the principles in action. Wildenberg and Danielson don't merely "tell" they also show how to use different parenting styles and techniques through common parenting scenarios. These gals speak from experience, but also share humbly as fellow sojourners who desire to be even better parents.

Kathy Howard, speaker and author of six books, including *Unshakeable Faith* and *Embraced by Holiness*

Raising Big Kids with Supernatural Love does just what its title suggests. It empowers parents to raise their children with Christ centered values. Lori and Becky have given us a gift of sound and practical advice on bringing up kids from a faith perspective. As a parent of two sons, I appreciated the questions and tips at the end of each chapter that allowed me to develop a parenting plan that fit my family. If you are looking for parenting books that are based on solid Biblical principles and values, The 1 Corinthians 13 Parent Series is it.

Pete Larson, Executive Director Family Fest Ministries

Raising Big Kids with Supernatural Love is practical, useful, and a very simple read for parents with not-so-simple lives. These books are tantamount to sitting across a table with two wise women discussing family challenges over your favorite coffee. What would you have in your parenting toolkit if you could break the chapter of love (1 Corinthians 13) into useable segments with practical action ideas? Well...you're holding it! Raising Big Kids with Supernatural Love brings love out of ethereal chatter and into your family room. Lori and Becky have taken sage biblical advice and massaged it into the stiffness all families encounter. Buy it. Read it. Use it. Then for goodness sake, share it.

Doug Herman, speaker and author of *FaithQuake* and *Come Clean*

An excellent and practical resource for parents. This book provides effective ways to coach our kids through life.

Margaret McSweeney mom, author, founder of PearlGirls.info, and host of kitchenchat.info

DEDICATION

To my husband, best friend, encourager, confidant, and
hiking pal, Tom, I am thankful we are doing this thing
called life together. And to my four former teenage
children— Courtney, Jake, Samantha, and Kendra,
our life has been full of the unexpected. God has used all
the comical, challenging, chaotic, and even crisis moments
to grow a love in our family that is without boundaries. I've
learned love never divides; it always multiplies. My heart is
full and I am beyond blessed to be loved by each of you.
I love you all.
Your not so normal wife and mom,
-LORI

To Scott my husband, best friend, and partner on this
journey of parenting and life. And to Ryan and Eric,
my reasons for wanting to do the journey well.
Life is a fabulous adventure!
XO BECKY (MOM)

LOVE IS PATIENT,

LOVE IS KIND.

IT DOES NOT ENVY,

IT DOES NOT BOAST,

IT IS NOT PROUD.

IT IS NOT RUDE,

IT IS NOT SELF-SEEKING,

IT IS NOT EASILY ANGERED,

IT KEEPS NO RECORD OF WRONGS.

LOVE DOES NOT DELIGHT IN EVIL

BUT REJOICES WITH THE TRUTH.

IT ALWAYS PROTECTS,

ALWAYS TRUSTS,

ALWAYS HOPES,

ALWAYS PERSEVERES.

LOVE NEVER FAILS.

1 Corinthians 13:4–8a

Contents

FOREWORD

Love is patient. Love is kind. It does not envy. It does not...

Well, you know the rest because you've been to your share of weddings. Reading verses from 1 Corinthians 13 is both popular and appropriate. This portion of scripture reminds the listeners of the attributes of love, of "the most excellent way." (1 Corinthians 12:13)

The hope is that the Love Chapter, the verses shared in the ceremony, will provide guidance for the new couple throughout their lives together. But what if at some point it isn't just the two of them? What verses of scripture should be highlighted when that same husband and wife become dad and mom? Lori and Becky suggest that when children arrive, it is time for 1 Corinthians 13 – Take 2.

That makes perfect sense. After all, the gift of a child is truly a gift of love. The encouragement and admonition found in those verses can apply to marriages and also to an expanding family.

When I first met Lori and she passionately shared the dream, the idea, the vision she and Becky had for this project, it brought a smile to my face. As the mom of three adult sons who were once "Big Kids," I knew the importance of loving them God's way – the "most excellent way."

As you read this book, I encourage you to take time to reflect on what your Heavenly Father desires for your child. Don't rush through each chapter. Instead, soak in the wisdom and accept any challenge presented, by the authors or the Lord himself.

In our household we believe everyone is born with a song inside, a song put there by God. As a parent, you have the privilege of helping your child discover, develop, and sing his song. And when he sings it back to God, he is glorifying the Creator. Let this book help you raise Big Kids who choose to glorify God with their song.

Kendra Smiley,

Author of *Journey of a Strong-Willed Child,*
Be the Parent,
Do Your Kids a Favor. Love Your Spouse,
and other popular titles.

Acknowledgments

First, we want to express our appreciation to our agent, Mary G. Keeley of Books and Such Literary Agency. A great big thank you for believing in us and in the importance of the 1 Corinthians 13 Parenting series.

With grateful hearts we want to thank our many class participants, readers, and prayer warriors. Your contribution to this project has been invaluable.

Thank you to the following individuals for your part in bringing this project to fruition: Julianne Adams, Marlene Bagnull, Maureen Behrens, Paul and Kym Benfield, Ed and Nancy Bock, Chuck Bolton, Vicki Brock, Keri Buisman, Becky Clark, Tim and Suanne Deskin, Jeannie Edwards, Ken and Kerry Ekstrom, Lori Hayda Felton, Jill Gillis, Tom and Lynn Halloran, Nina Hinds, Karen Hoops, Mary Heathman, Katie McElroy, Jim and Laurie Muehlbauer, Liz Manning, Karen Murkowski, Kathy Namura, Jerry and Kyndall Nixon, Carol Olsen, Amy Raye, Danielle Reeves, Melonie Richards, Darcy Roberson, Dwight and Lindee Sebald, Sara Silburn, Megan Stone, Chris and Ann Tillotson, Scott Turansky, Stacey Van Horn, Sheila Wilson, Chris and Kathy Wolfe, Stephen and Elsa Wolff, George and Cindy Wood.

Bible Study Fellowship has played a tremendous role in each of our spiritual lives. We thank God for Bev Coniaris (MN) and Tina Cotton (CO) for their faithful service and excellent teaching. You have stretched us heart, mind, and soul.

To our church families: Christ Presbyterian Church and WaterStone Community Church. With special thanks to John Crosby, Lynda English, Nick Lillo, James Madsen, Sarah Norton, and Larry Renoe.

We are blessed and honored to be ministry partners with: A Chosen Generation, The M.O.M Initiative, and National Center for Biblical

Parenting. And of course those ministries represented on our 1C13P team: 10 Great Dates (David & Claudia Arp, Peter & Heather Larson), A Father's Walk (Matt Haviland), Family Fest Ministries (Pete Larson), Family Time Training (Kirk Weaver and Jenna Hallock), Rising Above Ministries (Jeff Davidson), The Mom Café (Chris Carter), The Single Mom (Misty Honnold), Stone Foundations of Learning, Inc. (Megan Stone), and Tonja's Table (Tonja Engen). We want to be sure to include these outstanding team members: Sherri Crandall, Sommer Crayton, Laura Crosby, Doug Drake, J.L. Martin, D. W. Murray, Dale Skram, and Thomas and Karla Marie Williams. Thank you Jesus for these faith-filled and talented team members! We are blessed beyond words.

Many thanks to our publisher: Bold Vision Books. Karen, George, and Ginny working with you has been a pleasure! Thanks for sharing our excitement and our message!

Big appreciation to our editor, Katie McDivitt.

With great affection, thanks to our moms, Pat Appel and Carole Erickson. Your encouragement and interest in our writing inspires us.

Last but never least, we are grateful for the love and support from our husbands and children. Our combined kids, listed oldest to youngest: Courtney, Jake, Samantha, Kendra, Ryan, and Eric. And always and forever, our guys: Tom and Scott.

To the One who makes all things possible, Jesus Christ— the Author and Perfecter of Supernatural Love.

With faith, hope, and love,
LORI & BECKY

INTRODUCTION

LOVE IS HEART WORK
When I was a child, I talked like a child,
I thought like a child, I reasoned like a child.
When I became a man, I put childish ways behind me.

1 Corinthians 13:11

BETWIXT AND BETWEEN

"Stand up if you are a parent of a teen." All the participants in the parenting teen class stand.

"Remain standing if you were a pretty good teenager." Many, definitely not all, of the moms and dads continue to stand.

"Keep standing if you were completely and totally honest with your mom and dad about your entire teenage life?" The whole class laughs while they all sit; they know where I'm going with this illustration.

When parenting tween and teens, we need to keep a realistic perspective. I (Lori) have found it is good to take a stroll down memory lane when raising big kids. It is helpful to me to recall that I wasn't a perfect young person. I didn't do everything I was supposed to and... did some things I wasn't supposed to do. Many times I learned the hard way.

Our kids won't be perfect either. And they will not always do what they should and will sometimes do what they shouldn't. The teen years are filled with learning about and experiencing life. It is an exciting time, but it is not bump-free. Yet even when the going gets tough because bad choices are made, God can use those opportunities for the child's good. For instance, the consequence of poor judgment

19

leaves room for wisdom to grow. Remembering the spiritual perspective and God's love for the child provides hope to the parent of a young person.

Young adults are lots of fun to hang out with—great energy and interesting ideas and fun conversations. Teens are developing their sense of humor and seeking autonomy. Young people are enjoyable one moment and then annoying (or you may prefer to fill in your own word) the next.

This developmental stage in a child's life is dynamic and challenging. Becky and I have noticed the greatest number of parent class participants are the moms and dads of toddlers and parents of teens. These are the times kids begin to stretch their wings and test boundaries. It feels liberating for the child but emotionally constricting for parents.

"How are you enjoying the teen years?" one dad asked with a hint of sarcasm at a parenting event where Becky and I were speaking. He was bracing himself. He also had four children who were a few years younger than my four. "I love this stage," was my semi-naive answer. At that time my kids were seventeen, fifteen, thirteen, and eleven. Things were going pretty smoothly. I even wondered what the "parenting-of-teen fuss" was all about. Had I known the challenges that were waiting for me just around the corner, I would have qualified my response.

It has been said, "Once a child is fit to live with he[1] is living with someone else." We laugh, but we get the point. Even though tweens and teens live in an adult body, they are still kids. Young people need training and love from Mom and Dad. In the hard moments, a parent feels as if he is just surviving this stage in his child's life.

But then come the seasons of celebration: watching your child blossom into a young man or woman, noticing how your teen helps out an elderly person, or seeing his desire to participate in a mission trip. This generation of kids more than any previous generation wants, really wants, to make a difference in the world. The teen years don't just have to be endured, they can be also treasured and enjoyed.

Kids grow up and leave the nest. The parent's job is to raise a socially well-adjusted adult. A Christian parent would add faith-filled to that description. Tweens and teens are in the unique position of physically looking like an adult but behaving more child-like emotionally and socially. This is where the parental frustration, confusion, and exhaustion enter the picture. Becoming emotionally and socially adept takes life experience.

We need to demonstrate supernatural love during the common challenges we face raising tweens and teens. We'll look at how to support, encourage, train, guide, and pray for our kids when encountering adverse situations, while being cognizant of the fact that young people do not talk, think, or reason like adults. This book will show you how to do the following.

- ♥ Apply the four godly parenting styles for success
- ♥ Increase your tweens' and teens' self-worth by demonstrating patience
- ♥ Act in kindness to build family unity
- ♥ Foster sibling relationship rather than sibling rivalry
- ♥ Respond when your youth lies or steals
- ♥ Put respect back into the family
- ♥ Understand what drives your child's behavior
- ♥ Control your anger and effectively deal with conflict in the family
- ♥ Walk alongside your young person when he's suffering
- ♥ Give your tween or teen strategies to deal with temptation
- ♥ Present the concept of absolute truth to your child in a subjective world
- ♥ Support your adopted child
- ♥ Establish limits on media and technology,
- ♥ Help your young adult establish healthy boundaries in dating and other relationships
- ♥ Build a relationship with your kids that will last a lifetime

Each chapter focuses on one of the fifteen virtues of love presented in 1 Corinthians 13. By implementing each quality of love, parenting approaches will be more effective, character development in kids will result, and God will be honored in the process.

TOUGH LOVE

Parents of younger kids want to parent perfectly. Parents of tweens and teens are *way* over that idea. The phrase "get real" comes to mind. By this time the perfection bubble has burst; parents of older kids know perfect families don't exist. What moms and dads of young people do want to know is, "How do I deal with (fill in the blank)?"

True love is unconditional. If we choose to love only when the young person behaves or performs to our specifications, we will be disappointed and the child will believe love is earned. Unconditional love is love without exceptions. No strings attached; no exclusions. Granted, it's difficult to love when your teen is lying about the party he attended or is rolling his eyes at your "lame" comment. When the child displays oppositional behavior, we can choose to respond in love even though we may not like the behavior. There are times we're so angry with the behavior we may even feel as if we don't like the child.

With clenched teeth and glaring eyes, one class participant confessed she hated her sixteen-year-old. The father, with downcast eyes, nodded in agreement. The teen controlled the family with her emotional outbursts and unruly antics. The parents had lost control and the teen was in full-blown rebellion. Intense dislike and escalating negative behavior was tearing the family apart. Sadly, this situation is not uncommon and will only get worse if not addressed.

Parents struggling with older kids often feel hopeless. They don't know where to turn due to the element of shame when Christian kids exhibit certain behaviors. Parents ask how to deal with behavior, but the better question is how to reach the heart of the child. Becky and I say, *Hold on! It's never too late.* "What is impossible with man is possible with God" (Luke 18:27). God is not constrained by time.

In regard to the family mentioned above, by consistently applying the techniques mentioned in this book, the relationship between the parents and teen has improved. There is still a lot of work to do, but love is worth the fight. Unconditional love provides stability and models God's love. The Lord loves us at our worst, and that's when we need His love the most. "Do not remember the sins of my youth and my rebellious ways; according to your love remember me" (Psalm 25:7a).

Most parents of kids in the tween to young adult years are in agreement: parenting isn't for wimps. Thankfully we have a God who provides supernatural strength and love, so we can love when it is most difficult. Love matters.

BLAST FROM THE PAST

Our family history, current parenting styles, and family makeup are all relevant and have an impact on the raising of each individual child with whom we have been blessed. Before we can press forward, it is helpful to first fall back and look at our family of origin. Then with eyes wide open, we see the present position of our nuclear family.

Family patterns of sinful behavior have been an issue since time began. Recognizing them is vital to breaking the destructive chain. Abraham, even though he had great faith and God called him friend, had a propensity to lie when in a tight spot. He passed this character flaw on to his son Isaac and grandson Jacob. Dishonesty was one of this family's generational sins. We all have sinful patterns passed from one generation to the next. Habitual sins aren't pleasing to God. For that reason alone it's good to identify those habits and make a decision to not yield to familiar temptations. "Know therefore that the LORD your God is God; he is the faithful God, keeping his covenant of love to a thousand generations of those who love him and keep his commandments" (Deuteronomy 7:9).

The following assessment has ten questions to be used as an evaluation tool. This will help identify familial patterns, positive and negative, that you have taken from your family of origin into your nuclear family. These experiences are embedded in your mind. They are the tapes that play until you and your spouse create new ones. The past affects the present. This is why the observation "I sound just like my mom or dad" is common.

Start with a quiet time of prayer asking God to open your eyes, heart, and mind. Reflect on your family of origin's relationships, faith, values, discipline methods, communication patterns, generational sins, and division of labor. These experiences enter into the parenting equation in the form of unspoken expectations. Ponder these questions with this caution: this exercise isn't meant to be a blame game but a tool for recognizing the good and tossing the bad.

1 Corinthians 13 Parent:
Raising Big Kids with SUPERNATURAL Love
Family of Origin Assessment

1. Growing up, how were mistakes handled in your family (frustration, blame, patience, etc.)?

2. How was faith taught and lived in your family of origin?

3. Who made the major decisions in your home?

4. How would you describe the type of discipline your father used (train, punish, ignore, etc.)?

5. How would you describe your mother's approach to discipline?

6. How would you characterize your relationships with your siblings?

7. How was conflict dealt with in your family?

8. How were emotions expressed (freely, with restraint, repressed, etc.)?

9. What positive things would you like to pass along to your children from your upbringing?

10. What negative patterns from your upbringing would you like to change or avoid?

Differing family values are cause for potential conflict. One woman shared that her father's family of origin valued a college education for boys but deemed it unnecessary for girls. Her mother's family valued education across the board. This could have been a bone of contention, but once her parents married, they chose to raise all their children to value education.

Our expectations drive who we want our kids to become. Most of us expect a lot. We have the hope our children will be like us—only a better version, a perfected mini-me. This can lead to conflict, guilt, and a sense of failure on the parts of both parents and children. Identify and evaluate expectations. Are they reasonable and appropriate?

THE RUBBER BAND

Being the best parent we can be requires an ability to adjust when needed. Flexibility is a main ingredient in raising teens. On the first day of our parenting classes, Becky and I often pass out a handful of items contained in a small plastic bag. Parents relate these objects to parenting. A rubber band is included in the bag; it illustrates parenting is flexible. When used properly, the rubber band holds things together. If the band is too tight, the contents may break or the band may bust. If it's too loose, things fall out.

As your child moves into the tween and teen stages, you need to alter your previous parenting strategies. Frankly, this is where Tom and I struggled. We had our system down; then the kids began to mature. We needed to let go a little. Releasing can be mighty difficult when you're a highly involved mom or dad.

God is our perfect parent. He is who He needs to be at the perfect time, in the perfect way. The top four effective parenting types, when used correctly and at the right time, are Controller, Chum, Coach, and Consultant. These approaches are methods God uses when He parents His children. God is Father and Lord (Controller), Daddy and Friend (Chum), Encourager and Guide (Coach), and Influencer and Counselor (Consultant). He is never Clueless or Checked Out. He is all-knowing and ever-present. He never slumbers. Since we are not perfect parents, we are susceptible to falling into the last two undesirable and ineffective styles when dealing with teenagers.

Examine the following chart. Read over the characteristics of each of the various parenting styles. Each type described is exaggerated as a caution to the reader not to overuse any one technique. Look over the descriptions and determine which one is your default style—the style which tends to dominate your parenting.

1 Corinthians 13 Parent:

Raising Big Kids with SUPERNATURAL Love

Parenting Styles Chart

> **Relationship-based**
> **Child-focused**

The Chum
"I want to be my child's best friend."

Values:	child's happiness, friendship with parent
Parent Behavior:	high degree of warmth, acceptance, responsive, undemanding, indulgent, indecisive, weak, power relinquished, rescues, unable to say no, whines, begs, pleads, highly involved, makes excuses for child
Fear:	conflict, doesn't want child to get upset
Discipline Strategy:	permissive
Negative Result:	child is dependent, disrespectful, whiny, manipulative, demanding, insecure, resentful
Positive Result:	child feels loved, knows he belongs

THE CONSULTANT
"I'M HERE TO ADVISE."

VALUES:	child's decision-making skills, maturity, independence
PARENT BEHAVIOR:	actively observes, listens, evaluates, imparts wisdom when asked, may ask permission to give advice
FEAR:	wonders if child is ready for this. Asks self, "Have I said too little or too much?"
DISCIPLINE STRATEGY:	allows natural consequences to be the teacher, asks questions
NEGATIVE RESULT:	child may flounder and make lots of mistakes
POSITIVE RESULT:	child is independent, responsible, confident, knows parent is there for support

THE CLUELESS
"I BLINDLY TRUST MY CHILD."

VALUES:	child's independence and maturity
PARENT BEHAVIOR:	overwhelmed or stressed, weak, warm, relies on belief child is always good, unable to keep promises, uninformed, relies heavily on others to help raise child, undemanding, appears laid back, confused, blames others for child's behavior, feels helpless
FEAR:	"I won't know what to do, or I'll be more overwhelmed if I engage."
DISCIPLINE STRATEGY:	threatens but ultimately does nothing, avoids discipline
NEGATIVE RESULT:	child is rebellious, angry, prone to aggressive behavior, disrespectful, seeks structure, doesn't feel capable
POSITIVE RESULT:	child may become a risk-taker and is resourceful.

THE CONTROLLER
"I'M IN CHARGE."

VALUES:	order and good behavior
PARENT BEHAVIOR:	forceful, decisive, highly organized, controlling, demanding, overbearing, micro-manager, authoritarian, highly involved, points, preaches, threatens, instills guilt, takes over
FEAR:	loss of control, lack of respect
DISCIPLINE STRATEGY:	punishment
NEGATIVE RESULT:	child is dependent, resistant, rebellious, withdrawn, blames others, lies, sneaky
POSITIVE RESULT:	child feels safe and secure

The Coach
"I'm here to guide and lead."

Values:	family unity, rules, interdependence, co-operation, commitment, connection
Parent Behavior:	encourages and supports child in struggles, provides solutions, sets limits, authoritative, responsive, demanding, actively involved, able to make the tough call
Fear:	loss of family unity
Discipline Strategy:	prevention, training, retraining, redirecting
Negative Result:	child may lose some autonomy and individuality due to the family focus
Positive Result:	child feels capable, lovable, secure, accountable, responsive, respectful, cooperative

The Checked Out
"I'm busy."

Values:	own personal time and schedule
Parent Behavior:	busy, workaholic, distracted, may try to buy love with material items, unattached or disconnected, strong-willed parent, cold , uninvolved, unavailable, self-absorbed
Fear:	child will be dependent
Discipline Strategy:	none unless a big problem, then jumps to extreme punishment
Negative Result:	child is withdrawn, seeks attention from other adults, may try to prove worth through achievement, defeatist attitude, doesn't feel loved
Positive Result:	child is self-reliant and resourceful

Be aware of your usual style; note the positives and negatives. Know your child's abilities. Then parent to his age, stage, and personality. Adapt your approach according to the circumstances, and watch for the pitfalls of using only one technique. Note that four styles— Chum, Controller, Coach, and Consultant—have the most redeeming characteristics. It's the overuse of any style or misuse of a style that produces the negative results.

We need to exercise less control as the child ages and gains experience. When kids are younger and safety concerns loom, most parents fall into the Controller style. As children mature, a necessary parenting shift occurs to the Coach and Consultant. A young, less experienced child needs more parental involvement in terms of relational and directional intervention. The styles that fit those needs best are the Chum and Controller. These styles, when used correctly, produce feelings of belonging and security. The older, more experienced child needs less parental involvement. Backing off a bit will meet the tween and teen's need for respect, independence, and freedom. The two most effective approaches at this time in your child's life are the Coach and Consultant. Picture the job of mowing the lawn. If the child is twelve years old and has never operated a mower, he will need a lot of assistance and supervision. If he's fifteen and experienced in cutting the lawn, allow him the opportunity to push the mower with minimal interaction and instruction.

Misuse or overuse of any approach has its pitfalls. The extreme Controller dictates a home of rules without relationship. These controls can result in teen rebellion. The Chum exaggerated provides a home where there is relationship but no rules. This permissiveness could end in the youth's resentment of the parent. In combining the Controller and Chum styles, there will be rules with relationship. Then respect will reign in the family. After both love and limits are established, it is easier to transition into the Coach and Consultant modes of parenting. Parenting takes on different faces for different stages. Once we hold that baby in our arms, we're committed for the long haul. Our young people need both love and limits.

LOVE IS

When we understand God's transcending love and apply it to our families, it changes how we relate to our kids. Then it changes how

31

the children relate to us as parents and each other. This love is "the most excellent way" (1 Corinthians 12:31b).

Love Is

Love is patient, love is kind—a decision.

It does not envy, it does not boast, it is not proud—an attitude.

It is not rude, it is not self-seeking—outward focus.

It is not easily angered, it keeps no record of wrongs—self-control.

Love does not delight in evil but rejoices with the truth—a heavenly perspective.

It always protects, always trusts, always hopes—an action.

It always perseveres, Love never fails—a commitment.

The greatest of these is love—ultimate strength.

The knowledge of other parenting styles and the examples of the use and misuse of them provided within this book will enable you to appropriately implement them. From your past and present situations, accentuate the positives and alter the negatives. Love God and love your family members without condition and without exception.

Parenting well doesn't mean our tween or teen won't disappoint us (or even disappoint himself). Successful parenting means keeping the relationship intact by living a life that demonstrates truth and love no matter the circumstances. Love is a choice.

Prayer

Holy God,

I thank You for the gift of my earthly family, for the parents You graciously provided for me. I realize I've inherited the sins of previous generations in my family. Free me to make choices pleasing to You. Father, I am choosing to stop_____ and ask You to replace that thought or behavior with _____. Thank You for bringing this generational sin to light. Please help me to learn from the mistakes of my forefathers. Let me be convicted, but remind me I am not condemned. I am more than a conqueror over this pattern of sin because of Christ's work on the cross. I am covered in the cloak of the righteousness of Jesus. Thank You in advance for turning me from this sin and freeing my children and their children from this bondage. Guide me as I raise the children You have blessed me with for Your glory. Keep my heart strong and healthy. I thank You for being my Abba daddy.

In the precious name of Jesus,

Amen

AND NOW I WILL SHOW YOU THE MOST EXCELLENT WAY.

1 Corinthians 12:31b

SECTION ONE

LOVE IS A DECISION

CHAPTER 1   CHOOSE PATIENCE
CHAPTER 2   CHOOSE KINDNESS

Chapter 1

Choose Patience

Love is patient.

1 Corinthians 13:4a

Prescribed Patience

On a quiet Saturday afternoon, my husband and I (Lori) were working in the study. One of our daughters flew by, let out a growl, and stomped up the stairs. Tom and I exchanged glances. He shook his head.

"Ohhhhh." A barely audible sound came out of his mouth. He held up three fingers; three of our four kids are girls. I noticed his hair was standing on end, poor guy. Daughters with raging hormones can be hard for a dad.

Boys don't typically growl; they mumble. It sounds like teen boys have a mouth full of marbles. Who understands the secret language of grunts and groans? Other teens. It's a total mystery to me how they can communicate over the phone. Maybe that's why texting is so popular.

If your child displays any of the symptoms of impulsivity, impatience, indecision, moodiness, frustration, self-centeredness, irresponsibility, forgetfulness, poor communication skills, or little common sense, you live with a teen.

"I can't believe how crazy my teenager makes me." Many parents feel like this. The tween and teen years can really weaken the parental patience factor. Becky and I get it. At one point, Tom and I had four teens living under the same roof. Becky has two teenage boys at home.

Time and maturity are nature's cure for the tween-teen malady. If you don't feel like waiting for nature to take its course, you'll need some techniques to help you and your young person during this hormonally and emotionally charged time. Patience is the foundational quality upon which all the other virtues of love listed in 1 Corinthians 13 is built. Families who want to live and love well must begin with learning and demonstrating patience.

The typical teen or parent can't be kind, content, humble, respectful, unselfish, peaceful, forgiving, truthful, protective, hopeful, and tenacious—let alone flourish—without the common element of patience. While increasing our own patience, we can build patience into our young adults.

Scripture says patience is the result of wisdom—"A man's wisdom gives him patience" (Proverbs 19:11a)—yet practicing the desired discipline of patience is quite another thing. Patience is defined as bearing trials and annoyances calmly, being able and willing to endure others' mistakes. To be patient is an intentional response to wait rather than wail while in a difficult moment. It's self-control in an out of control circumstance.

Surprisingly, even good qualities may interfere with being patient: a desire for a child's success, wanting the best for a child, or having pride in his accomplishments. We are so anxious for our child to succeed, have the best, or get the best that we sometimes jump in, take over, or get involved in the thing the young person should be doing or experiencing independent of the parent. Of course other less desirable factors that contribute are more obvious and circumstantial, such as being hurried, tired, or over-programmed. Temperaments and past experiences also play roles in how we respond.

Growing up in a home where patience reigns will more often than not produce patient people. Self-worth and patience go hand in hand. When parents display patience, a child's self-worth will blossom. Conversely, living in an environment plagued with little tolerance for disruption or error diminishes a child's self-worth. Patience produces confident and content individuals. Insecure and envious people come from homes where impatience rules.

With this understanding we'll first explore developing patience in our kids, parenting with patience, and having patience while waiting for God's plans to unfold. Tom has needed to summon lots of patience being a father of three girls. His strength in living with the unpredictable wave of emotions is a testament to fatherly love…and a hope-filled perspective that this too shall pass.

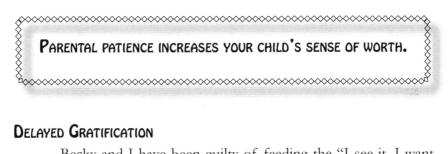

PARENTAL PATIENCE INCREASES YOUR CHILD'S SENSE OF WORTH.

DELAYED GRATIFICATION

Becky and I have been guilty of feeding the "I see it, I want it" beast. Most parents don't want their kids to experience discomfort or struggle. The concept of patiently working hard for something and then seeing the later benefits is especially foreign to the "entitlement generation." We parents are partly responsible for this attitude.

"Oh, he wants that so much. Let's just get it for him." We do this in the name of sympathy, love, or bonding. This generation is geared for immediate gratification, and we bear some of the responsibility. There are times Becky and I have been tough and done it right.

My (Lori) middle school daughter and I were out shopping for school supplies. An expensive calculator caught her eye. I was willing to buy a cheaper version, but she was determined to have the better brand.

"Buy me the calculator now, and I'll pay you back later." She was working a deal.

"If I can't get it today, we'll have to come back." She was appealing to my desire for errand consolidation. Clever strategy.

It wasn't easy, but I held strong. I determined that an experience of delayed gratification was worth more than my inconvenience or desire to please her.

39

Provide ways for your kids to experience delayed gratification. The knowledge gained will help later in life. Children who are typically characterized by an "I want it now" attitude have a greater potential to be adults who get into credit card and other types of debt.

> **PROVIDE WAYS FOR YOUR KIDS TO EXPERIENCE DELAYED GRATIFICATION.**

I Wanna Be Free

Frustration increases during independent phases of growth, often seen in toddlers and teens, due to the inner conflict between the need for freedom and the need for security. During this time of inner turmoil, kids are more likely to engage in impulsive activities and rash decision-making. Many young people are unaccustomed to waiting, planning, and thinking things through. Becky and I recommend using a step-by-step process to increase patience in kids.

First, ask, "Why is he reacting with impatience?" Then make a mental note of when patience is difficult for him. Begin by intentionally providing opportunities for waiting and planning. Developing any plan takes time and forward thinking; give your young person opportunities to practice. Experience is one way to strengthen the child's "wait" muscle.

A parent shared with me (Becky) how her teenage son developed patience. He devised a plan to accomplish a community service project. This mom admitted that she and her husband were tempted to step in to help because they were also excited about their son's project. However, by playing a supportive rather than an active role, they knew their son would reap great personal benefit. They watched as he spent time gathering information, evaluating how to raise money, and speaking with involved community leaders. The parents acted as the Consultant and posed questions during the process rather than offering solutions. Their boy diligently and effectively executed his project. The final result was a huge success—for the community and for their son.

As these parents did, be the Consultant when your young person is planning a project, activity, or outing. Becky and I have discovered that having the teen list the factors needed for a successful outcome is a good exercise: time, place, transportation, cost, and curfew. Then before the teen leaves with the car (this is the tricky part), have him lay out the *final* plan for the night. Specifically and clearly communicate expectations such as, "You will be (where he has said he'll be) and you will do (what he's said he will do)." Conclude by being the Controller saying, "If plans change, I need to be informed."

It's been my (Lori) experience that teens can be notorious for last-minute "no big deal" changes. Once they have the keys, they often believe they also hold the power to make all decisions after they drive off. This is *so* annoying. One afternoon I gave my eighteen-year-old permission to use the car to go shopping, and she returned home with a pierced nose. You can't anticipate all the different contingencies, but by asking questions, expecting clear answers, and clearly—very clearly—stating expectations, you'll have a better idea of what to expect.

> ### ASK GOOD QUESTIONS. EXPECT SPECIFIC ANSWERS. VERY CLEARLY STATE YOUR EXPECTATIONS.

DECISIONS, DECISIONS

We want our kids to make wise choices, right? Absolutely, but for that to happen they need opportunities to make decisions and live with their choices. So to those of us who are highly involved, it means we need to take our hands off the wheel. We can have some parental involvement and input but only when necessary. The big challenge is how much or how little. Be flexible and consider the particular child and circumstance. Don't worry about the fairness factor. When it comes to setting limits or letting go of limits, the child's maturity and trustworthiness are the determining factors. We will have to let go more than we want. Frankly, it is a little scary, but once we get past the fear, we find parental freedom in fewer restraints. Set up clear, safe, and appropriate boundaries. Then offer freedom within those boundaries for choice and decision-making.

Typical teen decisions such as what extra-curricular activity to be involved in, whether or not to get a part-time job, and when to save or spend money are all big decisions for a young person. Allowing the teen to make these choices is not too costly for the teen or the parent. Once the teen graduates from high school, decisions such as looking for a job, taking a gap year, going to college, or doing mission work are even bigger decisions. Allow him to practice making decisions before he needs to think through the really important decisions.

One mother was amazingly patient when her daughter was attempting to make a choice between colleges, one out of state and one in state. The daughter had the opportunity to play soccer at either one, and the cost was about the same.

However, the second school offered her desired major. It seemed like a clear-cut decision, but it wasn't easy because emotion was involved. The young woman had dreamed of going to college in California, which was out of state. Standing too close to a decision can make it difficult to see the wise choice. If her mom had weighed in, the daughter may have felt pushed toward a particular outcome and then resented her mom for appearing to make the choice for her. It must have taken mega doses of self-control to stay quiet, especially when the application deadline was only days away.

This wise mama allowed her daughter the time, space, and freedom to wrestle with the decision, make the choice, and own it. Mom was available if her daughter wanted to discuss the options. The daughter learned valuable decision-making skills, gained confidence, and was responsible for the outcome.

The mother had an opportunity to witness her child growing up and owning her life choices. This mom needs a standing ovation, don't you think?

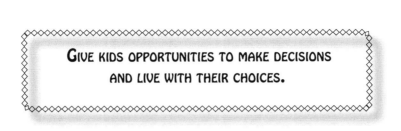

LIVE WITH IT

Although it may be frightening, we know our kids need to live with the choices they make. Sometimes they may fail. This is the part of parenting where we all cringe, hold our breath, and drop to our knees and pray. Many big decisions will be made between the ages of thirteen and twenty-five. The choices can be life-altering. "Teach us to number our days, that we may gain a heart of wisdom" (Psalm 90:12). We want our kids to be wise in the way they live out their lives.

Here's the balancing act: when to wait it out and when to speak up. Patience is not the same as permissiveness. Don't be afraid to add your thoughts into the mix when the stakes are high. If you don't, you can be sure someone else will. Surprisingly enough, even another adult—a teacher or a friend's parent with a different paradigm—may chime in. The world's voice is loud. Parents, speak up about decisions regarding sex, drugs, cheating, and alcohol. Talk with your kids about proper nutrition and wise fiscal principles. They may not always let you know they are listening, some teens may even argue a little, but keep talking. They may even heed your wisdom! "Listen to your father, who gave you life" (Proverbs 23:22a).

Our children will hear us. Our words will resonate in their heads, even if they choose the "wrong" way. (We know this because we can still hear our own parents' voices in our heads.) As parents, we have great influence in the areas of morals and values. Becky and I recommend wearing all the parenting hats when it comes to the core of the family's belief system. Be the Controller: speak up. Be the Consultant: ask questions. Be the Chum: listen. Be the Coach: present possible scenarios and assist the child in how to handle unexpected situations. Don't be Clueless, unaware of the choices your child is making, or Checked Out, ignoring the situation or clues. We want our kids to practice linking behavior to consequence. Then when the time comes to make a life-altering choice, they've had good practice making well-thought-through decisions and are ready and able to live with the choices they have made.

Hold Off

We have many opportunities to demonstrate patience in the home by the way we parent. Learning to wait before speaking or acting is hard for most people. Parents generally want things done quickly and completed in a specific way. Time is of the essence. We want to be effective and efficient. We're hurried and over-programmed, just like our kids.

Impatience may result when we're not satisfied with the process or outcome. In our rush to have a task completed, we may take over our children's jobs or household tasks. In order for young people to learn, they need to accomplish their tasks without parental intervention.

For the Controller parent, avoiding the hovering, "just checking" tactic requires great self-control. Explain or demonstrate what needs to be done—and walk away. If you return to check on, take over, or redo, the young person's motivation to do the task will melt away along with the satisfaction of doing the job independently. Go ahead and encourage and even retrain, but then step away. Allow the child to own the project by being the one to start and finish it. If he needs your help, he'll find you.

Learning a new task can be frustrating for kids. Hey, it's frustrating for Becky and me. We both get easily discouraged when learning a new technology. We've had many exasperating moments while writing this book and implementing various computer programs. Remember that learning a new thing can be difficult before you launch into teaching your child. As Coach, break down the new chore into smaller chunks. Be the Controller by demonstrating how something is done. If a best effort is exerted, give positive and encouraging feedback. Be specific about what was done well. If a half-hearted effort is given, tenderly provide constructive feedback mixed with some positive comments. Keep the child motivated to do his best. Then get out of the way. Move into Consultant mode to advise when asked. This same approach can be used with learning a new game, skill, or doing homework.

Jumping in and taking over sends kids the message that they aren't capable. Apply the slow-grow principle (It takes a lot of slow to grow.), not only to the little guys but to the older kids as well.

Have you seen the "Teenager changing a light bulb" cartoon? In the sketch the mother is standing by shaking her head while the teen is jumping up and down trying to switch out the light bulb. Kids need training and even retraining in the obvious chores. Remember that not all the synapses in their brains are wired yet.

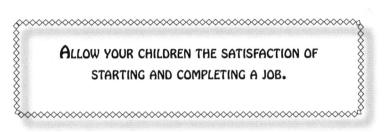

ALLOW YOUR CHILDREN THE SATISFACTION OF STARTING AND COMPLETING A JOB.

ZIP IT

As parents we may take over in action and in words. When my (Lori) dad was growing up, he felt frustrated when his parents would speak for him. As he grew older and eventually became a father, he realized his parents had a reason for answering for him. They were proud of him and were ready with a response before he could open his mouth. Having grown up with this experience, he determined to let his children answer for themselves. Dad understood from his own personal experience that, even though his parents were well intended, not having the opportunity to speak for himself undermined his confidence. Recognizing this, he was willing and able to be patient and allow his kids to express themselves verbally.

Solomon wrote that there is " a time to be silent and a time to speak" (Ecclesiastes 3:7b). Waiting through the awkward silence as our kids formulate an answer to a question asked by an adult takes a lot

45

of self-control. Remaining quiet encourages our children's confidence and maturity. As a disclaimer, there are some tweens or teens who are comfortable speaking up and might monopolize conversations. If your young person tends to take over, train him in conversational give and take. If his tendency is to hold back, allow times for him to speak up.

The quieter ones need help learning to draw out another in conversation. Give your child applicable ideas on how to ask questions to generate conversation. One mom shared a tip she gave her reserved nineteen-year-old daughter: "People like to talk about themselves. Ask them questions about their interests." Very practical.

A GROWL AND A MUMBLE

Conversation in the home takes on a whole different dynamic when kids enter the teen stage. (Side note: this is not as true for the tweens.) They typically become more private and less communicative in an attempt to separate and be independent. This includes sharing thoughts and day-to-day experiences. This is where Mom and Dad need self-control. Being patient, being present, and not forcing conversation set the tone and create a comfortable atmosphere in which the child is more willing to share.

You could say, "I noticed you weren't yourself when you came home today. I'm here if you want to talk." (This is where I almost need to physically bite my tongue. I say to myself, "Stop talking."). Let the child seek you out when he is ready. Once this happens, the child is all yours, ready to share and listen.

Becky usually has a snack prepared for her boys when they come home from school. She sets an informal, no-stress tone with food. In the comfort of this setting, her teen boys are more ready to converse.

LADY OR LORD IN WAITING

For child or parent, we can increase patience with experience. Learning to wait for God's plans to be realized, either short term or long term, requires spiritual patience. Life unfolds piece by piece. Our good God will help us learn what it means to be patient and still while waiting on Him to fulfill a heart's desire.

Mary Heathman, founding director of Where Grace Abounds, says, "Many times I pout rather than being still. I think I do this because I refuse to believe I live in a fallen world."[2] That's it! We falsely believe—and may even teach our children—that if we do the right stuff, everything should turn out just as we desire. A young man had done everything right in order to secure his first job. He went to college, studied, and received decent grades. He graduated and sent out his resume. A year later, he still could find no job in his field. It was beyond his control. The job market in his chosen field has been affected by the economy. No fault of his. It's a fallen world. But remember, God has a plan.

Having to wait for a passion to be realized is something your child will face. Encouragement in the midst of the difficult circumstance is some consolation. Help him move toward trust and hope rather than sit in discouragement and frustration. Remind him to not give up the dream and to not stop living. Encourage him to actively wait on God.

Patience is a quality we need every day. It is developed when we decide to put it into practice. Increasing opportunities for delayed gratification, planning, decision-making, and learning new tasks offers kids a chance to learn patience. By slowing down, being supportive, resisting the urge to take over, and sometimes by being quiet, parental patience will also mature. These practical experiences will be helpful in the spiritual realm when we are called to wait on God. Developing patience is a process. So be patient.

LOVE NOTES ON PATIENCE

LORI WRITES: My biggest patience challenge is to wait for my kids to come to me with their concerns. I want to jump right in, be in the know, and make things better. When I do this, I'm met with resistance. The involved approach worked great when my kids were little, but now that they are budding adults, my interest feels intrusive. This is hard for me, but I'm learning to wait for my kids to share their hearts.

BECKY WRITES: My level of patience is often determined by the calendar. When the schedule is tight, I'm impatient and easily frustrated leading to a domino effect with the boys, and even Scott. I'm learning that margin is necessary to keep me on track and to help me be patient with the ones I love.

QUESTIONS

1. When have you spoken too soon? What was the result?

2. Describe a situation where you allowed your child to experience the benefits of delayed gratification.

3. Describe a couple of scenarios in which you are typically impatient. What are the common threads? Do you see a potential trigger to impatience?

PARENTING TIPS

1. Zip it! Allow your child to speak for himself when appropriate.
2. Resist the urge to take over a job you've given your child.
3. Develop patience in your child by having him wait or work for a desired item.

PRAYER

Father,

You are patient, slow to anger, abounding in love. I pray I have the same patience with my family. Nudge me when I need to be quiet and still. Give me the strength to allow my child to wrestle through life's difficulties, knowing that You're sovereign over my child's circumstances. Give me the ability to be patient and trust You, knowing that You're

with him, developing his character. Help me to remember You value a patient peacemaker more than a skillful warrior. I pray You give me wisdom and opportunities to develop my patience. I pray my family abounds in love by showing patience during the challenging moments.
Amen

I WAITED PATIENTLY FOR THE **LORD**; HE TURNED TO ME AND HEARD MY CRY.

Psalm 40:1

CHAPTER 2

CHOOSE KINDNESS

LOVE IS KIND.

1 Corinthians 13:4b

SETTING THE TONE

In our marriage, Tom and I have developed some clandestine signals. I'll let you in on one of our secret gestures. If I have a crumb on my face, Tom will inconspicuously brush his own face so I get the nonverbal cue to wipe mine. I do the same for him.

Wouldn't it be awful to continue an evening or move to another venue with dinner clinging to an upper lip? The small mess is a distraction for others and a delayed embarrassment for the wearer. Being the crumb observer and saying something can be a bit awkward, but it's much worse for the unknowing soul sporting the "cling on."

Kindness embodies elements of boldness, meekness, and humility. It is not to be confused with enabling or permissiveness. Kindness holds firm in the face of adversity, responding in truth mixed with love. Kindness isn't passive; it's strong and tender all at once.

God is kind and demonstrates loving kindness to us just as we should with others. "Be kind and compassionate to one another" (Ephesians 4:32a). Looking past one's own needs to awareness of another's is the first step in creating a kind atmosphere. In the family, parents set the kindness tone.

Patience precedes kindness. A patient person has the ability to hang in there, and the kind person responds in love through action and words. Kindness is the quality that knits families together. The lack of it will tear families apart.

Check this out. It's the definition of kindness: *Demonstrating zeal toward one another in a good way, doing mutual favors, having compassion, the rendering of moral goodness.*[3] Sounds really pleasant, doesn't it? Becky and I want homes that embrace kindness. We're guessing you do, too.

> ## KINDNESS IS THE QUALITY THAT KNITS FAMILIES TOGETHER.

ACTS OF KINDNESS

Doing mutual favors sounds nice, right? Home should be a place where family members help each other out. God regularly presents opportunities in our families for each of us to care for and about someone else. The combination of the parental example of being kind and the expectation of kind interaction among family members is important. Use the Coach approach and be specific in your directions to encourage kindness. "Looks like Dad could use some help taking out the garbage. Please help him. I know he'd really appreciate it."

One parent, who typically fell into the Controller description, asked how she could move to the Consultant mode while trying to get her kids to pitch in around the house. The best way to move into less intense parental involvement is to take those good thoughts and ideas the Controller has and ask a question rather than give a directive. For instance the Controller states, "Load the dishwasher." The Consultant asks, "How will you help clean up after dinner?"

51

Kindness naturally flows from the highly relational Chum. The Chum is keenly aware of the child's feelings and innately knows how to respond in either word or action. By modeling tenderness and doing favors the recipient learns how to care for someone else. Kindness brings unity.

Lean On Me

Being a helper to a family member is important. God is often referred to as our helper. In Psalm 118:7a David says, "The Lord is with me; he is my helper." Incredible, isn't it? The God of the universe is our helper.

We can be our child's helper, too. If our child calls from school in need of an important forgotten item, we have a choice. We can take the logical consequence route and say, "Oh, bummer, so sorry. What will you do?" Or we can demonstrate grace and lend a hand. I (Lori) ask myself, "If I were in a bind, what response would I hope for?" I'd greatly appreciate it if I received the help. Just as this was being written, my youngest daughter was attempting to call me to bring a forgotten math assignment to school for her. I never got the call because I was conferencing with Becky regarding this very topic. Since I was unavailable, my daughter moved to Plan B. She called her oldest sister for help. (Cell phones have their advantages.) The older sister jumped at the chance to assist her younger sibling. I was pleased to witness one sister helping out another. That's what we want, isn't it? Being able to rely on family members when we need them, knowing with confidence we are there for one another? Unless the child needs the hard lesson of natural consequences due to habitual poor planning, being helpful is the way to go.

Within a family, each individual feels valued when assisted by another, knowing each person can be counted on in a crisis. There is security in the knowledge that family members care about the things another values. Love, demonstrated in the form of kindness, draws the family closer. Consideration and thoughtfulness grow and positive relationships are the result.

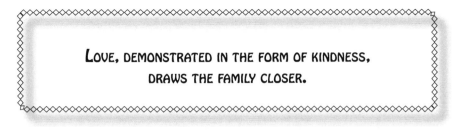

PACKING A PUNCH

Words are powerful. They can pull us together or push us apart. Our word choice impacts our kids. Sarcasm and condescension are unkind. Do children really get sarcasm? What's the receiver of the sarcastic remark supposed to do? Laugh or cry? Sarcasm is a hit below the belt, meant to harm. How often have we heard or even said, "What part of 'no' don't you understand?" Little kids don't get it, but the older ones do—and are shamed by this question. We need to say what we mean and be direct and specific rather than hurtful.

Our kids are growing up in a world full of sarcasm, from TV shows to conversations with friends. I (Lori) have even seen teachers use sarcasm as a means to control the classroom. I find this trend quite disturbing. Sarcasm is cruel and belittles the person to whom it's directed.

When I speak to various parent groups on effective communication, one of the main take-home points for the audience is to get rid of sarcasm. One single dad shared with me that he had decided to eliminate sarcasm. He admitted, "It's been difficult." Sarcasm had become a habit. He realized his caustic remarks were creating a barrier between him and his daughter. Now aware of the problem, he has made great strides in being positive. He says, "It's paying off." His relationship with his fourteen-year-old is improving.

We can be direct while being honest and kind. "Do not let any unwholesome talk come out of your mouths, but only what is helpful for building others up according to their needs, that it may benefit those who listen" (Ephesians 4:29). When kindness is shown in words, it looks like encouragement or empathy. A mother of three tells her kids, "If you can't be kind, be quiet." Making the choice to replace sarcasm with encouragement builds positive relationships.

MAKING FUN

Making fun of someone isn't fun for everyone. As with most types of character training, we need to start with ourselves first. Begin by putting a stop to mean-spirited jokes and harsh teasing.

As a family we (Lori) watch a popular TV reality show where talent is sought. Only a limited number of contestants auditioning for the show are accepted into the competition. I'll admit, we really enjoy this show and are so into it we even text in our votes. Unfortunately, it has an element of ridicule. The demeaning comments are seen as entertainment. This is the type of world in which our young people are being raised.

Our tween or teen may even be the ridicule recipient. Ignoring the comments usually works because the teaser eventually gives up when a response isn't given. Another tactic is to use humor. At thirteen, my (Becky) youngest son used this defense successfully. He was often teased because he was short for his age. When the taunting began, he responded, "Hey, I'm fun size!" This usually made everyone laugh. His quick, humorous comment deterred ridicule.

The tween years are especially difficult for kids on either end of the developmental scale. Physical appearance is a perfect target for the middle school meanie. Early or late blooming provides ample ammunition for a cruel joke. Ridiculing, making fun of, or laughing at someone else shows a person's true colors.

Not standing up for a ridiculed individual is cowardly. We often have an opportunity to put a stop to this type of cruelty. If you notice this kind of situation happening, speak up. I (Lori) recall a sporting event where the referee was getting heckled by a few parents. He was merely a boy, no more than fourteen. One mom spoke up and said, "Reffing is tough. He's doing his best. All I can think of is my son who's about that age. How would I feel if the ref were my child?" That small observation put a stop to the behavior of the vocal parents.

Speak to your tween or teen about incidents such as this. Explain how compassion moves people to stand up for the dignity of others. Elevate children's consciences toward this type of compassionate behavior. Real life experience and talent seeking TV shows are venues for this discussion. We can directly teach empathy by having the young person imagine he is in another's shoes. Although empathy is best learned through difficult personal experiences, parents can begin to foster it through discussion, demonstration, or role-playing.

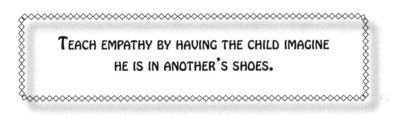

> ## TEACH EMPATHY BY HAVING THE CHILD IMAGINE HE IS IN ANOTHER'S SHOES.

ENCOURAGING WORDS

We can respond in kindness, and our kids can learn kindness through our words and actions. "The wise woman builds her house, but with her own hands the foolish one tears hers down" (Proverbs 14:1), and "Fathers, do not exasperate your children" (Ephesians 6:4a). To be fair, I (Lori) quote both verses when speaking to moms and dads about effective communication. (Otherwise, I notice lots of elbowing between parents.) Then I ask, "Do we want to encourage or frustrate our children?" Encourage, of course. What parent would want to purposely tear down a child? Yet sometimes we speak before we think. Deliberately speak encouraging words. While being sincere build up the child and be positive. Avoid overdoing it and giving false praise. False praise can prevent children from striving to do better.

We want our kids to have a real sense of self. Especially if the child is experiencing challenges, speak encouraging words just like a coach would. It's reassuring for a child to hear his parent cheering for him even in his trials. A child can be inspired to persevere when a parent, as the Chum, shares how he's struggled with certain things in the past. A parent sharing honestly, with humility, frees up the child from needing to do everything well in order to please the parent.

Becky and I thought it would be helpful to illustrate two different approaches and outcomes. Look at the contrast in the following interactions. (In this instance, the Controller approach is being misused.) Compare the Controller's threat to the Coach's guidance.

The Controller states, "You aren't working very hard at school. You have a D in science. You're capable of doing better. You will be working with a tutor starting Monday. If your grade doesn't improve, you can't_____."

Upon hearing this the child will shut down emotionally. He will not be motivated to do better. He'll feel defeated and misunderstood. He will feel shame or anger.

The Coach says, "I'm noticing that science is a bit of a challenge for you this semester. It looks like you need some support. I know you can do this. You're a smart kid. A tutor will be helpful in bringing that grade up."

Notice the problem and the solution are the same, but the delivery is different. Both the Controller and the Coach address the grade issue; that's positive. But the Coach's words soothe an already defeated and frustrated student. When kindness is factored into the equation, the child feels supported and loved. When he feels cared for rather than scolded or threatened, he will be more open to accept help.

When you recognize a child's problem area, begin with kindness. Training and supporting our kids moves them forward toward resolution. Use punishment as the very last resort. Punishment sits in the past, serving as a reinforcement and reminder of failure. Sharing both successes and struggles with our kids builds a bridge of understanding, compassion, and empathy.

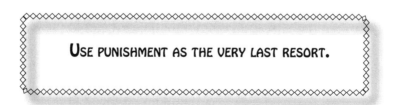

USE PUNISHMENT AS THE VERY LAST RESORT.

FIGHTING WORDS

I'm (Lori) sorry to say my words and tone can both be razor-edged. But I'm going to guess others struggle with this, too. Collectively, women probably own the Sharp Tone Store. But men, have an aisle in the store as well.

In Proverbs 15:1 God tells us that "A gentle answer turns away wrath, but a harsh word stirs up anger." Sometimes we try to blame the person on the receiving end when he responds to us in anger. The Proverbs verse shows how cutting words stir up rage. Each party bears responsibility for an argument. In the realm of physics, every action has an equal and opposite reaction. That holds true for interpersonal communication as well. If harsh words are delivered, an angry response is sure to be returned.

Wise planning involves carefully choosing the words, the time, and the place before engaging in a difficult discussion. Be aware of nonverbal cues and body language. Having a "talk" during dinner isn't the best time—unless indigestion is the goal. Typically, most of us want the family dinner to be a time of reconnecting after being apart. Dinner should be a pleasant experience. Also, keep in mind who needs to be included in the hard conversation. Keep certain issues private, between the parents and child. Siblings don't have to be in the know regarding their brother or sister's issues. Leave that up to the child concerned whether or not he wants to share certain information. This discretion also sends a message of respect for the individuals in the home.

Sitting side by side rather than standing facing one another is a better posture for potentially heated discussions. Standing face to face could be interpreted as more adversarial. Possible outcomes of this position are shutting down, walking away, or becoming physical. Rather, sitting together on the couch side by side will encourage a more positive and productive conversation. I personally can vouch for this technique. It works like a charm.

SPEAK SOFTLY

When our young people have behaved badly, the most helpful—but perhaps most difficult—first response is gentleness. A parent's accusing finger and angry words will create a brain freeze or will ignite defensiveness in the youth and fuel anger in return. When someone points an accusing finger at me, it fans the flames of my rage. Nevertheless, Scripture tells us to instead restore the individual gently (Galatians 6:1). Choosing to be gentle and respectful when we've discovered our child may be engaged in an unwholesome activity encourages communication.

Gentleness is often associated with kindness in Scripture. Gentleness is seen as a strong quality. In Proverbs 25:15b, "a gentle tongue can break a bone." Gentle words have strength. Most of us prefer a gentle touch to a firm tug. Paul even asks the church at Corinth, "What do you prefer? Shall I come to you with a rod of discipline, or shall I come in love and with a gentle spirit?" (1 Corinthians 4:21). Before speaking, ask yourself, "Is this truth meant to heal or hurt? Am I able to speak this truth with love?"

We (Lori) have had situations where we've handled this well and other times when we dealt with a problem poorly. When we have handled issues with gentleness and respect, the outcomes were even better than we had hoped. Of course, when parental emotions have taken over, things have gone badly. Keep in mind that the discovery of an issue and the ensuing discussion will more often than not produce discomfort in the child. If the discussion is anger-based, the child's discomfort will turn to defiance and rage.

I recall coming across something that created concern, and I told my husband what I found. We prayed together for guidance, "Lord let us handle this well. Give us Your words and love. Give our child a tender and receptive heart to hear our words."

Not only did God answer the cry of our hearts, but He also provided protection for the child. When we had the discussion, none of the other siblings were present. God gave calm hearts, clear minds, and privacy. He supernaturally covered the time, emotions, and words. Had we approached our child with elevated emotions, we would have failed in our goal of changing inappropriate behavior. Doing things God's way allows the child to know he's loved without compromising the truth.

JOY STEALER

Kindness begins in the heart. Kind plans begin in the mind and are then lived out in kind actions. Joy is produced in the helper when he helps another by demonstrating kindness. Sadly, I'm (Lori) guilty of being a joy stealer. On a number of occasions, my kids have had an idea for reaching out to help someone, and I have either dismissed or ignored the idea.

One of my girls had a coach who frequently broke his clipboard at soccer games. He was passionate about the game and would throw the clipboard down when upset with a call. My middle school daughter mentioned a couple of times she wanted to buy him a metal clipboard, one that wouldn't break. Great idea, yet it never came to fruition because I didn't assist her in the process. She needed me to drive her to the store in order to follow through with this idea. I did nothing except offer some unwelcomed comments. In my opinion the coach should have controlled his temper, but I'd missed the point. My daughter's consideration and humor should have been the focus. Kindness shouldn't be reserved for only when it's earned or deserved. I had an opportunity to encourage my child's kindness and instead stole the joy she could have experienced. A side benefit could have been the coach's response to the gift. Maybe he would have held onto it rather than thrown it down. Kindness is a gentle teacher.

How can you promote joy rather than rob it from your kids? Watch for moments when you can join your children in spreading joy. Listen for their ideas for blessing others with words and actions. Then assist them in carrying out the plan.

I Feel Your Pain

Our children need our time and our understanding. Compassion is true understanding of another person's feelings, and it's usually learned by a direct experience. Sometimes we have misplaced compassion. A mom of a teenage daughter shared with me how she hurt for her child. Her teen had made poor choices and was now having to live out the consequences of those choices. Her husband reminded her that the reason their young person was in that situation was due to unwise decisions. He advised his wife to let go of the sympathy she was feeling and hope their daughter had learned something in the process. The husband was suggesting that a Controller or Coach approach would be more helpful than the Chum parenting style in this situation.

Often big events can spur on misplaced sympathy. Maybe we don't want our child to be left out of a social gathering, so we compromise on what we know to be best. The compromise might look like a movie we aren't comfortable with him seeing or an activity in which we aren't certain he should be participating. Joy and obedience are linked. God desires us to be both joyful and obedient. He knows we won't be completely content unless we are obedient to His Word. God wants the best for His children, just as we do for ours. Obedience results in contentment. Standing up to peer pressure will build character muscles. Once those muscles are used and developed, the need to please peers over pleasing God shrinks.

Be prepared to respond when circumstances change. Ask, "When circumstances change, do my standards remain the same or do my standards depend on the situation? Do my standards fluctuate according to my child's feelings and reactions?" Romans 11:22 tells us, "Consider therefore the kindness and sternness of God: sternness to those who fell, but kindness to you, provided that you continue in his kindness." It's difficult not to compromise. Kindness isn't the same as compromise. However, when you stand your ground according to your faith, morals, and values, both trust and respect are fostered. This doesn't mean, however, that there won't be a battle of the wills. There most likely will be a battle, but important issues are worth the fight. Love your child, stand your ground, and be kind.

Our homes are a training ground to foster kindness in our kids as they relate to other people. Home is the first place our children learn kindness. When parents consistently model and expect kind words and actions, children will usually assimilate the quality of kindness into their personalities. What a great blessing it is to see kindness bloom in our children—to watch them learn how to stand up for the underdog and to show kindness even when it isn't deserved. Kindness draws families together. Family members feel cared for and loved when they are encouraged and helped. Demonstrating kindness takes a little extra thought. It may even interrupt the schedule, but the fruit is family unity. Kindness is a choice. 1 Thessalonians 5:15b advises, "always try to be kind to each other and to everyone else."

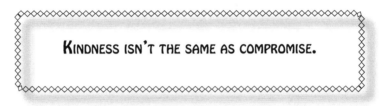

KINDNESS ISN'T THE SAME AS COMPROMISE.

LOVE NOTES ON KINDNESS

LORI WRITES: Being highly task-oriented, interruptions can make me bristle. When I view my husband's or kids' interruptions as an intrusion, I know my priorities are out of whack. I want to speak and respond with kindness because I know the fruit is a close-knit family.

BECKY WRITES: I *still* make my kids' lunches, not because they don't know how to pack a lunch but because I love to do it. At the high school open house, one of the teachers told parents, specifically moms, to quit making lunches for their children. Some of my friends think I'm crazy too. I do it as an act of kindness.

QUESTIONS

1. How do you model kindness to your children?

2. When have you "torn down" your family? Can you think of another way to communicate in a frustrating situation using the Coach parenting style?

3. How can you be both kind and strong in the middle of a disagreement?

PARENTING TIPS

1. Be direct and specific in communicating; avoid sarcasm.

2. Choose the best time, place, and position for an important conversation.

3. Give your child opportunities to help.

PRAYER

Father,

You are kind. Teach me to show love through kindness to my spouse, children, neighbors, and those who You place in my path each day. Give me Your love for them so I can love even when it's hard. Prompt me to speak gentle words. Give me strength to make the difficult decisions. Put a guard over my mouth so sarcastic comments and harsh words don't seep out. Change my heart so I desire to be kind and compassionate.

Amen

KIND WORDS CAN BE SHORT AND EASY TO SPEAK, BUT THEIR ECHOES ARE TRULY ENDLESS.

Mother Teresa[4]

Section Two

Love Is an Attitude

CHAPTER 3

CHOOSE CONTENTMENT

LOVE DOES NOT ENVY.

1 Corinthians 13:4c

PAUL'S SECRET

After much anticipation, the big day had finally arrived…the annual outdoor ski sale at the local sporting goods shop. My (Becky) youngest son sent me a text message during lunch reminding me to pick him up from school, "Don't be late, Mom." My older son and my husband were meeting us at the sale.

When we arrived, the parking lot was crowded, and the tent was jammed. People were everywhere, vying for the latest and greatest boots and bindings or for a good deal on last year's models. The negotiations going on between one mom and a teen caught my attention.

"Mom, can I get this really cool helmet?" the daughter asked.

"No, you already have a helmet."

"But it doesn't match my *jacket*!"

"Then your birthday money will come in handy," the mom stated as she walked away. Case closed. I thought, "Nice line, Mom."

I found my own brood ogling over ski boots. The boys and Scott had just finished their own negotiations, choosing boots within the price parameters. I was so glad Scott was the negotiator. After trying on a variety of styles, they had decided. All three were happy with the final choices.

Contentment is a state of mind, being happy with what one has been given. Unfortunately, what God provides and when He provides don't always meet our wants or perceived needs. We compare our situation or accomplishment to another's, and then determine we've come up short. Envy creeps in.

Lori and I have discussed envy and the entitlement generation at length. Collectively, we parents must be doing something wrong to have a whole generation of kids thinking "want" and "get" go together. Maybe, just maybe, we as parents feed into our children's feelings of discomfort or discontent. In our quest to keep our kids happy (even though making them happy isn't our job), we scramble to meet their needs as well as their wants and whims. Why wouldn't they feel as if life should be handed to them on a silver platter?

As parents we've witnessed firsthand discontent in ourselves and in our children. We've seen what someone else has and developed "green eyes." The apostle Paul understood the concept of contentment. "I have learned to be content whatever the circumstances. I know what it is to be in need, and I know what it is to have plenty. I have learned the secret to being content in any and every situation, whether well fed or hungry, whether living in plenty or in want" (Philippians 4:11b-12). So what's the secret to satisfaction? Paul reveals it in verse 13, "I can do everything through him who gives me strength." Dependence and trust in God were his weapons against discontent. Let's capture Paul's attitude and explore ways to combat envy.

The Power of Observation

"I compliment in private," a parent stated in my class one day. "I've found there's less conflict between my kids." There's a lot of wisdom in that suggestion. When others receive accolades, tweens and teens often take compliments of others as a personal put-down to themselves. (They are still a little egocentric even at this age.) "Aren't I doing a good job?" is the tween's question. The teen listens, remains silent, and feels slighted. They want attention and commendation too. Friends and siblings may be talented academically, artistically, or athletically, and the child may feel envy stir. Then jealousy rather than gladness for the accomplishments of others is the result.

We want our kids to be genuinely happy for one another's accomplishments. Model happiness for another's success and show your kids how to share another's joy. Words like, "I bet you feel really happy for your friend who got the part in the play," or questions like, "How will you help your friend celebrate his victory?" make a big impact.

When immersed in envious thoughts and jealousies, it's tough to be happy for someone else. There is a good reason Scripture tells us envy rots the bones (Proverbs 14:30b). We'd sometimes rather let our bones rot than be happy for someone else.

Look at what happened to Jesus. Pilate knew Jesus had been handed over because of the jealousy and self-interest of the Jewish leaders (Matthew 27:18). Jealousy can consume us.

Determine what motivates your kids and why that particular desire spurs them on. "And I saw that all labor and achievement spring from man's envy of his neighbor" (Ecclesiastes 4:4a). Solomon goes on to say these desires are like chasing the wind. I wonder if he was writing about tweens and teens. The new fad is always alluring; the old is cast aside. Solomon actually likens the pursuit of stuff to chasing the wind. A lot of kids are wind chasers, and maybe we parents are, too. I (Becky) fall into that category more often than I'd like to admit.

Lori told me about a convicting sermon her pastor gave on this very topic. He said, "Envy starts as admiration but over time turns green with competition or spite."[5] How does your child react to the accomplishments of his peers and siblings? What's done with the observation of another's success can be the place where sin enters as jealousy or admiration remains.

Mom and Dad, we can also fall into this trap. How do we react when we see a friend's kid succeed? Parents who are envious of other children's accomplishments may turn to their own kids and point out the child's lack of ability or effort. Lori reminds parents that this type of manipulation through guilt generally backfires big time. Subtly mentioning another's success, linking it to a specific child, results in feelings of low self -worth. What was perhaps meant as inspiration lands as a heavy load of condemnation.

The Controller in overdrive may say, "You'll never be as good as Johnny because he takes time to practice while you just play video games." Ouch.

If you use others as examples to encourage your children, take great care so your child doesn't feel tricked or shamed. Look at an example through the lens of the Coach. "Johnny's mom told me he spends a lot of time at the batting cage practicing his swing." Here the parent makes the observation, allowing the child draw a conclusion.

Better yet, be the Consultant and ask direct questions so the child can problem solve. "Sounds like you'd like to improve your swing. What could you do?" Notice this was done without bringing another child into the equation.

Someone else's accomplishments can be motivational when the child makes his own observation and applies it to himself. This has occurred at my (Becky) house. When my younger son heard about the praise his brother received for completing his Eagle project from friends and college reps, he started planning his own project. He was learning from his older brother's example.

Lori's daughter is a cross-country runner. Her coach has a great motto: "Hard work beats talent when talent doesn't want to work hard." The message of extra effort needed is best left to the child's power of observation.

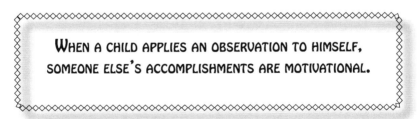

WHEN A CHILD APPLIES AN OBSERVATION TO HIMSELF, SOMEONE ELSE'S ACCOMPLISHMENTS ARE MOTIVATIONAL.

RIVALRY OR RELATIONSHIP

What was your own family like growing up? Was there respect between siblings or was there rivalry? Parents want their children to be friends rather than foes, enjoying a relationship into adulthood. There are two ways to foster a good relationship between siblings. First, don't play favorites. Second, avoid comparing kids. Comparison leads to competition. And in competition, there's always a winner...and a loser.

At an award ceremony, a father was keenly tuned into both of his kids. His son was receiving many accolades, while his daughter had had a pretty difficult school year. It is possible that this wise and sensitive dad knew, in his daughter's mind, she saw herself as an invisible failure. When the dad took the podium to say a few words, he acknowledged that it was his son's special night, but he also shared that he was proud of both of his kids—his son and his daughter. The daughter tried to contain her smile. A small gesture of recognition can draw siblings together rather than cause rivalry and conflict.

Relationships grow as children learn to get along with each other. Little kid squabbles are annoying; teenage quarrels are aggravating. Disputes are a normal part of development, but children need to learn how to handle disagreements in an effective way and work through conflict. This sets the stage for children to develop acceptable social behaviors. Conflicts in the family are opportunities for teaching kids to fight fair. Being respectful while disagreeing is a necessary life skill.

When my boys get into it with each other, it's usually a noisy ruckus. I'm the one who *really* doesn't like conflict. The funny thing is they have their tiff and then one initiates, "Friends?" The other will shoot back, "Yeah, friends." They're over it while I'm still frustrated with the hollering. They've learned to fight, forgive, and move on, confident in their friendship.

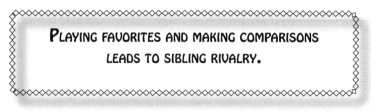

PLAYING FAVORITES AND MAKING COMPARISONS LEADS TO SIBLING RIVALRY.

THE THIEF

An interesting thing happened at the ski sale I told you about earlier. As we waited in line to check out, we noticed sales people carrying box after box of goggles from the tent back into the store. One of my kids asked why when we made it to the register.

"Oh, we had to take the goggles and other small items back in the store. Too many were getting stolen." "For where you have envy and selfish ambition, there you find disorder and every evil practice" (James 3:16). Internal covetous feelings can shift to external actions quickly. Stealing is wrongfully taking or keeping something that doesn't belong to us. For tweens and teens who struggle with this, they usually commit theft at a friend's house or in retail stores.

If a parent discovers his child is stealing, swift action is necessary.

The first step in addressing a theft is to determine why the child stole the item. Is a need not being met? Is the child looking for attention? Does he feel he needs something to fit in with his peer group? Does he need more control or freedom to make his own purchases? Was the act of stealing motivated by seeking a thrill or taking a dare? Does he think it was no big deal?

Once the reason why is identified, the next step is to return the item to the individual or the store. Expect the child to explain his actions and apologize. If appropriate, the child should pay for the stolen item.

Lori and I recommend these general guidelines in dealing with theft:

1. Return the item to the owner with a verbal and written apology.
2. Ask for forgiveness.
3. Discuss in private how your family and God value honesty and trust.
4. Create a plan for what to do when the child covets.
   A. Talk about why he wants the item.
   B. Help the child determine how he will pay for the item by earning and saving money.
5. Pray that God will guide your child, giving him the desire to be honest and trustworthy.

Theft can result in legal prosecution. There are serious consequences for illegal activities.

Discuss dares and how to say no to activities that are against the law. If dabbling in theft is part of a friendship or relationship, help the child make new friends. Pray that the child always gets caught. The legal stakes get higher as the child gets older.

Parents can make a big impact by modeling honesty. Explain that God desires honesty and that the family pays for what it needs and wants. Include a brainstorming session to help the child figure out ways he can earn money to purchase the things he desires. Most importantly, love unconditionally, expect the best, and deal with the worst.

HOME TURF

In the home remove the temptation to steal. It can be enticing to pinch a few dollars when money is left lying around. Put cash and credit cards away. When a child runs an errand, get the receipt and change to keep the expectation high for honesty. If you think he may be stealing, take a deep breath and stay calm. Try to catch him in the act rather than accuse him. We don't want to take this violation personally. Kids usually steal to get what they want, not to hurt Mom and Dad. Some kids view money in their parents' wallets as "family cash". It seems obvious to parents but not necessarily to kids. Some teens need to hear that the money in Mom's purse or Dad's wallet belongs to the parents; it's not free for the taking.

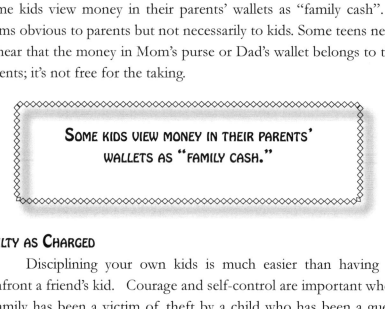

SOME KIDS VIEW MONEY IN THEIR PARENTS' WALLETS AS "FAMILY CASH."

GUILTY AS CHARGED

Disciplining your own kids is much easier than having to confront a friend's kid. Courage and self-control are important when a family has been a victim of theft by a child who has been a guest in the home. This type of theft is not uncommon. Items that often go missing include cosmetics, clothes, toys, sports equipment, liquor, high-tech devices, and cash.

Okay, so you know Billy took your son's tennis racket. What do you do? Get all the facts before proceeding. There are some teens who prefer to solve this on their own. If that is the case, have the child detail his plan to solve the problem. Include in the conversation what to do if the item is not returned. Ask the child when he would like you to step in and assist. Consider the age of the thief. If the child is under fifteen, go directly to the parents. For children fifteen and older, speak to the child first and give him a limited opportunity (no more than one day) to confess to his parents. (The teen can do this if he thinks that would be preferable. Let him choose who makes the initial contact.) Then make the phone call or visit, asking the parents to help in solving the problem. Restoring the relationships of all people involved hinges on addressing the elephant in the room. The child needs to confess and apologize to the victims, and the parents of the thief must also express their regret regarding their child's actions. The final step is necessary so the victims are not left with a feeling of unfinished business, creating a barrier in the relationship. If this restoration doesn't occur because the child's parents are Checked Out, Clueless, or don't believe you, the adult relationship will be strained and may even become severed. At this point, it's necessary to redefine that adult relationship. If the child is unable or unwilling to express remorse or regret, as a family, discuss and decide how to move forward. Is the child welcomed back into your home or not? Will limits be put on his access to rooms in the home or not? There is no right answer. Families will handle this situation differently.

A couple discovered that a young person, a close family friend, had been forging their son's name to gain access to a private country club for a full month. He racked up all kinds of charges, including inviting guests and ordering food for them. Once the couple discovered what was happening, they confronted the young man. He was given time to confess but chose to keep silent. The father arranged a meeting with this boy's dad. They came to an agreement regarding paying back the charges. The young man had to go face to face with the victims and take responsibility for his actions. He apologized. The relationships were restored; the friendship remained intact.

Lori and I encourage addressing any type of theft, even if it appears minor. If a child has stolen from someone outside the family and is unable to pay it back, lend the child the money to make things right with the violated person and set up a plan for reimbursement. Then the person hurt by the crime is made whole and can put the incident behind him. In all stealing scenarios, respond the same: confess, apologize, and pay back.

All people are tempted. God knew we all would be tempted to steal. Coveting the new electronic gadget, expensive snowboard, or cool track shoes happens. It's when the temptation of coveting turns into theft that we have a problem on our hands. Even illegal behavior, as shocking as it can be, is an opportunity for learning about honesty.

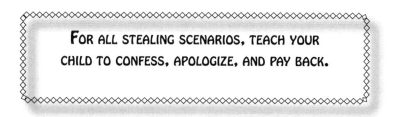

FOR ALL STEALING SCENARIOS, TEACH YOUR CHILD TO CONFESS, APOLOGIZE, AND PAY BACK.

I BOUGHT IT MYSELF

How do your kids get the cash necessary to buy what they want? Kids generally have four sources: allowance, additional chores, jobs outside the home, and gift money. We call the jobs that warrant pay in addition to the weekly duties "above and beyond chores." Additional work such as mulching flower beds, reseeding the lawn, and washing windows are "above and beyond chores" at the Danielson home. The Wildenbergs' paid chores include washing the wood floors, staining the outdoor furniture, and weeding. The additional income provides for special purchases.

My (Becky) then tween-age son wanted an iPod. He'd saved gift money, allowances, and pay from extra chores in a special jar, not spending his precious savings on frivolous things. He worked hard for months to accomplish his goal. With his savings and an additional discount coupon, he was able to make his purchase and also buy a case to keep his new gadget safe. He took very good care of his iPod, better than if Scott and I would have purchased it for him.

When kids desire a particular item, parents can assist them in learning to be savvy in money matters. Here are a few ideas Lori and I share with moms and dads. Require the child to pay for the item or split the cost with the child. Create a place for them to keep funds safe (a savings account, a piggy bank, or even a pickle jar). Teach them how to research products and prices to determine the best buy. Working for and making the most of every dollar earned are important experiences for children.

Financial lessons in childhood will instill in tweens and teens the principles they need to make wise financial decisions as adults.

THE SIMPLE LIFE

My friend and I were walking on a beautiful autumn day, the bright sun illuminating leaves of red, yellow, and orange. "When I stop and look at how much I already have, it humbles me. God is so good," she said. She's right. God is good and freely gives to His children. A state of contentment feels good. We experience warm feelings of love and happiness when we are settled, satisfied, and at ease with life.

The desire for happiness is innate. Happiness in some Christian circles has received a bad rap. Good character and continued spiritual growth are emphasized in teachings about successful parenting and honorable living. Have you noticed how these qualities tend to be presented as serious? Why is that, since one of God's character traits is joy? C. S. Lewis wrote, "Joy is the serious business of heaven."[6] I want joy to be serious business for me! Joy in my circumstances, joy in my relationships, and joy in my work.

SATISFACTION GUARANTEED

As our tweens and teens mature and begin to choose a career path, most hope to find a job that makes a difference, somehow contributes to society. Millennials desire to make the world a better place. They want to touch lives. Not a bad goal! One twenty-something said, "I could make more money doing something else, but I chose to be an elementary school teacher because I want to make a difference." This young woman experiences satisfaction in her job because she is using her gifts to serve the community by teaching kids.

When God finished creating the universe, He was pleased with His work. "It is good," sums up His thoughts on His creation. God was content with the job He had done.

"A man can do nothing better than to eat and drink and find satisfaction in his work. This too, I see, is from the hand of God, for without him, who can eat or find enjoyment?" (Ecclesiastes 2:24-25). A teen's work includes schoolwork, chores, and participation in activities. Putting forth his best effort honors and glorifies the Lord. And the benefits are great! "To the man who pleases him, God gives wisdom, knowledge and happiness" (Ecclesiastes 2:26a). Contentment is the blessing for a job well done.

To train your child to be joy-filled in his work, be the Coach. State what you've observed, "Wow! You spent a lot of time on that project. Your PowerPoint presentation is amazing. You must feel happy with your hard work." This type of guidance will encourage job satisfaction and develop intrinsic, rather than extrinsic, rewards. When your child puts forth his best effort just to feel good, you'll know he's developing a healthy attitude toward work. One of the benefits of instilling this quality in your young person is that he will have the desire to do things well even if there's no visible reward. A child driven by internal motivation will become the type of worker who will perform to the best of his ability with little or no supervision. He won't choose to slide by with the least amount of effort or ask, "If I do this, what's in it for me?"

As our kids grow up we want to help them find their sweet spot--the place where they can use the gifts God has given them to serve God and others. Work can be a form of worship, doing what the Lord created them to do. Maybe that is why the feelings of contentment and joy can be derived from a job well done. That is the satisfaction of success. Asher (whose name means happiness or happy) was the eighth son of Jacob. He is a biblical example of a person discovering his sweet spot, doing what he was created to do. Before Jacob died, he blessed this son by saying, "Asher's food will be rich; he will provide delicacies fit for a king" (Genesis 49:20). Asher and his descendants were blessed with fertile farmlands and experienced success in their vocation.

> **HELP YOUR CHILD FIND HIS SWEET SPOT--THE PLACE WHERE HE FEELS HAPPY AND SUCCESSFUL IN WHAT HE DOES.**

COUNT YOUR BLESSINGS

Rather than allowing ourselves or our children to stew in envious thoughts, count God's blessings. A strategy my (Lori) son uses when he begins to feel discouraged is to remember a child from his youth group who is wheelchair bound. This boy has a positive attitude about life, a strong faith, and is up for the challenges facing him as a paraplegic. My son says, "I try to remember, no matter what I'm going through, my outlook needs to be like my friend's." This viewpoint keeps struggles in perspective and adjusts negative attitudes in order to appreciate blessings.

The best way to get rid of envy is to be thankful for what God has already given. Spend time in praying with the kids, listing the gifts God has given. It's surprising what children will offer up in thanksgiving. Pot roast, flannel sheets, and snow have all made the thank you list at my (Becky) home. Make a list to refer to during moments you see envy creeping into the scene. Consider the tangible and intangible blessings. A family list of blessings is a good place to start when encouraging contentment. Satisfaction and joy are the results of recognizing God's blessings. "Contentment is not the fulfillment of what you want but the realization of how much you already have."[7]

Draw close to God when feelings of envy strike. Ask the Lord to remove envious feelings and replace them with feelings of gratefulness. Mirror Paul's contentment in all circumstances, his "It's all good" attitude. Parents want to give their children the desires of their hearts. So does God. He always listens and provides what He knows is best. Look for joy in the small things of life. When we start to count, the blessings multiply.

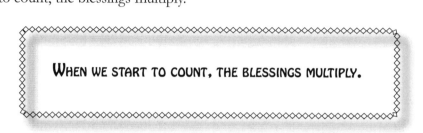

WHEN WE START TO COUNT, THE BLESSINGS MULTIPLY.

LOVE NOTES ON CONTENTMENT

LORI WRITES: I'll be the first to admit, and Tom would second this, I want my kids to have something if they *really* want it. It takes a lot of self-control to firmly stick to a budget when I take them shopping. If I don't leave the house with a plan in place and a determination to stick to it, I'm an envy and entitlement enabler.

BECKY WRITES: What am I envious of? Just to name a few: 20-20 vision, mathematicians, and racecar drivers. I wish I could see better, calculate correctly, and drive faster. I know… surgery, practice, and a racetrack -- not the highway. Truly, envy makes me focus on things other than God, not a good place to be.

QUESTIONS

1. How can you assist your child in counting his blessings as opposed to coveting the talents and possessions of others?

2. Characterize your children's relationships. What can you do to foster a healthy, lasting relationship between your children?

3. How do you model honesty?

PARENTING TIPS

1. Promote sibling relationships by avoiding comparisons and playing favorites.

2. Encourage your child to congratulate another child for an accomplishment.

3. Provide opportunities for your child to do "above and beyond chores."

PRAYER

Heavenly Father,

You are the giver of all good things. You provided Your Word so I can learn about You and teach my children about You. I confess I'm often ungrateful for what You've given me. I'm envious of the possessions, status, and accomplishments of others. Please forgive me. I thank You for the many blessings You've so abundantly provided for my family. Help me to be content with what I have and thankful for Your lavish provision. Help me to pass along this attitude to my children. Fill me with Your Spirit of appreciation and contentment.

In Your generous name I pray,

Amen

BUT GODLINESS WITH CONTENTMENT IS GREAT GAIN.
FOR WE BROUGHT NOTHING INTO THE WORLD, AND
WE CAN TAKE NOTHING OUT OF IT.

1 Timothy 6:6-7

Chapter 4

Choose Humility

Love ... does not boast, it is not proud.

1 Corinthians 13:4

It's All About Me

"Our Father, who art in heaven, hallowed be *my* name, *my* kingdom come, *my* will be done..." When my (Becky) youngest son first learned the Lord's Prayer, he misunderstood the word "thy." It's not preschool vocabulary. Scott and I would chuckle at the innocent pronoun mistake. If you think about it, his prayer accurately captures the human condition. We really do live in an *all about me* world.

Pride, like envy, begins to grow when we demand our own way or assume we are better than others. While envy thinks someone else has it better, pride believes, "I am better." Pride means we want to be noticed for accomplishments or attractiveness, hoping to foster envy in another. Pride seeks to elevate status and create jealous desire for that status in others.

Humility, on the other hand, is the lack of sinful pride. It's the attitude, "We're all in this together." Credit is honestly given or deflected to others. Humility is the virtue that draws people together; it's a cousin to kindness. Pride is in all of us. In tackling the issue of sinful pride in our families, we'll take a look at ourselves and learn to encourage and value humility in our kids.

78

WALKING IN PRIDE

Paul cautions, "Do not think of yourself more highly than you ought, but rather think of yourself with sober judgment" (Romans 12:3b-c). Boasting and pride go hand in hand; it is more than healthy confidence. Boasting is full-blown pride in self--and self alone.

You know the look, the one we gave or received in our teen years. (Even if you didn't experience it, you know what I'm describing.) The haughty eyes, the tilt of the head, the not-so-subtle glance that says, "I'm better than you." This look brings back that awful feeling of inadequacy.

A mom told of her daughter's dismay in not getting a leading role in the school play. "She studied for the part and didn't get it. The disappointment was bad, but the actions of the girl who got the part were worse. It's all she talked about: how fabulous she was at the audition, how she deserved the role, how she knew she would be chosen." It felt like she was rubbing the daughter's nose in her success.

While Becky described this mean-spirited situation, it struck me how this difficult and disappointing time was an opportunity. When going through difficult and even hurtful times, the heart can become soft and pliable, if handled gently. This young girl on the receiving end of another's prideful actions could see how hurtful boasting can be. Through this event she could develop empathy for others who might find themselves in a similar spot. Proper timing and words of compassion must envelop the discussion. If the daughter were able to gain empathy and swallow her own pride by saying a gracious, "Congratulations," she might discover the bragger holds less power over her own disappointment. Not getting the part in a play is a bummer, but it's only a momentary disappointment. Developing graciousness and empathy in our kids will last a lifetime.

God gives us many lessons on the detriment of pride in the Bible. Few are as poignant as the story of Nebuchadnezzar, the braggadocios king of Babylon, and Daniel, a humble Hebrew captive. The prideful ways of the king are compared to the God-glorifying ways of Daniel. This account, found in the book of Daniel, is worth noting personally and sharing with our kids because the principle holds true today. We possibly have more in common with Nebuchadnezzar than Daniel. I've (Becky) often told myself, "I deserve this." God has taught me that when I think I'm all that, I'm really not. When I act like it's all about me, I will fall. Pride comes before the fall, and fall I will.

MIRROR, MIRROR

Achievement in the arts, academia, and athletics can stir pride. Appearance is another trouble spot for pride. But it only counts if someone else notices our success or beauty.

How many mirrors do you have in your home? I (Lori) counted ours. Including handheld mirrors, mirrors over dressers, bathroom mirrors, and decorative mirrors, my house contains an embarrassing sixteen. That excessive number answers the question, "Where is my focus?" Apparently, my household is more externally focused than I'd like to admit.

Our attention is often geared to things more external in nature. We compare and boast about our bodies or physical appearance. We're competitive, comparing the skinniest, the strongest, the tallest, the best looking, etc. This competition leads to unhealthy diets, steroid use, and elective surgeries. Teens are even getting plastic surgery for graduation gifts. "In 2006, procedures performed on kids ages 13 to 19 totaled 244,124, including about 47,000 nose jobs and 9,000 breast augmentations, according to the American Society of Plastic Surgeons (ASPS)."[8] Graduation gifts include breast augmentations, nose jobs, tummy tucks, liposuction, and teeth whitening. What's the underlying reason? Physical perfectionism. Parents want their kids to have the advantage, and kids want to be physically perfect.

Perhaps we send subtle messages, stressing value of truly unimportant things. I (Becky) was certain my son was colorblind. He consistently wore clothes that didn't match. It bothered me so much I was convinced there had to be a physiological reason. I took him to the doctor to have him screened for colorblindness. Really, who would put orange and red together? According to the doctor, "An eleven-year-old boy who doesn't care about being color-coordinated would." It turned out just as the doctor said. My child was perfectly able to distinguish colors. I decided not to worry about the mismatching.

"The LORD does not look at the things people look at. People look at the outward appearance, but the LORD looks at the heart" (1 Samuel 16:7b). God looks at the inside not the outside. He knows the heart. This doesn't mean parents can't assist a child in looking his best or address issues that make a child feel self-conscious. For example, braces can straighten a crooked smile and increase confidence. We should teach our children about healthy diet, skin care, and exercise. These fall under the category of self-care. Knowing how to care for themselves prepares our children to one day take care of someone else.

Many children, especially teens, struggle with self-image. They are often hypercritical of themselves. "Oh, I'm so dumb, ugly, skinny, fat…." Pride, the quality of being self-focused, isn't only manifested in bragging. It can show up in lamenting.

This is when being "your best self" doesn't feel good enough. Our culture tends to focus on the beautiful people. Many times magazines showcase these beautiful people, but their pictures are Photoshopped and airbrushed. Body figures and shapes impossible to copy can become an obsession. Anorexia and bulimia can be birthed from this fixation on perfection and control. *(Note: Eating disorders and the reasons for them are complex and need to be discussed with a doctor and a therapist.)*

Sometimes teens gain attention through their attempts to achieve physical perfection, and, for a short time, self-esteem rises. However, finding one's value in external changes is only a temporary way to increase self-worth; the satisfaction won't last. We want our teens to have a healthy sense of self-worth. This comes from knowing who they are in Christ. When a tween or teen becomes too self-focused and then feels a sense of defeat, it is time to remind them of who they are in God's eyes: adored, beloved, cared for, a conqueror, delighted in…and much more! Now those are true bragging rights. One pastor on Becky's and my 1 Corinthians 13 Parenting team reminds his tweens of their value daily. He prays blessings over them each night.

Even parents are prone to buying into the focus on the external. One mom expressed a concern about her daughter's figure.

"My daughter's getting chubby. What should I do?"

"What is your daughter's age?" I (Lori) asked.

"Twelve," was the reply. Prepubescent. Prior to a growth spurt or menstruation most kids are a little chubby. Often children first grow out then up. The mom and I discussed this growth pattern, and she felt more at ease.

Most parents are tuned into their kids' physical wellbeing. Good diet and regular exercise are the components to a healthy body. Unless your child's physician tells you otherwise, focus on healthy foods and activities rather than weight loss or gain.

Piercings and tattoos are in vogue right now. Both may be the result of a poor self-image or a desire to replicate Hollywood stars. It can be just an attraction to the "style". If your child is interested in pursuing any of these things, put on your Consultant cap and ask questions that will help you get to the heart of why the child wants the adornment: Why do you want the piercing? What result are you looking for after you get a tattoo? How will you feel about that piercing in a year, five years, ten years? The answers will give parents insight in determining the child's motivation. Is it fitting in, self-expression, or rebellion? This will help the parents decide whether to support or oppose a desired permanent body adornment. Hopefully, this will become a self-questioning technique used by the child when he turns eighteen and no longer needs parental permission to have a medical procedure.

One mom suggested that the child sketch the tattoo he may want a year prior to getting it. That would give the young adult twelve months to think about it. This is an excellent idea. The parent, as the Consultant, has not acted as an obstacle to the procedure but instead has encouraged delayed gratification, avoided the impulse action, and moved the child to think before making a physically permanent decision.

Just because it's legal to get a tattoo at eighteen doesn't mean it should happen. In Leviticus 19:28, God's people weren't permitted to get tattoos. Tattoos were permanent signs of apostasy and many pagans were tattooed. The focus of a person's beauty is to be internal not external. In 1 Corinthians 6:12, Paul states, "'Everything is permissible for me,' you say—but not everything is beneficial. 'Everything is permissible for me'—but I will not be mastered by anything." There is potential for tattoos and piercings to become addictions. One or two may lead to more. Be wise in advising your child. *Can* does not translate to *should*.

Sometimes the focus isn't on changing our bodies but on what drapes over them. Designer or name brand clothes are important to many kids, from elementary school through college. Before heading to the mall, be the Coach. Start a conversation regarding what type of style and cost is appropriate. As the Controller, specifically address the amount of skin and number of insignias displayed. If a company name or logo is important to parents, it most likely will be to children, too. Parents need to decide where they stand on the name brand craze.

1 Peter 3:4 states that a "gentle and quiet spirit" is unfading beauty. How can we encourage our kids to have a healthy self-image and a pleasing spirit? One technique is to avoid continually complimenting them on looks. It's especially important for a father to exercise caution when giving his children, particularly his daughters, attention for superficial things like appearance. Often children look to their father for direction. If the attention they receive from their dad is based solely on physical features, this will increase the kids' focus on looks. The messages we want to send need to promote the values we hold dear, such as being kind-hearted or patient, having a good sense of humor, or being a hard worker. Think of the virtues your family esteems. Those are the character traits that are worth calling to attention. Physical beauty is fleeting, but good character runs deep.

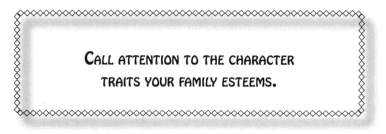

Court's in Session

A person's character is shown in how he acts in competitive situations. Both pride and humility can be observed in athletic, musical, artistic, or academic competition. I (Lori) attended a high school state tennis tournament where, of course, there were winners and losers. What stood out to me was the graciousness or lack of it in the winning and losing. In one match the loser became very upset and wasn't able to shake the winner's hand. Rather than leave with dignity, he chose to hurl insults. Following the game, a reporter, having knowledge of this player's behavior, questioned the winner of the match about the incident. The athlete took the high road. He gave no words of condemnation, only empathy. He said he understood why his opponent was upset. "It was the state tournament, and it was his senior year," was the reply.

At the same event I saw another player win with grace. Each time his opponent made a point, he would say would say, "Good point. Nice shot." Winning or losing isn't the most important part of athletic competition; we win some, we lose some. But to win or lose with grace and humility demonstrates quality of character.

Share the Love

Good sportsmanship is revealed in any competitive circumstance; it doesn't have to be athletic. A good sport usually has a team or group mentality, sharing the spotlight and credit for success. "Honor one another above yourselves" (Romans 12:10b). Teams rarely win due to one star player. Most victories are the result of teamwork, each working with others toward a common purpose and doing his job to the best of his ability.

One band director was especially gifted at fostering this type of team spirit. She would debrief the band following every competition. She emphasized band unity and teamwork. She would acknowledge how all the individual band members worked as a unit. The result of setting this tone was a unified band. The musicians all believed, "We're in this together." Fostering a teamwork attitude is one way to encourage humility.

We can do this in our homes as well. Affirming group effort fosters graciousness and a spirit of unity. My (Becky) family lives in an old house with a big lawn. With mature oak trees dropping mountains of leaves and acorns, raking is a major chore. One fall day when the boys were tackling the yard work, I peeked out the window and saw only one kid on the job.

"Why is he working alone?" I fumed, assuming the other brother had ditched his duty. Marching out the door, I was ready to read the riot act to the AWOL brother.

"You're hard at it. Where's your brother?"

"He's in the garage looking for more bags," he said cheerfully. "I rake the leaves into piles. We both load the bags. Then he hauls them to the side of the garage." He gave his brother credit where credit was due. They had a system, an arrangement of congenial teamwork, both humbly assuming their duties. I was peeved with myself for assuming the worst, but I was pleased with their teamwork. (The yard looked great at the end of the day, too.)

THE COMPETITIVE EDGE

Society's theme of proudly touting personal success is the antithesis of a team mentality. Our society tends to emphasize individual performance. The cultural measuring stick of success and significance includes being or possessing the best of the best and then proclaiming it to whomever will listen.

Our kids are pushed to play hard, often practicing one sport year-round, including Sundays. Why is this? Is it motivated by pride? Thoughts of needing to be the best? Is there some need to win every game?

Sports and participation in them have become an all-encompassing endeavor. We are paying the price in terms of time, injury, and financial cost. Sometimes teams travel great distances for extended periods of time to compete. The lack of rotating sports and instead zeroing in on one sport has increased the incidents of child injuries such as stress fractures. Student athletes are experiencing injuries similar to pro athletes. Should kids be that competitive at an early age? This is a family choice. Knowing the pluses and minuses will help a family make an educated decision regarding the appropriate level of competition for their child. Having full knowledge of the financial sacrifice, injury potential, time commitment, and an understanding of diminished family time may or may not be problematic. Realize that most student athletes won't play in college, in the pros, or in the Olympics. Many won't receive a scholarship. For those who do get stipends, the amount may not equal the cost poured into the sport by the parents. If the child loves the activity and the noted issues aren't a concern, then there's no problem. If the family is a single-child family, it may not be an issue. Conflict is inevitable if there happens to be more than one child in the home. Don't misunderstand; performance and enjoyment are good. God calls us to finish well and to do all things for His glory, but He wants our best combined with a proper focus.

Any extra-curricular activity has potential to overtake a family, sometimes without anyone realizing it. Music, Scouting, the arts, sports, and even church activities are all excellent, yet time-consuming, activities. As parents, we need to ask ourselves a few questions.

1. Does my child *really* want to participate or is he doing it for me?
2. Am I living vicariously through my child?
3. Is the activity consuming too much time or money?
4. Is my child's life balanced?

By evaluating each individual child's goals and activities, we are better able to determine what to emphasize and what may not be worth the time.

Humility at Its Best

Parents may decide that full family support is necessary for one child's activity. One teenage girl described her discomfort when raising money for a mission trip to Guatemala. "It's not easy to come up with a list of people to ask for money. Then you actually have to ask them for money." The parents were uncomfortable, too. They were able to pay for the trip, but part of the learning experience was to live the life of a missionary, needing to develop financial support to fund the trip just as missionaries do. "My daughter couldn't solicit her friends, so we came up with a list of our friends. Asking for money was humbling for my daughter, my husband, and me." The daughter added, "It was a humbling experience for both the students asking for money and for the friends and family members donating. People are willing to buy candy bars and gift wrap for school fundraisers because they get something tangible in return. This was different. We were asking people to just give us money and prayer. They began to ask questions about the trip concerning the goals, logistics, and opportunities we would be experiencing. Through the curiosity of friends and family members, the Lord blessed me with the opportunity to share my faith by explaining our mission for the trip. In the end, I learned that God wasn't only humbling me and allowing me to share my faith while on the trip, he was revealing himself to people here at home as well."[9]

The goals of the trip were accomplished: planning, raising money, and delivering God's message to an impoverished part of the world. The experience also gave this teen and her family a beautiful lesson in becoming humble servants of the Lord.

Here Comes the Judge

Lori and I intimately understand the phrase, "Parenting keeps ya humble." Many moms and dads have come to our parenting classes with stories of children's extreme behavior and unwise choices. The parents feel hurt and confused, wondering why they're in this position when they've loved their kids, loved God, and given their best to both. These parents go on to describe a second wounding from fellow believers, even friends. They feel attacked and abandoned in their time of need. They feel shame and embarrassment in their situation. Sometimes in the Christian community, we don't leave room for the grace and mercy we've personally experienced through Jesus. Why do we do this to our brothers and sisters in Christ? We need a comrade in arms, not a judge.

When I was teaching, before I (Lori) had kids, I had great wisdom to impart to parents. When I became a parent, I thought, *I've got this down.* God had enough of that prideful attitude coming out of me. He's allowed me to fully experience real-life parenting. I didn't "have it down." As a family, we've gone through some challenging times. Some of those moments have been innocent suffering, some my doing, some my husband's, and some our children's. God can use the things we struggle with to help others.

Let's help each other out by speaking words of comfort rather than condemnation and truth without judgment. Everyone appreciates love and support.

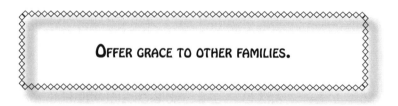

OFFER GRACE TO OTHER FAMILIES.

THE BEST MEDICINE

Laughing with another person is so much fun. Being able to laugh at oneself is a great quality. Life doesn't need to be so serious. When we take ourselves too seriously, pride is often the culprit. Raising kids in an environment where life can be more light-hearted and mistakes aren't the end of the world will promote humor in the home. Laughing together is great bonding.

A high school teacher was telling me (Lori) about the day a chair broke while my daughter was sitting in it. She landed bottom first on the classroom floor.

"Oh no! How embarrassing." She must have been mortified. Teens don't like to look foolish.

"She wasn't embarrassed at all. She was a good sport and laughed with the rest of the class."

I was glad to hear that. I thought of all the times I've done goofy things, and the kids and I have laughed. Looking for my keys while holding them, putting on a pair of sunglasses while I had another pair on my head, hitting the car alarm when I meant to unlock it. You get the idea.

Not making a big deal over things and being able to let down your guard by being a little silly is the light side of humility. This is the Chum at his best. Laughing at a situation or ourselves is good pride prevention. Laughter and love, these are two beautiful human experiences.

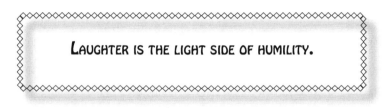

LAUGHTER IS THE LIGHT SIDE OF HUMILITY.

ONLY GOD DESERVES THE GLORY

We spend hours observing and coaching our children in their endeavors. From the first baby steps to the first chemistry test, we walk beside our kids. When they are little and they fall, we pick them up, dust them off, and encourage them to keep going. As they grow, we allow them to pick themselves up, shake off the dust, and persevere. Humble servants give God the glory, acknowledging that all that we can do and all that our children can do is because of what He has given and what we have chosen to do with those gifts.

So how is a Christian parent to teach a child to respond to a compliment without taking any of God's glory? Two words, "Thank you," often followed by, "I appreciate your encouragement. God is good!" In doing this, the encourager is affirmed and the receiver glorifies God.

Our God is holy. He is the One to receive praise. Bible study teacher Beverly Conaris said, "Once you touch the glory of God, your power is gone." Give Him the credit, and He'll give you the power to do the job for Him.

I (Becky) smile every time I see an NFL player hit his knees, bow his head, and point to the sky after scoring a touchdown. Why don't I do that for my successes? Maybe I'm too busy to notice or too selfish, thinking I did it all by myself. God is in control. The things I can do well are because He has given me what I need to do the job. The same is true for my children. The Lord uniquely prepares us for the journey, knowing exactly what we will need and when we'll need it. He knows before we know.

There will be a day when all pride will move aside, and on that day every knee will bow and every tongue confess that Jesus is Lord (Romans 14:11, Philippians 2:10-11). Until that day, be like the NFL player who hits the ground after a touchdown: point heavenward and give credit where credit is due. (Being a Tebow fan when he was a Bronco, I (Lori) picture Tim Tebow "Tebowing".)

Love Notes on Humility

Lori writes: Frankly, I struggle with pride. I don't care about designer stuff, but I sure have the corner on stubbornness. My pride prevents me from both forgiving and accepting help. It's about time this changed. I can see Tom cautiously nodding in agreement.

Becky writes: I have to admit, I like compliments. To hear, "Good job," "Great dinner, Mom," or "You look fabulous, Honey," elevates my mood. Does it make me proud? No. It makes me feel good. (Plus, Scott wakes up with me every morning: messy hair, no make-up…not pretty. Looking in the mirror can be a quick reality check.)

Questions:

1. What is your greatest area of pride? In what areas are your children prideful?

2. How can you develop a more humble attitude in yourself and your children?

3. What teachable moments concerning issues of pride have you experienced? How did you handle the situations?

PARENTING TIPS

1. Have a sense of humor when you could appear foolish.

2. Value good sportsmanship in your child both at home and on the field.

3. Encourage desirable character traits more than appearance, ability, or academics.

PRAYER

Lord Jesus,

Only You are King. You are sovereign over all things. Forgive me for thinking and acting like the world is all about me when it's all about You. I before You to worship Your holy name. I confess my stubborn pride. Please wipe me clean to be a vessel You can fill and use for Your glory. Help me to teach my children to be humble when they succeed. May my spouse, children, and I use the gifts and talents You have so graciously given us for Your glory. Amen

WHEN PRIDE COMES, THEN COMES DISGRACE, BUT WITH HUMILITY COMES WISDOM.

Proverbs 11:2

SECTION THREE

LOVE IS AN OUTWARD FOCUS

CHAPTER 5

CHOOSE RESPECT

LOVE IS NOT RUDE.

1 Corinthians 13:5a

SAY WHAT?

Teens and tweens appear to have a very limited memory when it comes to following through with a parental request or expectation. The words "I forgot" are spoken on a daily basis. The current brain research does support the "I forgot" excuse. If it's not important in the teenage world, the requests or expectations seem to vanish into thin air. Here's an everyday common sense reaction from two seasoned moms to the synapsed-challenged teens, *You can do it!* (I wanted to say, "Deal with it," but Becky wouldn't let me.)

"I can't get my kids to listen to me." Translation: "My kids don't do what I tell them to do." This is one of the most common complaints we hear in our parenting classes.

Other forms of disrespect are big sighs, huffing, rolling eyes, tongue clicking (mostly tweens), and hands on hips. The young person's nonverbal displays can reduce a parent to the same level.

Have you noticed rudeness has become socially acceptable, even justified? We experience impoliteness on a daily basis both in and out of our homes. Our kids deal with incivility constantly in the crowded school corridors: pushing, bumping, and shoving. This constant exposure to rudeness creates immunity to it.

Being polite, punctual, and complaint-free (or at least reduced) are ways to show respect in the home. When anger comes in the form of the silent treatment, guilt, power struggle, or a surprise attack we feel "dissed." Rather than doling out or accepting crass behavior, let's respond with and expect respect. Let's start by addressing parental behavior and then discuss training our children to be respectful. Being created in God's image is worthy of r-e-s-p-e-c-t.

If Looks Could Kill

Remembering that each person is created in God's image should make an impact on how we live. I (Lori) often forget that the person who has cut me off in traffic is made in God's image. This concept should transform the way I react to people, even in busy traffic.

"Whoever has haughty eyes and a proud heart, him will I not endure" (Psalm 101:5b). Uh, oh. This verse shakes me to the core. I've been the giver and receiver of haughty eyes. Proverbs 6:16-19 lists things the things God hates. On the top of the list are haughty eyes, which are a reflection of a prideful heart. When I've been angry with my children, I have had haughty eyes. When my kids were little they dubbed this "The Mad Face." Now it's just known as "The Look." My facial expression is often followed by someone saying, "Mom, relax." (Grrrr....)

A while back, my mom, who has been married to my dad for more than fifty years, gave me a tip. She told me, "When I feel irritable, I go and give your father a kiss. I do this for me. That kiss changes me."

Let's relate my mom's advice to being a parent. When I'm really frustrated with one of my kids, I deliver my comment with respect and love (remembering this child is created in God's image) by first saying, "I love you very much. I try to treat you with respect. I feel disrespected when you (fill in the blank)." When I start this way, my comment is better received and a resolution comes more swiftly. One small act or word of love changes hearts--my kids' and mine.

The Surprise Attack

Nasty looks are overt. They don't often come as a surprise since they are usually the result of anger. Surprise attacks, on the other hand, come out of the blue. Life interactions can be going well when all of the sudden, zing.

Picture this, a parent having a nice conversation with his teen. Both enjoying a meal together. The teen is letting down his guard and allowing the parent into his world. He's telling about a recent time when he demonstrated some good judgment. Then suddenly the parent hits him with, "You aren't all that smart. Last week you made a really bad choice when you decided to hang out with Melinda." That's the surprise attack. This type of pattern causes mistrust in a relationship.

It's hard to feel safe if the person you love lashes out when time together is going well. It's difficult to feel secure when the person you've trusted with personal struggles or private information suddenly uses it as a weapon.

When we use the surprise attack, we foster a closed spirit in the person we attack. A teen with a closed spirit shares little to nothing. He has learned that sharing isn't safe and that shared thoughts can come back to bite him. By keeping short accounts, addressing situations as they occur, relational frustrations will be reduced.

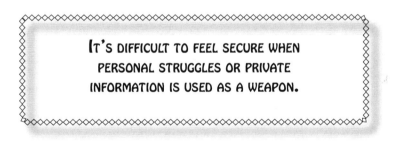

It's difficult to feel secure when personal struggles or private information is used as a weapon.

The Guilt Trip

Being honest and direct is much less confusing than attempting to gain cooperation through guilt. The guilt from the Holy Spirit that tweaks our conscience is good. This message is a result of God speaking directly regarding a choice, behavior, thought, or feeling. Hopefully, the conviction moves to correction. But guilt can be twisted. Being stuck in guilt, frozen with it, controlled by it are all ways guilt can be damaging. Our Father forgives as far as the east is from the west (Psalm 103:12). Let's follow the Father's example.

The exaggerated Controller uses guilt to manipulate kids. Kids mirror the behavior, "Everyone else gets to go, why can't I?" Or the parent may say, "Your sister doesn't act like that." These words drip with shame. Using "I" statements—phrases that begin with, "I feel…" or "I think…"—will typically help avoid instilling guilt and will assist in eliminating the temptation to use guilt to control behavior. "I" statements don't leave us wondering what someone really meant. When noticing a sink of full of dishes, state, "I see the sink is full of dirty dishes. I feel discouraged since I just cleaned the kitchen. What's the plan to take care of this?" Versus, "Wow! No one seems to care about how hard I work." Guilt causes confusion. If we say what we mean and mean what we say, there will be fewer misunderstandings and more cooperation.

BLAH, BLAH, BLAH

Effective and efficient communication leaves little room for confusion, and it paves the way for cooperation. Message repetition is irritating for both the speaker and receiver. "I've told you a thousand times. Do I have to repeat myself again?" The teen or tween responds with, "Huh?" to these questions. Becky and I have a solution for this round robin of frustration. Say it once. That's it. Once. Think of it this way: It's disrespectful to repeat the instruction a tenth, fourth, or even a second time.

The responses you hear when you repeat instructions could sound like, "You already told me," or "I know," or "I get it!" If your child verbalizes these statements, what he has heard is, "You aren't smart enough to get it the first time." Whether you mean to communicate that or not, it's implied.

Of course, sometimes the child has been trained to wait for the fifth time before he thinks the parent means business. So adult retraining needs to happen first. Say it, leave it, and wait. If the child isn't able to follow through with the given direction, continue to wait. This can be hard, but persevere. When you hear a request such as, "Can I use the car?" The next step is to use a follow-up line such as, "Sure, once the dishwasher is unloaded." Or another version, "I would love to say yes. Are all your jobs completed?" Two more options are: "Yes, when…" or "After you _____, you can _____." Stay positive and leave the responsibility with the child. We want our kids to know they are both lovable and capable.

This scenario has played out in our (Becky) house:

"The garbage needs to be taken out," I stated to my son.

"Okay, Mom, in a minute." More than a minute elapsed. The trash was still in the bin.

When dinnertime rolled around, everyone converged around the kitchen table, ready to eat.

"When the garbage is out, you're welcome to join us for dinner," I whispered to the "I'll do it in a minute" kid. It's amazing how fast a hungry boy can take out the trash. It has taken me a while, but I've learned to say it once and then use a follow-up line later if necessary. He knows he's capable of getting the job done, and he will only be asked once.

SAY IT, LEAVE IT, WAIT.

WAH, WAH, WAH

Guarding our own mouths will be helpful in training our kids to be careful with theirs. It's always easier to see what we don't like rather than what we do. It would be difficult to work in a complaint department. I sure don't want to *live* there. The Bible tells us, "Do everything without complaining or arguing" (Philippians 2:14). Complaining is disrespectful. Dialoguing with kids about their frustrations assists them in moving toward a solution.

A CONSULTANT ASKS:
1. What can you do to change the situation?
2. What action can you take now to improve the situation?
3. What have you learned?

These questions steer the complainer toward a resolution. Encourage your complainer to do a complaint fast. Here's how it's done:

1. Begin by asking God to forgive your complaining spirit.
2. Ask Him to help you stop the obnoxious habit of complaining.
3. Then repent from complaining when it happens.[10]

The success of the complaint fast will be determined by the obedience you demonstrate when the desire to complain rises in you. Have your child make an effort to substitute complaining words with positive words. It's worth a try. Nobody wants to live with a complainer.

MSA

Do you speak tween? You know, communication that comes in the form of mumbling, a condescending tone, and big sighs. Add to that the favorite word, "whatever," or the favorite phrase, "That is SO annoying." In our (Lori) home this is known as MSA (middle school attitude). How should we parents deal with MSA? Before we can deal with it, we need to acknowledge a basic turning point for parents: we lose our "cool." Recognize that you aren't hip like you were when your kids were younger—and that's okay.

I remember the day it happened at our house. Our tween-aged son wanted to change from briefs to boxers.

My husband agreed, and then inquired, "What's going to happen to the tightie-whities?"

"I'll get rid of them."

"You're getting rid of perfectly good underwear?"

This question was followed by peals of laughter from our son and his sisters. I told my husband, "Today is the day we've lost our 'cool.'"

After accepting your un-cool state, you need to readjust your thinking. If the MSA results in out-and-out defiance or disrespect, you must deal with the problem. Start by asking the child to restate the question or response with a respectful attitude. Keep the end goal in mind, and train and retrain as needed. Don't focus on the offense.

Young people tend to speak authoritatively, and they often think the adult's input is pretty lame. Most teens discount parental ideas and disregard sound advice. A father of two teens said he's only going to hire teenagers at his office since teens know everything. Funny. This attitude is developmental; don't take it personally. Unless a child is flat-out defiant or disrespectful, let it go.

Reinforce positive rather than negative traits. A tween or teen may need to go to his room to think about how he can communicate respectfully. Have him think about how he will talk differently next time, "When I communicate my ideas to my parents, I need to speak in a respectful tone," rather than replaying what he did wrong, " I am grounded because I spoke disrespectfully and rolled my eyes at my mom." This helps to reinforce the trait you want instead of reinforcing the negative trait. This training works well if the teen has an open, moldable spirit. Teens are generally capable of coming up with appropriate verbiage. When disrespect enters the conversation, have the child restate his comments with respect.

First said with disrespect: "I'm using the car. You're just going to hang out and do nothing anyway."

Restated with respect, "I'm sorry, here's how I should have asked, "May I borrow the car?"

MSA on Steroids

However, if the child has a closed spirit, characterized by anger, defiance, or defensiveness, the restating approach will backfire. It will only teach him how to be manipulative, like the proverbial Eddie Haskell. A defiant child is the kid with MSA on steroids. If the child has the attitude, "You're bugging me," that isn't a major issue. If the attitude seems to state, "I hate you. I don't want to talk with you. I don't really want to be a part of this family," the child is controlling the family with his moods. Kevin Leman recommends the "bread and water treatment."[11] Stop all perks such as paying for things and driving him places without warning. After the child notices the perks have ceased, Leman says this is the teachable moment. Say, "It seems like you want to drop out of the family, so that's the way it'll be for a while.

99

Being a member of this family has some perks, I think, but you've got to live your life the way you want to live it. I can't force you to do things, but there will be changes in how the family will function."[12] Dr. Leman's method works especially well for tweens and teens. But he does warn that things will get worse before they get better.

If this approach makes you feel uncomfortable and disrespectful, you probably don't have a young person ruling the roost with his attitudes and actions. This strategy is only for the parent of a highly defiant child. For the parent struggling with this heart-breaking and exhausting situation, this technique is effective but often difficult to implement. So hang in there.

Living with a tween or teen in full-blown rebellion is painful for the entire family. Often, the parent closest to the child bears the brunt of the verbal or physical abuse. This leaves the parent feeling betrayed and deeply wounded. In coaching parents in troubling times, I (Lori) have found a few basic guidelines to be helpful. First, parental unity is critical. Dad must act as Mom's protector. "My wife, your mother, is deserving of respect and you will not speak that way to her." Referring to the marital relationship first demonstrates the family hierarchy. Mom must back up Dad's ultimate decision. "I'm in agreement with my husband, your father." This tactic creates an impenetrable force of two leading the family. The way the child responds will dictate the outcome: If he threatens to leave, say, "We love you and want you to stay. If you leave, you go with the clothes on your back. (No family property goes with the child.) If you decide to stay, respect is nonnegotiable." If your child does take off, is under eighteen, and you want that child home, you can call the police. The child can be listed as a run-away and be brought back home by law enforcement when he's found. (Be forewarned, there is the risk that the teen will be arrested.) If there has been a physical altercation and the parents so choose, charges can be pressed. It may be that having this child removed from the home is the best way to go. A volatile situation needs to be considered carefully. There is no perfect formula. All the decisions you and your spouse make need to take into account what is best for the family unit not just the individual causing the problems. Seek help and support from a pastor or trusted counselor.

MANNERS COUNT

Respect is shown in good manners. As our children grow, we tend to be more lax in this area. It's still important to encourage our young adults to say the "magic words" and to write thank you notes. In Paul's letter to the church in Corinth he expresses his appreciation. "I always thank my God for you" (1 Corinthians 1:4a). Honoring people and their acts of services or gifts is important in developing a grateful heart.

When my (Lori) kids were younger, my husband and I told our children, "The person is more important than the gift." We still use that strategy today. "Wow, your uncle made a DVD for you. Think of all the time and effort he put into your gift. You must be pretty special to him." Verbalize the gift-giving scenario to allow your young person to see the love behind the action and to encourage the development of a thankful heart. Reinforce the relationship between the gift giver and receiver through the lost art of a thank you note. Young and old alike ought to acknowledge another's thoughtfulness and generosity. One mom told me she discovered her son's unfinished graduation thank you notes hidden under his bed. When this young man returned home for his fall college break, he had a job to complete. Expressing appreciation acknowledges the giver's service or gift.

Thankfulness can be expressed in actions as well as words. Our (Lori) family spends a lot of time at my parents' cabin in northern Minnesota. We demonstrate thankfulness by mowing the lawn, doing the dishes, and cleaning. This behavior says, "Thank you," in a tangible way.

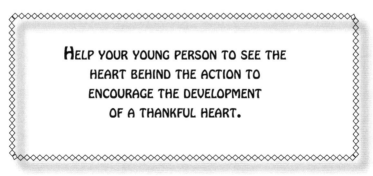

HELP YOUR YOUNG PERSON TO SEE THE HEART BEHIND THE ACTION TO ENCOURAGE THE DEVELOPMENT OF A THANKFUL HEART.

I'm Late, I'm Late!

Being punctual also falls into the politeness category. Tardiness can be an issue for school-aged children, but the greater the age, the bigger the problem. High schools and middle schools deal harshly with lateness. Coaches are famous for punishing late arrivals. Unfortunately, I (Lori) know this because I tend to run late, and my kids have suffered the consequences. If you are like me, make strides to be on time. However, if the child is to blame, allow the natural consequences to play out rather than covering for the teen.

"Mom, just call the school office and excuse me for being tardy." This would have been an easy solution from my already-running-late daughter.

"What am I going to say? You will be arriving late? I don't think that will be acceptable." I feigned confusion.

"You want me to get a tardy mark on my record?" My commitment to honesty was being tested.

"No, but I can't make up an excuse either. What do you want to do?" As the Consultant, I threw the ball back in her court.

"Ah! I guess I will just be marked tardy since you won't excuse me." Clearly annoyed, she tried to toss the blame in my direction.

"Have a great day. See ya later," I disengaged.

Because this child cared about her school record, that was the first and last time we had that dilemma. Most high schools have a late policy enforced by after-school detention or in-school suspension. Experiencing the fallout of tardiness is tough, but it teaches a valuable lesson.

Dirty Dancing

Punctuality demonstrates respect, respect for another person. We tend to think of respect more in terms of how we treat another human being. Equally important is self-respect how we present ourselves, treat ourselves, and talk about ourselves. A lack of self-respect gives others permission to treat us disrespectfully.

We want to honor other people, just as we want others to respect us. Our behavior often dictates how others respond to us. When kids respect themselves, they generally are treated with respect.

A few years ago, I was in Mexico with my newly graduated daughter. The two of us, along with her friends and their families, went to the hotel's discotheque so the girls could go dancing. I noticed a couple almost "honeymooning" on the dance floor. One of the older brothers in the group noticed my expression and said, "Yes, the dancing is *highly* inappropriate!" He got a good chuckle over my culture shock.

Sexual dancing is very public and socially acceptable today. Even stripper poles have entered the mainstream dance and exercise scene. This type of display demeans both girls and boys, objectifying their bodies. One mom said her son was invited to a graduation party, paid for and supervised by the graduate's parents, where a stripper pole was included as part of the "fun". Unbelievable!

The grind, juking, or twerking are popular teenage dance moves, way beyond the Bump of the '70s. Ask your daughter how she will deal with a young man who approaches her from behind and wants to grind. A couple of tactical actions are to grab both hands that the boy has placed on her hips and throw them down, then walk away. Another idea is to remove the boy's hands from her hips, continue to hold onto one, turn around and face the boy and dance face to face without grinding. A third reaction is to grab one hand and lead the boy off the dance floor and get a soda while explaining that grinding isn't her thing. None of these responses will feel easy or comfortable, but they're effective.

Surprisingly, young girls are often the initiators of this dance. If you have a son, he also needs training on how to respond to a girl grabbing his hands and placing them on her hips. Show him how to twirl her around so she is facing him or grab her hand and walk off the dance floor to get a beverage or to talk. This is a difficult position for a young man in which to find himself. Use positive prevention by talking about common scenarios. Help your young person be proactive.

"Therefore, prepare your minds for action; be self-controlled" (1 Peter 1:13a).

Grinding, freak dancing, or juking are not the only way kids can dance. Becky told me about a proactive and creative principal in Minnesota. The slogan "Dance like Grandma's Watching"[13] accompanies videos created to remind students that grinding is not okay for school dances. The purpose is to establish a new culture with new rules. Some schools are now offering dance classes as a way for kids to learn "new moves." Parents can enroll their kids in a ballroom dance class or have them participate in Cotillion. Let's support our kids and schools by suggesting programs such as these.

The human body is a temple of the Holy Spirit, worthy of respect. We respect ourselves by expecting respect.

We show respect to others by the way we speak to them and about them. The same holds true for our respect for God. Do you use the Lord's name in vain or casually use "omg" as a part of your family's vocabulary? Using "Jesus" as an expression of surprise or displeasure has become commonplace. The third commandment requires us to respect God's name.

Once when my husband and I (Becky) checked the kids' text messages, we found one that included the abbreviation "omg." When questioned, the response was, "Mom, it means, *oh my gosh*." This was a time to discuss the holiness of the name of God as well as text messaging etiquette. Even if the phrase is common, it isn't appropriate.

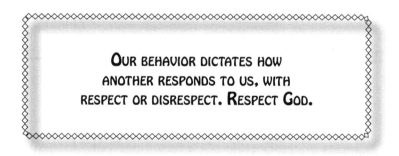

OUR BEHAVIOR DICTATES HOW ANOTHER RESPONDS TO US, WITH RESPECT OR DISRESPECT. RESPECT GOD.

THE 'TUDE

A respectful attitude is a choice. We can't change others, but we can change ourselves. A bad attitude is a bad habit. We've heard it said that attitudes aren't taught but caught. Proverbs 15:15b reminds us, "The cheerful heart has a continual feast."

Think of how you show respect for others through your words and actions. Teach your child to treat the waitress, clerk, cashier, grocery bagger, or others in the service industry with dignity and graciousness. Rude and disrespectful children grow into rude and disrespectful adults.

People are worthy of being treated respectfully simply because God created them. We honor God when we respect others with our words and actions. We show respect to God when we worship Him with our actions and praise Him with our words. Respect is outward focused; it's all about others. Wait, actually, it's all about God!

LOVE NOTES ON RESPECT

LORI WRITES: I've realized disrespect often creeps into our home due to an unrelated situation. When my kids are upset or frustrated by something else, their response to me can be tinged with a lack of respect. I can be guilty of doing this too. I've found the most effective response to a caustic attitude is to calmly state, "I show respect for you, and I expect the same in return." Usually an "I'm sorry" follows that statement.

BECKY WRITES: Scott and I have a phrase that follows a disrespectful remark made by our boys, "Say it again, respectfully." This has helped our kids learn to think before they speak. We will not put up with rudeness.

QUESTIONS

1. How do you demonstrate respect for family members?

2. How do you respond to disrespectful behavior from your young person as a Coach or Consultant?

3. Why is respect a loving behavior?

PARENTING TIPS

1. Say directives once.

2. Speak honestly, directly, and with grace when stating expectations or concerns.

3. Have your tween or teen restate disrespectful demands and responses.

4. Have the family participate in a complaint fast.

PRAYER

Father, Heavenly King,

I pray that out of my mouth come words that are tender and tactful. Please give me the sensitivity to anticipate how my words might be received. I desire to show respect to my spouse and my children. Help me see the positives and not focus on the negatives. Remind me to treat others the way I want to be treated. I want to communicate to my children that they are both capable and loved. Let our home be one that overflows with respect and love. Start with me.

Amen

RESPECT IS LOVE IN PLAIN CLOTHES.

Frankie Byrne[14]

CHAPTER 6

CHOOSE UNSELFISHNESS

LOVE IS NOT SELF-SEEKING.

1 Corinthians 13:5b

EGOMANIA

Recently I (Lori) witnessed a perfect example of selfishness. I was traveling alone by plane, it was open seating, and the flight was full.

"Would two people seated next to each other be willing to separate so a father and his six-year-old daughter can sit together?" The flight attendant's question was met with silence.

She asked the question one more time before saying, "Where's the love, people?"

Finally, a husband and wife raised their hands and offered their seats. Because I was unable to help in this situation, it's easy for me to pass judgment. I hope if I'd been flying with my husband, we would have relinquished our seats.

The slow reaction to the family's plight on the plane is typical today. We tend to weigh the personal cost of the sacrifice rather than care about another's predicament. While working on this book, it occurred to me that respect and unselfishness are closely linked. Both are outward-focused. In direct contrast is the self-seeker who looks out for Number One.

Sometimes our parental vision is skewed when we encounter difficult parenting situations. We see how each circumstance affects us rather than the possible reason for the child's behavior. The focus is entirely on me rather than my child. A wise, unselfish mom or dad seeks understanding and sensitivity to a child's needs. This parent realizes that his child is not an extension of himself but rather a unique individual complete with foibles.

When we're unselfish, we act with empathy rather than apathy in terms of relationships and resources. Becky and I know that people can't be selfless unless they themselves are in a place of wholeness. When true personal needs like security, belonging, respect, power, freedom, spirituality, and fun are met, we are filled and in a better position to serve others. Also, evaluating and modeling our own use of time and possessions will help our children be unselfish. Selfishness, manifested in child or adult, is the quality most detrimental to the family.

ACTING WITH EMPATHY RATHER THAN APATHY IS UNSELFISH.

ME, ME, ME!

"Live in harmony with one another, be sympathetic" (1 Peter 3:8b). Empathy is the ability to put self in someone else's shoes. How do we move from the natural bent of egocentric thought to selflessness? Let's face it, we may never get to that perfect altruistic state, but we can at least move in that direction by asking, "Am I loving my family members and other people in a way that I would want to be loved?" Pitching in without being asked, adjusting plans to accommodate another, or remembering a birthday are simple examples of ways to think of others.

I'm highly task-oriented, which is a good quality as an employee but not so good as a parent and wife. It's hard for me to look past my own agenda. Once I get started, it's difficult to stop until the task is completed. My husband has helped me to see how this can be destructive; he gently points out what I have not observed. My family had a busy weekend of sports and errands, yet I was anxious to help our daughter reorganize her room, even though she had a lot of homework. She'd stated clearly that the reorganization project should wait. She had too much work to do. Stubbornly, I went ahead and began hanging things on her wall. This was fun, at first. My husband and daughter even got into it. Unfortunately, this small project ended up expanding into closet cleaning and drawer organizing. My daughter was exasperated. She wanted to finish the room, yet she had mountains of homework. My husband saw her frustration and discussed this with me. My daughter had verbalized her needs, but I hadn't listened. I needed to put myself in her shoes to appreciate her priorities.

It's Golden

Treating others the way we want to be treated is the Golden Rule. Matthew 7:12a states, "So in everything, do to others what you would have them do to you." Choosing unselfishly to look at life from another's point of view combined with showing others proper respect will change the way we interact in our homes.

The paradigm shifts from "My child's behavior is upsetting or inconveniencing me" to "I wonder what is driving him to behave this way." Looking deeper for behavioral motivation is the long-term fix for the short-term annoyances in parenting.

"God created mankind in his own image" (Genesis 1:27a). Because each of us is made in God's image, we have the qualities of being rational, volitional (decision makers), relational, emotional, and spiritual. These characteristics generate legitimate needs in every individual. Being created to be rational, we need for others to treat us respectfully. The quality of volition brings out the individual's need for freedom and independence. We are innately geared for relationship, so each person needs to feel that he belongs. Our emotions are a reflection of God's. We need to know they are valid. We are even wired to laugh and have fun. God is spirit, and humans have a spiritual vacuum that must be filled. The needs of respect, freedom, belonging, fun, and spirituality all must be met in the context of relationship with God and fellow human beings.

We gain much insight into our kids when we examine their actions and reactions through the needs lens. Their behavior is the key to what needs are not being met.

Behavior is usually driven by need. Personality, developmental stage, and gender will influence the amount of need in each of the following six categories. Notice how being made in the image of God creates the following legitimate needs. These are needs that must be met in a godly way, or they will be filled in an ungodly, sinful way.

God's Image	Human Need Generated
Rational (God is logical, thinking)	Respect
Volitional (God has a will, is powerful, and independent)	Freedom
Relational (God is relational in the Trinity)	Security/Belonging/Love
Emotional (God has emotion)	Joy, Fun
Spiritual (God is spirit)	Spiritual Fulfillment

Your child will provide insight into needs that are lacking. Listen for the cues your child may give while speaking to you. The examples below are extreme cases where time after time a need is not met.

Child's Statement (Cue)	Translation	Ungodly Filling
"You treat me like a baby."	"I need respect."	selfishness, bossiness

Solution

Give the child more responsibility and an opportunity
for more independence. Be the Coach and Consultant.

Child's Statement (Cue)	TRANSLATION	UNGODLY FILLING
"You never let me choose."	"I need more freedom"	"I need more freedom"

SOLUTION

Allow your child to have more of a voice and a little more flexibility. Let him enter into some decision-making situations. Be the Coach.

Child's Statement (Cue)	TRANSLATION	UNGODLY FILLING
"You love _____ more."	"I need love."	sexual activity

SOLUTION

Spend more time with your child. Watch for ways that you may appear to be playing favorites. Be the Chum.

Child's Statement (Cue)	TRANSLATION	UNGODLY FILLING
"You never do what you say you will do."	"I need security."	anxiety

SOLUTION

Let your child know that no matter what, you will never leave him. Talk about and even post the day's schedule. If you promise something, be true to your word. Be the Controller.

Child's Statement (Cue)	Translation	Ungodly Filling
"You're always so serious."	"I need some fun."	risky behavior

Solution

Loosen up a bit. Go and have fun with your child.

Laugh. Be the Chum.

Child's Statement (Cue)	Translation	Ungodly Filling
"I can do it myself."	"I need respect/ freedom."	explosive anger

Solution

Resist the urge to take over. Let the child own the task

or project. Be the Consultant.

Child's Statement (Cue)	Translation	Ungodly Filling
"I'm interested in horoscopes."	"I need the Holy Spirit"	dabbling in the occult

Solution

Play worship music. Talk to you child about spiritual

things. Pray together. Be all four!

Have a conversation. Ask your child what would help fill the lacking need.

- State the observed problem:
- ♥ "You mentioned I (treat you like a baby)."
- ♥ Ask what he thinks can be done to fix the issue:
- ♥ "What can I do to correct this so you feel more (respected)?"

Chances are good the tween or teen will want more than you feel ready to give. Together arrive at a solution, one that fits within your family value system.

Watch for the things the child is drawn to naturally. Consider if a need isn't being met, resulting in discontent. There is potential for the hole to be filled in a counterfeit or an illegitimate way. If a child is drawn to horror novels or movies, it's possible he's looking to fill a spiritual need. If the child *always* has to have a boyfriend or girlfriend, it could be the belonging or love need hasn't been satisfied. One mom reflected on her teen's pregnancy, "I guess she needed love. She got pregnant hoping the baby would fill that emptiness." If we are students of our tweens and teens, we will be able to identify the depleted need. Then we can help them replace the negative substitution with a God-honoring filling; add prayer to this replacement approach to strengthen the strategy. Pray for the child's mind and eyes to be renewed and to see a better choice.

Young people are motivated to behave a particular way in order to feel whole. If the parent is able to look past the behavior, he may be able to see a child who is seeking respect, freedom, security, love, fun, or spirituality. Each child is in the process of developing as a person. Behavior that tests the water such as hair and clothing styles, messy rooms, and music choices are usually not problematic. But you know your child, and if something elevates your concern, look into it. Home should be a place where each kid is free to be who he is, warts and all. Belonging to a family and being accepted are basic needs.

Home should be the safe haven. The social, emotional, and physical climate of the culture is shifting as quickly as the child is changing. The child needs a place to feel safe and secure. One mom described to me (Becky) her son's transition from elementary school to middle school. During this turbulent time, her son called home his sanctuary. Don't we all want our children to see home as a place of peace, security, and belonging?

God is the ultimate One to meet and fill human needs. We all need to take our eyes off ourselves and keep them open to notice the kids' needs. Be on the lookout for possible counterfeit fillings, and be ready to assist the kids in finding God-honoring ways to meet those innate needs.

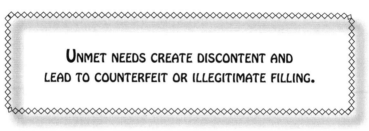

UNMET NEEDS CREATE DISCONTENT AND LEAD TO COUNTERFEIT OR ILLEGITIMATE FILLING.

His Needs, Not Mine

To determine if an action or inaction is self-centered, we need to examine our motivation. While writing this book, I (Becky) was given an opportunity to practice what I preach. My husband and I feel strongly that we should volunteer in our children's activities. Not only do we feel a sense of duty, but also we really enjoy being involved in our boys' lives.

A student ministries staff member called to see if I would be interested in helping with the eighth-grade Commitment Class. A couple of years earlier, I volunteered in my oldest son's class. It meant a lot to me to play even a small part in his church experience. My first impulse was to say, "Yes!" again. But I resisted my urge and decided to run the idea past my eighth-grader.

"How do you feel about me helping with your Commitment Class this year? Would you like me to be there?"

"Mom, you always volunteer for everything. I think I want to do this one on my own."

Initially, I felt a little deflated. I wanted to be a part of this special time. But I honored his desire to go through the class on his own. Saying no to volunteering met my son's needs for freedom and respect.

Remain sensitive to God's leadership to be wise about participation and volunteering in your kids' extra-curriculars. Be selective and pray about volunteer opportunities that involve or revolve around the young person. Before saying yes or no, take the tween or teen's needs into consideration.

THE CALENDAR

Busyness takes a spiritual, emotional, and physical toll. One day I (Lori) was frantically shuttling my four kids to three different activities, hurrying home in between drop-offs and pick-ups to make dinner. I picked up my fifteen-year-old from band, dropped my thirteen-year-old son off at football, and then left the two younger girls at a horse stable to wait for their riding instructor. Normally, I would not leave my twelve- and ten-year-old girls in the barn without their teacher present, but she typically ran late and I was busy. My oldest child needed to get home to start her homework, and I had to get dinner going. I was confident the teacher would arrive momentarily. Shortly after I got home, the phone rang.

"Mom, our instructor never showed up."

How could the teacher have spaced out the riding lesson? I was upset with myself for leaving my girls alone in the barn. I picked them up and drove straight to the riding instructor's home. Firmly and rapidly, I knocked on her door.

"You didn't show up for the lesson. The girls were in the barn waiting for you."

"What?" Her confusion was followed by, "Their lesson is next week."

Whoops, my mistake. I assumed the problem was someone else's fault. Aside from my obvious pride problem, the main issue was we were over-programmed.

My family isn't the only one that struggles with the overscheduled mode. Becky and her gang found they have a similar problem. She came up with a solution that works well in her home. Becky color-codes her calendar. Each family member has a different color for daily activities and appointments.

As a family, the Danielsons decided to add a fifth color. This additional color identified their family priorities: church, Bible study, dates, and family fun nights. This plan has made their household schedule easier to manage and they have found their calendar better reflects their family values. The calendar is now under control.

WALK THE TALK

In freeing up our time from activities that don't reflect our priorities, we have more opportunity to slow down, experience less stress, and help out another. God gives parents many opportunities to demonstrate unselfish and empathic actions. Unfortunately, we often don't take Him up on it.

My heart has always hurt when driving past a homeless person. I want to show my children how to love, but I feel conflicted. You might ask the same questions. Do I give this man money? Do I ignore him? Do I continue on my way then feel guilty the rest of the day? How would I like my children to respond to someone in a difficult circumstance? What does God want me to do?

I received an answer to one of my questions a few years ago. Hopefully, this will help you, too. Jeff Johnsen, director of Denver Mile High Ministries and Joshua Station, alternative housing for those who would otherwise be homeless, gave this great advice: "When driving past the person flying a sign on the corner, most of us struggle to know the right thing to do. But the place to start is to recognize their humanity, and that their day's pursuits matter as much to God as do your own. And it sure won't hurt to make eye contact, wave, or even smile."[15]

Listen to the Lord, and He will move you if you're to go beyond just acknowledgment.

Sometimes a small and easy gift can be a blessing to someone in need. Becky's family stashes gift certificates to local fast food restaurants in the visor of the car. They write a message of encouragement, include a Bible verse, and paste the note inside the packet of gift certificates. Their goal is to nourish the body and the soul of the recipient. Her boys are able to reach out the car window to deliver a practical reminder of God's love to the person on the street.

HONOR IN SERVICE

Teaching our kids to honor God by meeting someone else's needs is critical in developing unselfishness. Many churches have programs where older kids can take part in a life-changing mission trip. Local soup kitchens and homeless shelters provide opportunities for families to serve together closer to home.

An experience of service and gratitude happened at a soup kitchen not long ago. After serving a hot meal, volunteers were encouraged to eat dinner with the guests. My (Becky) boys filled their plates and headed to a table with a family who had kids about their ages. They sat down and started talking. A few minutes into the conversation, they realized the young man seated next to them was not part of the group. As he was drawn into a conversation, he told the boys how great this night was and how much he'd been looking forward to this dinner. He explained how he carefully kept track of the nights this particular church was open for dinner because it was the only time he ever had a hot evening meal.

"Why? Doesn't your mom cook dinner for you?" my son asked.

"Nope, she's either drunk or high when I get home from school. I make my own dinner when there's food in the kitchen."

He thanked them and was out the door. The church was a haven for that young boy. For him, dinner was a delicacy, being served was a luxury, and experiencing the love of Christ was a comfort. My boys have been moved to pray for this young man. God has grown their compassion and thankfulness through this experience.

We don't have to go downtown to serve others. A kind word to a tired spouse, an offer to shovel the elderly neighbor's sidewalk, or a sibling offering to help with math homework is service in the eyes of God. Serving others is our response to God's grace and everlasting love. It should be a way of life, "just as the Son of Man did not come to be served, but to serve" (Matthew 20:28a). When we care for someone else, God smiles.

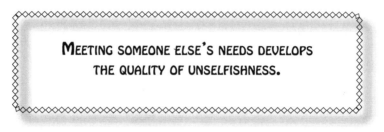

MEETING SOMEONE ELSE'S NEEDS DEVELOPS
THE QUALITY OF UNSELFISHNESS.

TIGHT-FISTED OR OPEN-HANDED?

Often we are asked to serve others or make a monetary contribution to a cause. Not everyone can be a missionary, but many can contribute to the mission. If we're discerning with the money the Lord has blessed us with, we'll be more likely to be generous with it. Saving money, giving money, and spending money wisely are the components of money management. The way in which those three disciplines are handled tells us a lot about an individual. Wildly and haphazardly spending or selfishly hoarding are both unhealthy ways to handle money. While teaching our kids to be generous givers, we also need to train them to be wise spenders and savers. The lessons will pay off when our young people go off to college or move out of the house. Kirk Weaver of Family Time Training shares these three ideas in money management for tweens and teens.

1. Talk with your children about the *who, what, where, when, why, and how* of your giving.
2. Help your child understand budgets, balance a checkbook, manage debt, and use money to help others.

3. Experience giving by going on a mission trip, deliver meals to friends who are in need, or bring food to a homeless shelter.

Kirk goes on to say, "Giving is important to Jesus, and he calls us to be givers. The Bible includes 500 verses on prayer and 500 verses on faith but more than 2,000 verses on money and possessions."[16] Those verses are often accompanied by a warning like, "Watch out." Attitudes about money are often inherited, so we must be aware and be intentional.

House Rules

Attitudes are seen in our actions. House rules can enforce unselfish behavior. Selfish people are cavalier about other people's possessions and don't like to share their own. If we want our kids to be unselfish and respectful, we should implement some basic standards. First, the borrower must ask prior to using or taking someone else's things. Then follow these common sense principles:

♥ break it, fix it;

♥ borrow it, return it;

♥ lose it, replace it;

♥ dirty it, clean it.

Always return the item in the same or better condition. This shows respect and appreciation for the lender.

Being responsible should be the status quo. Consider this example. If a teen borrows the car and returns it with the gas gauge in the same place, that's good and responsible. The car is returned in the same condition it was borrowed. If he returns the car with a full tank, this demonstrates respect and appreciation. It's a step beyond what's expected. If the young person returns the car washed and vacuumed and tank full, he shows deep gratitude and honor. Unselfish behavior takes service a step farther. Discuss and demonstrate how to go beyond being an even-steven.

119

A Yielding Outlook

Unselfishness isn't only demonstrated in sharing or giving but also in attitude. There are times when compromise is good. "I like the room clean, but my roommate leaves it messy." There is no right or wrong in this instance. However, deferring to another, compromising, or dialoging about those preferential choices shows respect. It's an opportunity to problem solve and reach a mutually acceptable solution. Teaching our kids deference and compromise are good people skills when it comes to noncritical things.

In helping our children learn how and when to compromise and defer, we also need to give them skills to deal with someone who does not exercise these traits. One way to deal with a demanding and aggressive person is to call the bluff. The aggressor may say, "I won't hang out with you if you don't do what I want." That's a threat. The child who is learning to set boundaries could say, "That's okay. I'd like to chill with you, but it's my turn to choose." If the bossy friend isn't able to back down, your child needs to be ready to walk away. The next interaction over what to do will most likely end differently. Discernment is needed when deciding to defer or compromise. Strength is necessary when taking a righteous stand. Saying no when being taken advantage of isn't selfish, it's smart.

DEFERENCE AND COMPROMISE ARE GOOD PEOPLE SKILLS WHEN IT COMES TO NONCRITICAL THINGS.

Whole Heart

Unselfishness is marked by empathy and generosity. Foster God-chasing rather than self-seeking behavior in your relationships and resources. We can show our love for God and others by the way we use our treasures, time, and talents. Let's look for ways to be God's instruments to meet the needs of our children and others. When we do, our children will be blessed by our example. An unselfish heart loves whole-heartedly.

Love Notes on Unselfishness

Lori writes: Time is the thing I covet most. I can be very selfish with my agenda. When I have stopped to help another, I wonder why I hold on to my schedule so tightly. I am blessed when I let it go and follow God's plan for my day. I'm learning life happens in the interruptions.

Becky writes: As my boys have become older and are busy with activities and friends, I cherish the times we are together, especially dinnertime and family road trips. While I have the tendency to be selfish with my time with Scott and the boys, I've realized the need to become less selfish, giving the boys opportunities to be independent. This gives them a chance to spread their wings.

Questions

1. Does your family calendar reflect your priorities?
2. How does your child handle his money? Is he able to be generous and responsible?
3. What type of service project could your family do together?

Parenting Tips

1. Identify your child's current needs and find godly ways to meet them.
2. Include worship and Bible study in your family calendar.
3. Train your child to compromise in noncritical and preferential situations.

PRAYER

Heavenly Father,

Thank You for Your love and for teaching me how to love others. Align my ways to Your will. Give me a heart to act as the Good Samaritan. Unclench my fists, and show me how to give generously of my time and money. Provide opportunities for my family and me to serve others. In Jesus' Name I pray,

Amen

TURN MY HEART TOWARD YOUR STATUTES AND NOT TOWARD SELFISH GAIN.

Psalm 119:36

Section Four

Love Is Self-controlled

Chapter 7

Choose Peace

Love ... is not easily angered.

1 Corinthians 13:5c

The Many Doors of Anger

"Anger enters through many doors," my husband, Scott, said. I'd been discussing this chapter with him and was struggling with the many facets of anger. He hit the nail on the head. Anger does find its way into different emotional passages, making it complex.

Lori and I recognize that impatience, frustration, irritation, jealousy, envy, or selfishness open the doors. Other entryways are a reaction to another's unkindness or disrespectful attitude. Anger moves into our relationships, hearts and minds, expressing itself in a number of harmful ways. It slips in quietly in the form of implosion, passive aggressiveness, and silence. Or it blasts into our lives as an explosion or rebellion. And in our own minds it's justified. Can you relate?

"Of the seven deadly sins, anger is possibly the most fun. To lick your wounds, to smack your lips over grievances long past, to roll over your tongue the prospect of bitter confrontations still to come, to savor to the last toothsome morsel both the pain you are given and the pain you are giving back in many ways is a feast for a king. The chief drawback is that what you are wolfing down is yourself. The skeleton at the feast is you."[17]
At the onset, Fredrick Buechner's quote is tantalizing but reveals truth.

124

Anger and its antithesis, peace, are choices. Scripture speaks about anger over and over again, often in the context of self-control and wisdom. People who are quick to become angry are categorized as fools. Anger is a secondary emotion, triggered by a primary emotion. Anger isn't sinful in and of itself; it's a God-given emotion. It is a heads-up indicator that something is amiss.

In this chapter, we will examine the different expressions of anger. To do so, we need to determine our primary emotional catalysts and hot spots. Together we'll discover ways to interrupt the rage, resolve conflict, and bring peace back into our homes. In order to change the tone in the home, we first begin with ourselves and then train our children.

ANGER IS A HEADS-UP INDICATOR THAT SOMETHING IS AMISS.

ANGRY WORDS

James lays out how we are to behave. "My dear brothers, take note of this: Everyone should be quick to listen, slow to speak and slow to become angry, for man's anger does not bring about the righteous life that God desires" (James 1:19-20). Just three responses: quick to listen, slow to speak, and slow to become angry. You might agree that anger management is a necessary skill in parenting tweens and teens.

Learning to manage my (Becky) feelings constructively when my boys lash out at me is an ongoing challenge. Years of praying and practicing have paid off in the "thick skin" department. And...I'm still working on it.

My son was upset. Because the school project was not finished, he couldn't go to a movie with the guys

"You always freak out, Mom. You just don't want me to be with my friends," he shouted.

"I love you. Do your homework." I chose not to take the *freak-out* anger bait.

Not reacting to an angry outburst takes self-control. Here are a few other strategies that could prove helpful in situations like this. A parent could say, "I'm not going to argue with you. I love you." Or "I can see why you're mad. If I were you, I'd want to go, too. I would love to say yes. I wish your homework was done so you could go." Anger is defused with a combination of empathy and self-control.

IMPLODE, EXPLODE, RELOAD

So, what causes mad? What are the primary emotional catalysts? The feelings of being out of control, jealous, fearful, frustrated, ignored, hurt, or disrespected are some of them. It's natural to jump to an angry response rather than deal with the main issue or feeling. There are two types of hurtful ways anger is expressed: implosive and explosive. Implosive is seething anger. It's rarely dealt with and festers like an infected wound. The silent treatment and stuffing the anger are examples of implosion. Nothing can be resolved. Resentment, indifference, and bitterness increase. Pushing the anger aside rather than dealing with the problem at hand is physically and relationally unhealthy. Lori and I know how hard it is to speak up and state what's bothering you. We have also discovered waiting allows the problem to grow. We've learned (and are still learning) to keep anger accounts current and short by dealing with issues as they arise.

Explosive anger is what the world sees when the emotions are not controlled. Yelling, screaming, fist-shaking and finger-pointing anger frightens everyone. When expressed in this way, the angry person feels the situation is out of control and is posturing in an attempt to control it. The person on the receiving end may or may not immediately retaliate, but he will certainly rebel. Explosive anger is a misuse of power. Any valid message that needs to be expressed is lost in the nonverbal expression, negative tone, and loud delivery. Explosive venting hurts as words and actions cannot be repealed. When you feel an outburst coming, use what we call a *rage interrupter*, a phrase or action to stop the fury. Some parents may count to ten, others may take a deep breath; one dad shared he bites his knuckle. Our two favorites are repeating, "Love is patient, love is kind," (Becky) over and over and the *silent scream* (Lori), making a quick turn away from the escalating situation, pretending to scream silently, then turning back. *Rage interrupters* replace the anger with a sense of control, calm, or humor. Find something that fits your personality; use it to replace the anger and renew your mind. Practice identifying and verbalizing the main emotion that is driving the anger, using "I" statements to reload your message. For example, "I feel frustrated when you don't put the scissors back in the drawer." This kind of statement is a constructive way to get across your message. A short fuse short-circuits the message. Reload constructively, not destructively.

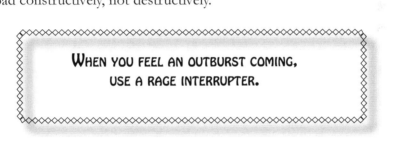

WHEN YOU FEEL AN OUTBURST COMING, USE A RAGE INTERRUPTER.

HOT SPOTS

Nowhere in the Bible does it tell us not to be angry. Anger is an indicator something is amiss, but it is a poor solution to the problem. What's your hot spot, the thing that just tweaks you? I (Becky) can get mad at my children when they purposely do, or neglect to do, what I've told them to do or not do. Not picking up dirty laundry and leaving homework unfinished are two of my hot spots.

I've asked my boys to put dirty clothes in the hamper repeatedly. At times the task is dutifully done, and other times clothes are left on the floor. Each one has a hamper, yet dirty socks and the like are often strewn across the floor. Even the logical consequence of no clean socks doesn't seem to make a difference. Lori shared a terrific strategy that can help deal with the frustrations of the "teen tornado." (It's very beneficial to have a mentor who can share proven strategies.) She calls her strategy "The Maid." The day before "The Maid" arrives she

(Lori) puts a notice on each bedroom door saying, "The Maid comes tomorrow. She charges ten cents for every item of clothing, personal belonging, or garbage she picks up." This way the kids have twenty-four hours to get their rooms in order. Then, as planned, "The Maid" arrives, cleans, puts things away, and leaves her bill on each bedroom door, expecting payment that day. The following week when "The Maid" shows up, she gives herself a raise and increases the fee per item. (Here's a little side note from Lori: You can always choose not to let the mess bother you and shut the bedroom door. Personally, I can be inconsistent with the problem of the messy room. When the clutter begins to make me crazy, "The Maid" gets rehired.)

Homework is another typical hot spot for parents of tweens and teens. Whether a child is learning the ABCs or preparing for the ACTs, our tips will prove helpful.

Establish a workable location for homework. This location may change as the child matures. It may be somewhat dependent upon the assignment, how much parental supervision is needed, and the personality of the student. The best location depends on the child's personality and his need for help. Introverted personalities will need a quieter spot with limited distractions. If more adult assistance is needed, the introvert may need to get up from his workspace and come to the parent for help. Or the parent can schedule a check-in time with the child. A desk or table off in another room would be best for this student. Extraverted kids need to be in the family fray in order to focus. An extravert will find it hard to concentrate if he doesn't know what is going on with the rest of the family. Sitting at the kitchen table or counter would meet this child's need.

Think through each child's schedule to decide the best time to do homework. It may vary during the week given extracurricular activities. There is no best time. Some kids do better right after school. Some, after dinner. Others have activities like sports, band, or a part-time job, so the best way to choose a time is just to find a time! Plan with the child. If consistency is possible, great. If not, flexibility is the way to go!

Recognize how the child handles responsibility. If he's successful in managing his obligations and workload, put on your Consultant or Coach hat. Be more of a support person and encourager. If he's less responsible, the Controller's ability to organize and schedule will come in handy.

Help the tween or teen get organized by providing the necessary supplies.

ADD and ADHD kids may need background noise. An iPod with classical or techno music to drown out the distracting household commotion has been proven beneficial.

Your child's age, ability, and experience govern your involvement in the homework process. Younger, less able, and/or less experienced equals more parental involvement and supervision. Older, more able, and/or more experienced equals less parental involvement and supervision.

If your child develops good study habits and handles responsibility well, be flexible with the schedule. Show confidence in his ability to manage his work.

By identifying hot spots, being proactive, and deciding to keep cool, we will reduce the number of parental angry outbursts.

HARMONY IN THE HOME

Effective communication is the best way to ensure peace and cooperation in the family. Encouragement, empathy, and efficiency are the main tenants of communicating effectively. When the Coach speaks words of encouragement and then blends in some Chum-like empathy, the recipient feels loved and appreciated. A more cooperative spirit is fostered. Efficiently-given directives, directions that are clear and concise, are easier to follow. Too many words are confusing. A quiet voice, eye contact, and the parties being in close proximity are all that are needed. When training for the desired behavior, speak about what you want rather than what you don't want. Say, "Put the dishes in the dishwasher," instead of, "Don't leave the dishes on the counter." Clearly stating expectations and modeling behavior increases

129

cooperation. Watch for opportunities to catch your kids being good. Be "gracious and compassionate, slow to anger and abounding in love" (Nehemiah 9:17c).

Disunity is contrary to God's character. Make the words of Ephesians 4:26a a family motto for conflict resolution. "In your anger do not sin." The rest of this familiar verse says, "Do not let the sun go down while you are still angry." The preferred way is to resolve conflict quickly and solve problems before the day is done. But there are times the issue may need to be set aside if exhaustion is taking its toll and the conflict is escalating with no resolution in sight. When this happens, get some rest, and revisit the issue the next day.

Positive Communication Tips to Use During Conflict

1. Use "I" statements rather than "you" statements.

2. Avoid using "always" and "never."

3. State the hoped for outcome, "I appreciate your help cleaning up the kitchen after dinner," rather than, "You never help me clean up after dinner."

4. Stay calm, stay focused, and grow thick skin.

5. Avoid bringing up past offenses. Deal with the present issue.

6. Sit next to one another; touch each other to decrease defenses.

7. Keep respect intact.

8. Use a *rage interrupter*.

9. If your approach to conflict isn't working and issues continue to recycle, try a "new dance." (For example, if you clam up, speak up. If you explode, try listening first.)

10. If possible, keep your sense of humor!

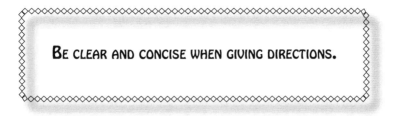

A Peaceful Palace

We desire peace-filled homes, yet we save our worst behaviors for the ones we love the most because home is usually a safe place. If your home is one where feelings are expressed, be encouraged because you have set up a safe environment for your children. Within the security of family, honest opinions can be stated. Begin by helping children learn no one is perfect. People are going to disappoint us. An attitude of grace and understanding goes a long way when we're let down by a loved one. Recalling our own personal imperfections and sinful behaviors is a "grace and mercy" reminder and gives us a proper perspective.

Most parents expect their children will view life from a similar perspective. When the teen or tween challenges the family values, arguments may ensue. This is a perfect time to recall the verse in Matthew 5:9, "Blessed are the peace makers, for they will be called sons of God." Peacemakers are relationship builders. Agitators are relationship busters.

The young adult is coming of age. He's trying on different philosophies to see how they fit. During election time we (Lori) have had some lively debates at our home. My husband and I know that allowing our kids to express their opinions in a respectful way and listen to an opposing view are important skills for teens to develop. Even though it can be difficult to hear the teen state something contrary to what's been taught in the home, everyone is entitled to an opinion. We've had many lively discussions about politics, the environment, religion, and gun control around the kitchen table.

Even though it can be difficult, leave room for differences of opinion. And imperfection. We don't all have to look at life the same way in order to love each other and get along.

ICY ANGER

Minnesota winters can be bone-chilling cold, but a wind-chill factor of forty-five below zero is nothing compared to the dismissive cold shoulder. "I don't care. You no longer exist in my life. Leave."

A mom told me (Becky) she would never forget the first time she heard, "Go away, Mom. Leave me alone." The mom was deflated and hurt. Her teen had wanted to attend a party and was told no. The teenager's mom shared the rest of the story. The teen refused to join the family dinner. Bedtime prayers were said while the teen remained in stony silence. There was no response to Mom's, "I love you." The next morning, hunger was too much to bear, as was the load of anger. The daughter came down for breakfast and was greeted with a cheerful, "Good morning." The daughter was remorseful for her actions even though she was still upset. In spite of the child's poor behavior she was confident in her mother's love. The warm food and her mother's unconditional love thawed the emotional ice, and the relationship was restored.

Acting indifferent to another's existence is the opposite of love and perhaps the cruelest emotionally. This style of anger uses cold unconcern as revenge. Kindness is a good course of action. The mother in the example above didn't play into her daughter's emotional blackmail. The mother realized her daughter was attempting to punish and manipulate through anger and indifference. She held her ground and continued to act as she normally would. Even though it must have been difficult, this mama stayed the course. It took a little while, but her daughter came around. This young teen discovered her mother wouldn't be held emotionally captive and that her theatrics didn't

132

control the family's evening routine. This mom acted in wisdom and self-control.

Paul quoted Proverbs 25:21 when he wrote how we are to treat those who hurt us, "'If your enemy is hungry, feed him; if he is thirsty, give him something to drink. In doing this, you will heap burning coals on his head.' Do not be overcome by evil, but overcome evil with good" (Romans 12:20-21). It's difficult to be angry for too long when the anger is doused with kindness and love. Think of it as burning coals to melt icy anger.

SILENT TREATMENT

Words and attitudes are powerful. The lack of words is an attempt to control. Usually the silent treatment begins with an announcement, "I'm not speaking to you." Then it screams with attitude. When the silent treatment begins, ask three questions: What precipitated the silence? Is this a power struggle? Have I hurt my child in word or deed?

When a parent sets a consequence and the teen reacts with the silent treatment, ignoring it as the mother did in the previous example is wise. It can be difficult, but stick with the plan. We don't want to be manipulated. Kids have staying power, sometimes more than parents have, so stand firm.

On the other hand, we need to take ownership of our words or actions, too. If needed, ask for forgiveness. It may take a while for the teenage ice to melt. But saying, "I love you, and I am sorry I hurt you," will begin repairing the relationship.

If a child is using silence because he has been hurt, be the Chum and encourage him to talk. Communication is so important, especially in the tough times. Demonstrate how families work together through thick and thin toward a solution rather than shut each other out. Model behavior that says, "We are in this together."

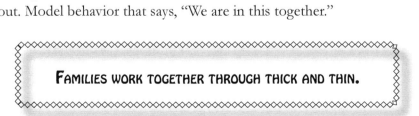

FAMILIES WORK TOGETHER THROUGH THICK AND THIN.

Target Practice

What happens when an arsenal of angry words is launched directly at the parent? Proverbs 12:16 says, "A fool shows his annoyance at once, but a prudent man overlooks an insult." A calm, quiet response can squelch an impending quarrel.

There are times direct action, not reaction, is necessary. Anger can turn physical. Abuse is much more likely to occur between family members than between strangers. One couple shared with me (Lori) a concern regarding their two tween-aged children. The brother was getting physical with his sister, hitting her when the parents weren't at home. As we conferenced about this situation, we came up with a strategy. A babysitter would be hired if the parents weren't present. Following a few weeks of using a babysitter, the family would meet to discuss possible scenarios that lead up to the rough behavior and brainstorm alternative behaviors with clearly defined expectations. If all parties agree the babysitter can be cancelled, the parents would then allow the tweens to be home, unsupervised for a limited amount of time, followed by individual conversations with each child. The parents were smart to take action and deal with a harmful situation in a constructive way.

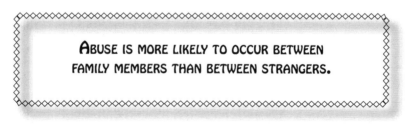

ABUSE IS MORE LIKELY TO OCCUR BETWEEN FAMILY MEMBERS THAN BETWEEN STRANGERS.

Teen Tantrums

Teenage anger is an interesting phenomenon. One moment a teen is happily sharing a story and after one seemingly innocuous parental comment or question there's an explosion. Think back to the toddler days when "no" became the most powerful word in a child's vocabulary and "I can do it myself" was the most common phrase as the child moved from total dependence to becoming independent. This is the teen version.

The tween and teen years are a time of tremendous growth, not just physically but emotionally and socially. Kids are trying to determine who they are, where they fit in, and what they think about life. They are forming an independent identity, separate from parents. As teens mature, they develop opinions that may or may not coincide with what Mom, Dad, and other authority figures think.

Anger is part of the mix as a result of these power struggles. Add in the newest research in brain development which has determined the adolescent brain may not totally mature until age twenty-five and there's no wonder kids experience frustration and anger. Teens want to spread their wings and make their own choices. Guidance is necessary from a parent's point of view but not from the teen's perspective.

When kids feel out of control, angry tantrums are the result. We can assist our teens by watching for trigger events or behaviors. For example, the death of a loved one, difficulty with friends, poor grades, or a move to a new home can all cause kids to feel like the control they have over their lives is slipping away. Teens may slam doors, use inappropriate language, strike out at siblings, or isolate themselves from the family. The anger is okay; the way the anger is often exhibited is not okay. Helping teens identify the emotions leading up to the boiling point is a good place for us to start helping teens handle anger. Asking questions like, "I see you're frustrated, do you want to talk?" or, "That must have been a difficult situation at school today, do you want to discuss it?" will assist the child in talking about his feelings. Sometimes they need time to cool off, so space is a good option. When they do come to us, a listening ear makes all the difference.

Righteous Anger

God desires for His children to be righteous, living a life of holiness. There are times righteous anger, anger in defense of another, spurs on necessary change. Jesus exhibited this type of anger when He confronted the moneychangers and those who sold animals for sacrifice in the temple (Matthew 21:12-13). So anger can be righteous and can have a positive result. Because of anger at specific situations, people have changed the world. For example, losing a sibling to cancer spurred one young man into choosing oncology as a career. Many social justice organizations have been formed as the result of anger at injustice. In regard to righteous anger, Dr. Scott Wenig, professor at Denver Seminary, recommends asking the following questions:

1. Is the cause of anger due to injustice, pain, or sin of some kind?
2. Is the expression of the anger without explosion or silence (venting or shutting down)?
3. Is the desired outcome something that God wants to happen?
4. Is the level or depth of anger appropriate to the situation?
5. Is there grace to be given regardless of the person or situation? In other words, can there be some sort of redemption?[18]

God understands anger. Here are a few places in Scripture that demonstrate God's righteous anger:

God had appeared to Solomon twice and still he turned away from the Lord (1 Kings 11:9-10).

Jesus was angered by lack of compassion and healed a man's shriveled hand (Mark 3:4-5).

Jesus drove the merchants and money changers from the temple courts (John 2:13-16).

Mankind suppressed the truth with wickedness, choosing not to glorify or thank the Lord, which resulted in depravity (Romans 1:18-32).

God responded in anger to unjust circumstances. Righteous anger handled without sin is godly anger.

Peace and Quiet

Is there anything more peaceful and satisfying than watching your kids enjoy each other's company? These moments are treasures. Hopefully the tips in this chapter will help you to reload constructively, identify hot spots, and come up with a plan to handle tough situations. Falling back on *rage interrupters* promotes peace. Growing thick skin and knowing "this too shall pass" gives perspective in the difficult times. Arming children to handle their anger constructively is helpful now and in the future. The whole family benefits when we choose peace over anger.

Love Notes on Peace

Lori writes: Tom and I try to help each other following a conflict with one of the kids. With his input and support, I am able to see the situation from a different perspective. Often I have contributed to the problem. Thankfully, we usually don't get angry at the same thing or at the same time.

Becky writes: When Scott and I have discussions with the boys regarding disciplinary matters, I tend to make my point over and over. I think they'll understand if I say it eight different ways. Scott has a signal for me to stop before the boys' frustration level hits a peak. I appreciate his help in keeping the conversation focused.

Questions

1. How do you resolve conflict, express anger, and communicate more effectively?

2. What are your hot spots? What *rage interrupter* would work for you?

3. How can your child's righteous anger be expressed in a positive manner?

Parenting Tips

1. Pray for thick skin. Don't be easily offended.

2. Use a *rage interrupter* rather than exploding in anger.

3. Assist your child in determining what primary emotion led to his anger.

Prayer

Lord Jesus,

Thank You that You forgive my angry ways. "I will praise you, O LORD. Although you were angry with me, your anger has turned away and you have comforted me" (Isaiah 12:1). You are slow to anger, abounding in love. Help me to develop and use *rage interrupters* as a control valve for my anger. Allow me to model how to use anger effectively to promote change. Guide me in teaching my children to control their anger as well. Forgive me when I blow it. Bless me with thick skin as I raise my children for You.

Amen

An angry man stirs up dissention, and a hot-tempered one commits many sins.

Proverbs 29:22

Chapter 8

Choose Forgiveness

Love ... keeps no record of wrongs.

1 Corinthians 13:5d

Broken Record

With homework and grades posted on the Internet, parents know when kids are doing a good job…or not. When I (Becky) see missing assignments, my most common reaction is anger born out of disappointment. Exasperated, I'll ask, "Why do you keep forgetting to turn in your homework? You do it and leave it in your binder." Then I threaten to cancel the kid's weekend plans. Later I regret my outburst and the extremely harsh consequence.

Does this type of thing happen in your home? How many times have you played a bad parental moment over in your head, running through the scene in your mind's eye and beating yourself up for a lack of wisdom and self-control? Like me, you may have regrets.

Forgiveness is a matter of self-control. It's mind over emotion. It is characterized by determination and humility. Lack of forgiveness can eat away at us, affecting our mental health. When wronged, we want to punish and withhold forgiveness. When in the wrong, we hang onto our pride to save face. While unforgiveness holds us captive, forgiveness sets us free.

Jesus was so serious about forgiveness, mercy, and grace He willingly gave His life. That's radical love. God calls us to take responsibility for our actions and to forgive as He forgives. If we forgive, forgiveness infiltrates our homes. Our children learn to give and to accept forgiveness. Our homes will be places where there is no record of wrongs.

I apologized and asked for forgiveness for my sinful reaction to the homework situation. I changed up the consequence. Rather than have him be on house arrest all weekend, he came up with a plan to help himself remember to turn in his work. This was his problem to solve.

JESUS WAS SO SERIOUS ABOUT FORGIVENESS, MERCY, AND GRACE HE WILLINGLY GAVE HIS LIFE.

REMEMBER WHEN

Remorse is a deep emotion, a sense of extreme pain and overwhelming regret. Wishing we had chosen to act or speak differently due to the consequences of our behavior characterizes regret and remorse.

A dad described this scene. He was in the unenviable position of confronting his sixteen-year-old daughter about a lie.

"It's not my fault. My friends chose to do it. I just stayed quiet and watched."

Here was an opportunity. The dad proceeded to explain the culpability in being a bystander. She respectfully listened.

"Well, I hope that doesn't change your view of me." Her discomfort was evident by the squirming.

"You know I love you no matter what. If there is anything else I need to know, now is a good time to get it out there," he prompted.

With tears streaming down her cheeks she confessed to some recent poor choices. The guilt was overwhelming. Remorse and regret

140

had set in. Her conscience, which had been nagging her for weeks, was now satisfied. The dad was wise. Rather than reacting in anger he responded in love. He gave her a hug and told her he loved her. (See the Goodness and Trust chapters for more information about temptations and telling lies.)

Psalm 38:4 says, "My guilt has overwhelmed me like a burden too heavy to bear." Remorse and regret can be paralyzing or precursors to action. Developing responsibility and taking ownership for wrongdoing are the first steps toward healing. Sitting in guilt only proves to be destructive. When our consciences are piqued and the still small voice of the Holy Spirit whispers to us, we move from conviction of guilt toward making the wrong right.

WHAT'S THE PROBLEM?

If we ignore the Holy Spirit's convicting voice, we choose complacency over responsibility. Complacency is settling into our sin, convinced that the sin isn't so bad or "It's just the way I am." We may not want to admit our wrong doing, yet we're quick to demand justice when we are the injured party. In Psalm 139:23-24 the psalmist asks God to reveal his offensive ways. "Search me, O God, and know my heart; test me and know my anxious thoughts. See if there is any offensive way in me, and lead me in the way everlasting."

A mother described to me (Lori) how complacency seems to be a part of the teen culture. She's right. It ties in with relativity, "It's not so bad. What's the big deal?" Her young adult had invited two other girls to the family cabin. While staying at the cabin one of the girls took a lawn decoration from a nearby resort. Apparently there were many trinkets in the yard. The other two girls participated by laughing and going along with the theft. Upon discovering the stolen property, the mom told the girls they needed to return it. The girls were dumbfounded.

"It's a cheap little thing. They have a million of them."

These young adults needed to move from the position of complacency to confession.

THE GREAT DIVIDE

Once we have moved from complacency, our next step is confession. Admitting a wrong to the injured party is the beginning of relational restoration. Until acknowledgment occurs there will be a chasm in the relationship.

A mom described a recent altercation that took place between her two teen daughters. The elder sister was constantly "borrowing" things from the younger one.

"Usually she'd ask, but sometimes she would take whatever she wanted without permission," the mom explained. "My younger daughter was willing to share, that is, until her favorite shirt was missing. She was furious with her sister."

A heated discussion ensued.

"The three of us sat down to talk, with me as the mediator." Good Coach/Consultant practices.

The mom said, "My younger daughter explained why she was so mad. 'I'm willing to share with you, but some things are off limits.'"

The big sister understood, apologized, asked for forgiveness, and immediately washed the shirt and hung it back in her sister's closet.

Confession, restitution, resolution, and reconciliation; the complete forgiveness package.

Healing begins with confession. Deliverance comes from the confession and repentance of sin. Teaching children to admit mistakes trains them how to confess. Confession is good for the soul, creating a new beginning. Modeling confession is critical. Admitting sin takes guts. The brave act of admission of guilt has the supernatural power to bring about relational wholeness. By providing a nonthreatening atmosphere in our homes our children will feel safe confessing mistakes.

NO EXCUSE

Generally speaking, most parents want to make things easier for their children. Lori and I understand it's hard not to fall into this trap. This natural inclination turns sour when it becomes excusing or enabling sinful behavior. A mom of a nineteen-year-old young man resisted the temptation to make his discomfort more comfortable. She received a phone call in the middle of the night. Her son, who had consistently made poor choices over a two-year span, was arrested for disorderly conduct and underage drinking. She courageously told her son, "Well, think of your night in jail like camping." She didn't bail him out. He learned a hard lesson that night. Her tough love approach, in the appropriate form of the parent as Controller, allowed him to experience the consequences of his choices. By her response she helped him move from complacency in his sin to conviction and then ultimately to the burden of responsibility.

My Bad

After the problem is confessed, there is a personal choice to be made: claim responsibility or give-up and give-in. Freedom comes in owning mistakes. Giving in and giving up lead to apathy and hopelessness.

Demonstrating to your children of any age the process of moving from guilt to sin ownership to forgiveness brings psychological, physical, relational, and spiritual healing. Taking responsibility is a mature act. When, yes when, your teen comes to you and confesses he dented the car, he's claimed the mistake. Not only has he moved from regret, he's taken responsibility.

"I'm glad you confessed you dented the car. I appreciate your honesty. What are your ideas for getting the car repaired?" The Consultant approach passes the responsibility back to the child, involving him in the process. Here are a few ideas: He could gather estimates, pay expenses, or find temporary transportation. This moves the young person from taking responsibility to the next step, restitution, fixing the problem.

Healing Balm

Restitution, making a wrong right, soothes both parties. It's easy to figure out consequences for material problems. Replacing, fixing, or repairing a damaged or lost item is common sense. With restitution it's important to have the punishment fit the crime so to speak. Or better said, let the natural consequences play out. This establishes the connection between the action, outcome, and righting the wrong. When the wrong is righted, restitution occurs.

Relational or emotional restitution is much harder. It's more than making the person "whole" regarding material items, it is repairing the hole left by a broken relationship. An attitude of forgiveness is critical. Everyone makes mistakes.

A dad described an unhealthy relational pattern involving his two sons. He felt he needed to squelch the bad habits forming between them.

"It's the same course of events every time. Something happens to irritate my youngest. He mutters a mean name or makes a derogatory comment directed at his brother. My older son then challenges, 'What did you say?'"

The dad stopped to let out a sigh. "My younger son, not about to back down, repeats his words in a voice loud enough for the whole neighborhood to hear. This leads to a shouting match. Finally, when I can't take it anymore, I send both sons to their separate rooms to calm down.

"When we sat down to talk, I gave each brother an opportunity to speak without being interrupted. My youngest said he was tired of always being bossed around by his brother. The look of surprise on my older boy's face revealed he hadn't realized he was being bossy. He encouraged his brother to speak up. On the other hand, my older son was hurt by the nasty comments and cruel name-calling. He asked his younger brother to please stop.

"Both boys apologized, claimed responsibility, and brainstormed ways to circumvent this situation before it gets heated. My younger son agreed to express his opinion, keeping the nasty vocabulary at bay. My older boy is making efforts to be less domineering."

This dad used his skills as a Coach to lead his boys to an amicable solution, while helping them communicate effectively, empathize, and forgive each other. Restoring the sibling relationship was number one. The experience of working through relational challenges in a respectful way was a nice side benefit.

Turn Around

Repentance is a little harder than restitution. A repentant heart chooses to turn from the sin and not make the mistake again. Think of Peter. He denied Jesus three times, yet he was the one Jesus chose to be instrumental in building his church. Peter learned from his mistakes. His heart was soft and humble, moldable clay in the Father's hands. Just as Jesus knew Peter would fail, He also knew Peter would follow (John 13). Knowing Peter's history makes his words in his first epistle so sweet. "Humble yourselves, therefore, under God's mighty hand, that he may lift you up in due time. Cast all your anxiety on him because he cares for you" (1 Peter 5:6-7).

No one likes to fail, but failure is the best opportunity to learn and implement change; it's when we are most teachable. In the first moments of a newly discovered indiscretion, let's try to recall our own flaws, especially as a teen. Reacting in anger won't solve the problem. Let each child know that no matter how great the mistake, sin is sin. No one sin is bigger than another, and there is no sin bigger than God's forgiveness. Drinking, premarital sex, drugs, homosexuality, attempted suicide, eating disorders, etc., can all be dealt with. With forgiveness and repentance comes hope. Encourage the young person to recommit making choices and living life God's way.

Mistakes, big and small, are great opportunities for training. Avoid sugar coating, excusing, or enabling sinful behavior. During trials, God will help parent and child alike because He has a vested interest in us.

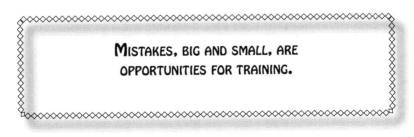

MISTAKES, BIG AND SMALL, ARE
OPPORTUNITIES FOR TRAINING.

Kids, like adults, say mean things when angry. A mom shared with me (Becky) how angry she was at her teen for getting another speeding ticket. "When we talked about it, he became defensive. He also reminded me of the speeding ticket I received not too long ago. I wanted to tell him this was his *second* ticket and he'd never drive my car again because he was such a lousy driver. Thankfully, I didn't."

Getting the child back by shaming or retaliating is not helpful. Don't repay the offense. The attitude of "You do this to me, so I'll do this to you" trains the child to seek revenge.

The mother in the story stopped herself from the tit-for-tat exchange. Very wise. But let's take it a step further. The reason the teen got defensive was because the parent was most likely expressing anger rather than empathy. (Easy to do under the circumstance.) Here's a way to handle this problem with grace:

"I see you received a speeding ticket. That's a bummer." (Controller-fact, Chum-empathy)

"So what? You just got one, too." (Child challenging the parent)

"You're right. I should have driven the speed limit. I deserved it. Now I have to pay my ticket. What's your plan?" (In control Controller plus Consultant. Note how the parent admits she deserved the ticket and has to deal with its consequence.)

"Guess I have to pay it."

"Yep. What have we both learned?" (Chum and Coach combo)

"Drive the speed limit."

The parent's words are laced with an attitude of forgiveness. Although not specifically stated, the underlying message is, "We all make mistakes, I understand, and mistakes need to be fixed."

After setting the tone of grace, move into the next phase.

"With this second violation, you could be in danger of increasing insurance costs or having your license revoked. I'd hate to see that happen. (To be effective this statement must be made without emotion, containing elements of truth and grace.) What can be done to help you remember to have a lighter foot on the gas pedal?" Have

146

the new driver think this through and come up with a consequence. Consequences may include no driving for a period of time or only driving to a particular location. A parent's forgiving attitude doesn't negate training, natural consequences, or punishment.

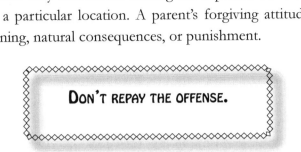

DON'T REPAY THE OFFENSE.

I'M OFFENDED

Just because we feel angry doesn't mean we cannot forgive or respond in love. "Forgiveness is not an emotion. Forgiveness is an act of will, and the will can function regardless of the temperature of the heart."[19]

Being easily offended and holding grudges complicates life. Harboring anger slows us down and affects other relationships in a negative way. When the anger basket is already full, it takes little to make it spill. When you and your child have worked through a situation that requires forgiveness, give your child the benefit of the doubt and avoid jumping to mad the next time something similar comes up. Don't replay the offense by reminding him of past mistakes. Look for effort exerted toward positive change; validate that effort and the resulting maturity. Then verbalize your appreciation.

DON'T REPLAY THE OFFENSE.

SURVIVAL OF THE FITTEST

Broken relationships marred by sin can be repaired, redeemed, and restored. One young teen felt convicted following a church lesson on forgiveness. She shared this insight with her mom. Realizing the importance of the moment, the mom put down what she was doing and provided practical support. She immediately drove her fifteen-year-old to the friend's home. Her daughter asked her friend for forgiveness. She had no expectation of a mirrored response from the other person. Not expecting the other person to respond in kind is vital. She was prepared for the possibility that the other person might not reciprocate. She was okay with that outcome. A beautiful thing happened that night. The friendship was restored when forgiveness and responsibility for the breakdown were given and owned by both parties. The teen obeyed that still small voice and was blessed by a loving interaction followed by great peace.

Try these steps to restore a relationship. Forgiveness is a gift that can lead to reuniting. "Be kind and compassionate to one another, forgiving each other, just as in Christ God forgave you" (Ephesians 4:32). Be bold to be blessed.

STEPS TO RESTORATION

1. Address the problem.
2. Determine where things went wrong.
3. Apologize and ask for forgiveness.
4. Refuse to blame the other person or to defend yourself.
5. Ask what can be done to repair the relationship.
6. Be committed to following through.[20]

Rick Warren, author of *The Purpose Driven Life*, says this about restoring a relationship, "When a fellowship is strained or broken, plan a peace conference immediately."[21] He goes on to say, "The success of a peace conference often depends on choosing the right time and place to meet. Don't meet when either of you are tired or rushed or will be interrupted. The best time is when you are both at your best."[22] Focusing on feelings not facts, beginning with sympathy rather than solutions, seeking reconciliation as opposed to resolution is recommended.

It takes one to forgive but two to reconcile. Robin Chaddock quotes Charles William in her *Soul Snacks* blog, "Many promising reconciliations have broken down because while both parties came prepared to forgive, neither party came prepared to be forgiven."[23] To accept forgiveness we need to realize we contributed to the problem. But we can only be responsible for ourselves. We can't own another's response. This is a tough place to be. Typically, when there's discord, each person involved views things from his or her own perspective. When we're vulnerable, we hope the other people will respond in kind. Sometimes they don't. Reconciliation isn't always possible.

Forgiveness doesn't mean automatic trust. If the offender is showing patterns of change, true repentance is occurring. It's foolishness to be exposed emotionally if there is no visible change. The authors of *Boundaries*, Drs. Henry Cloud and John Townsend, recommend forgiveness and guarding your heart until you see sustained change. They warn not to open up to the other party until you see "fruit in keeping with repentance" (Matthew 3:8).[24]

> **WHEN WE'RE VULNERABLE, WE HOPE THE OTHER PEOPLE WILL RESPOND IN KIND. SOMETIMES THEY DON'T.**

BITTERSWEET

I (Lori) know a remarkable young woman who has experienced much ridicule and bullying from preschool through high school. Had I experienced this I'd be a bitter person, angry at the world, unwilling to forgive, and hardened to love. Somehow God has supernaturally turned her horrible experiences into compassion and strength. She has a tender heart for the underdog. She forgives easily and quickly. Scripture says that when we are weak, God is strong. He's taken her brokenness and moved it to tenderness.

So on a smaller scale, when promises are broken and expectations are left unfulfilled, how do we respond? Heal or hate? What do we teach our kids? Hurt that is transformed into hate is all-consuming resentment. A grudge against another results in bitterness in the soul.

Kids will all experience a time when their circle of friends excludes them. Being there to support the young person during this painful time will help him get through it. Belonging and being loved are needs that are close to the heart and when not met, cut through the heart. We can listen to, comfort, and distract the tween or teen if this is an infrequent occurrence. Parents can normalize the child's predicament by sharing a their own left out story. If the situation becomes more consistent or is filled with harassment or bullying, the child will most likely need the parent to remove him from the situation. Continue to talk with, listen to, and observe the child while watching for signs that the problem is continuing or escalating.

There is a silver lining in the heartache. God does some of His best work in the brokenness. Knowing what it feels like to be left out or to be on the receiving end of meanness can be the best producer of empathy.

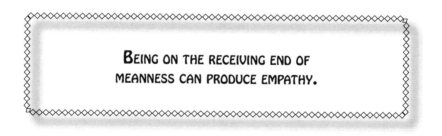

BEING ON THE RECEIVING END OF MEANNESS CAN PRODUCE EMPATHY.

Fruit of Forgiveness

Forgiveness is sweet, true fruit that frees us from the bondage of bitterness. Forgiveness is a healthy choice. When we experience forgiveness, we are unfettered from the past and free to move forward. Forgiveness is a present God gives.

Mary Heathman shares her epiphany about a sinner's relationship with the Lord. "Confession and repentance are gifts from God for our deliverance; they aren't punishment and humiliation for our sin. Confessing and repenting are the means to close the gap when sin has driven a wedge between relationships. Through confession and repentance, our relationship with God is restored. Whether I need forgiveness for something I've done or for something I've left undone, confession takes me back to God." Mary prays Psalm 51:1-3, "Have mercy on me, O God, according to your unfailing love; according to your great compassion blot out my transgressions. Wash away all my iniquity and cleanse me from my sin. For I know my transgressions, and my sin is always before me."[25]

Forgiveness brings a supernatural peace and healing to the heart, mind, body, and soul. Victory isn't winning a battle of the wills; that's stubborn pride. When reconciliation does occur, it's a sweet reward. Victory in the realm of forgiveness isn't being the last man standing; it's the first one kneeling. Forgiveness is G.R.A.C.E:

God's love,

Relationship reaffirmed,

Attitude of forgiveness,

Commitment to repentance,

Evil is not replayed or repaid.

Forgiveness is our grateful response to others for Christ's radical love for us.

LOVE NOTES ON FORGIVENESS

LORI WRITES: Recently, I went to a class on conflict resolution. The therapist leading the class said, "The issues you have trouble with, your children will, too." That thought was pretty convicting. My pride gets in the way of seeking or giving forgiveness. I don't want to leave this legacy for my kids, so I'm upping my game in the forgiveness department.

151

BECKY WRITES: I hate to say it, but my boys are far better at forgiving than I am. I sit and stew rather than forgive and forget. I am learning both from Scripture and my kids.

QUESTIONS:

1. What stops you from forgiving or receiving forgiveness?
2. How do you foster an attitude of forgiveness in your child?
3. How do you model a forgiving attitude?

PARENTING TIPS

1. Ask for forgiveness when you've acted badly.
2. Avoid excusing your child for his behavior.
3. Have your child make the wrong right by putting restitution into practice.

PRAYER

Father,

You are full of grace and mercy. I know I'm to forgive seven times seventy. Help me to have a soft heart and forgive those who have wronged my children or me. I desire to have an atmosphere of forgiveness in my home. I want to forgive as I have been forgiven. Help me to recognize who I need to forgive and where I need to be forgiven. Help me to recall what Your Son did on the cross for me. Free me from the bonds of bitterness. Give me a heart for repentance and reconciliation. Thank You for Your amazing grace.

Amen

LET THE WICKED FORSAKE THEIR WAYS AND THE UNRIGHTEOUS THEIR THOUGHTS. LET THEM TURN TO THE LORD, AND HE WILL HAVE MERCY ON THEM, AND TO OUR GOD, FOR HE WILL FREELY PARDON.

Isaiah 55:7

SECTION FIVE

LOVE HAS A HEAVENLY PERSPECTIVE

CHAPTER 9

CHOOSE GOODNESS

LOVE DOES NOT DELIGHT IN EVIL.

1 Corinthians 13:6a

BLIND SPOT

This chapter was a tough one to write. I'm sure you've noticed the previous ones contain many personal anecdotes. This chapter is crafted differently. Becky's boys and my four are not perfect. All six kids have sinned and fallen short. Just as Becky, Scott, Tom, and I have. (All six kids would heartily agree.) But because our young people are still in the throes of growing up, we want to be respectful and maintain an element of privacy. Therefore, our personal stories will be omitted in this chapter. Rest assured, like you, we have them.

Also by leaving out private struggles we believe you, the reader, will be more able to concentrate on your own tweens' and teens' sinful natures. You'll focus on developing strategies to help them conquer their temptation bents. (On that note, let's get down to business.)

Some parents are in denial (They are most likely not reading this book.); *my child would never do that*. When it comes to our kids, we often have a blind spot. We can easily be Clueless. Expecting the best is good. In fact, there is a phenomenon called the halo effect. When we expect good behavior and are confident our tween or teen will act accordingly, he often does.

Yet we want a clear vision of who our young person is so we can prepare him to deal with inevitable temptation. We want the right heart to love our tween or teen when he confesses he has succumbed to temptation. We pray sin will show itself so it can be addressed. Each child will be tempted and will make mistakes.

We'll explore the seven deadly sins and our adversary (the devil). We'll discuss where and when our kids are most vulnerable in the areas of expected testing, compromise, rebelliousness, and typical teen temptations. We'll address how to help the teen avoid or resist temptation while having an attitude of mercy and grace.

Observe your child. Notice areas where it's natural for your tween to demonstrate goodness. Conversely, make a mental note of times your youth appears to be tempted. In our Corinthians passage, Paul first speaks about forgiveness (no record of wrongs) prior to addressing evil. Perhaps he does this in preparation for the inevitable.

Sin happens; we all need to be ready.

WHAT'S YOUR PLEASURE?

Sin can appear pleasurable. Desires become needs. What previously was enough no longer satisfies. Cecil Murphey defines sin as the "confusion between what I need and what I think I need."[26] That perceived need grows because desensitization has moved in. Just like a fish, we take the bait, barbed hook and all. We are captured and reeled in. We may not even put up a fight. "Temptation—any temptation for any forbidden fruit—comes from two places. My first enemy is my own weakness, and giving in creates a craving for more forbidden fruit. The second is outside sources hitting on those weaknesses. The desire originates in me, and sin results from giving in, thereby increasing that desire to a need. Not giving in to the internal temptation in the first place will prevent the sin."[27]

Temptation creates a battleground between what's right forever and what feels good temporarily. Physiologically, our brain produces oxytocin when aroused. Sin can actually give a person a natural physical high. Sin is pleasurable, but only for a short time. The battle against it is exhausting, physically, mentally, emotionally, and spiritually. It's a messy war yet one worth fighting. Sin is our nature and the enemy's business.

SIN CAN ACTUALLY GIVE A PERSON A NATURAL PHYSICAL HIGH.

THE ENEMY

As much as we try to escape the influences of evil, we can't run from it any more than we can run from our own bodies. Isolation from evil is impossible. We aren't immune to sin because we carry the Adam and Eve gene.

The enemy is old, so he's a great historian. The adversary has seen our families one generation after another and knows what has tempted previous family members. He's prowling around, watching, taking note of what tempts each person individually. As it says in James 1:14-15, "…but each one is tempted when, by his own evil desire, he is dragged away and enticed. Then, after desire has conceived, it gives birth to sin; and sin when it is full grown, gives birth to death." The temptation itself isn't sinful; it's the action that follows. Feelings and emotions can rule over body and mind. If we know God and His Word, His Spirit is strong in us. The Holy Spirit and God's words are the tools we have to fight sin. We can't conquer the enemy or our own sin on our own.

Luke tells us the devil waits for the opportune time to tempt us. (See Luke 4:13.) Teach the tween or teen to identify vulnerable times and to avoid temptation. The enemy strikes when an individual is ill equipped and least prepared. He fights dirty.

THE DEVIL FIGHTS DIRTY.

The Big Seven

There are seven deadly weapons the adversary uses to entice our children and us. The traditional seven deadly sins aren't compiled in one place in Scripture but addressed in the sweep of the entire Bible.

Opposite the seven deadly sins are the desirable godly characteristics, including the fruit of the Spirit (Galatians 5:22-23). These are the traits to replace an individual's sinful nature. When you pray for these traits to counteract the sins, you will effectively renew your mind. Becky and I have dubbed this the *Replacement Technique*. This technique focuses our prayers and training efforts. Often we know what behavior we don't want but can't quite come up with what we do want. The list will assist in that direction.

Replacement Technique

The First Deadly Sin: Greed

Godly Traits/Fruit of the Spirit: Kindness, Generosity

Replacement Prayer: Lord replace my child's greed with generosity and kindness.

Training: Seek out opportunities to care for "the least of these." Find a charity to donate to shovel an elderly neighbor's driveway for free give up a seat for a pregnant woman.

The Second Deadly Sin: Lust

Godly Traits/Fruit of the Spirit: Love, Unselfishness

Replacement Prayer: Father, take away my child's lust for temporal satisfaction and give him the desire for true love and unselfishness.

Training: Work on delayed gratification, help another person, talk about the difference between love and lust. Discuss what self-respect looks like.

THE THIRD DEADLY SIN: Anger

GODLY TRAITS/FRUIT OF THE SPIRIT: Gentleness, Joy

REPLACEMENT PRAYER: God, my child is quick to become angry. Please replace his anger with joy and gentleness.

TRAINING: Identify anger triggers. Discuss ways to get to the solution side of the problem using gentleness and respect. Teach your child to look for the rainbow in the storm.

THE FOURTH DEADLY SIN: Envy

GODLY TRAITS/FRUIT OF THE SPIRIT: Compassion, Peace, Thankful

REPLACEMENT PRAYER: Abba, remove envy from my child's heart, and give him a heart filled with compassion, peace, and thankfulness.

TRAINING: Continually model a grateful attitude. Have your child list all the things for which he is thankful. Celebrate another individual's success. Make a meal and bring it to a sick neighbor.

THE FIFTH DEADLY SIN: Sloth

GODLY TRAITS/FRUIT OF THE SPIRIT: Servanthood, Perseverance

REPLACEMENT PRAYER: . Heavenly King, replace my teen's laziness and sloth with the desire to help others, be physically active, and to persevere when the going gets tough.

TRAINING: Turn off the TV or shut down the computer and have the young person get some exercise. Assign household chores. Have him complete homework prior to engaging in media activities. Show appreciation for his help or ability to complete a task.

THE SIXTH DEADLY SIN: Gluttony

GODLY TRAITS/FRUIT OF THE SPIRIT: Self-Control, Patience, Discernment

REPLACEMENT PRAYER: . Lord, take away the desire for more and replace it with self-control, patience, and discernment.

TRAINING: Give away excess items. Put out smaller plates and have the teen start with one spoonful of each dish. Wait before eating more, buying more, gathering more. Talk about the difference between wants and needs.

THE SEVENTH DEADLY SIN: Pride
GODLY TRAITS/FRUIT OF THE SPIRIT: Humility, Meekness
REPLACEMENT PRAYER: . God, remove the sin of pride from my child and give him humility and meekness.

TRAINING: Approach family life like a team. Have each family member recognize and appreciate other family members. Have the siblings teach one another a skill.

Here are a couple other common issues a parent of a teen may want to pray using the *Replacement Technique*:

- ♥ If your child lies or steals, pray God replaces the dishonest heart with an honest heart.

- ♥ If your child is doing drugs or drinking alcohol, pray the Lord replaces the need to use substances to feel good with contentment in all circumstances.

When reviewing the deadly sins list, it's easy to rush to judgment, noticing others' shortcomings before our own. This isn't to say we aren't to be discerning. It is important to know right from wrong. Being judgmental is judging hypocritically or self-righteously. "Do not judge, or you too will be judged" (Matthew 7:1). With the right heart we're able to demonstrate love while training our children in the war against sin.

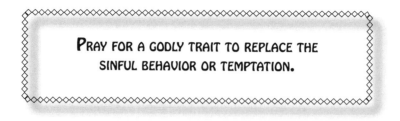

THE SLIPPERY SLOPE

One of the best gifts we can give our kids is to teach them how to effectively pray against temptation. In combining the best of the Chum, tenderness, with the Coach's guidance, we can train our tweens and teens to pray specially against the things that tempt them using the *Replacement Technique.* If he's tempted sexually, have him pray that he has enough self-control to flee from situations or avoid circumstances that could lead to sexual activity. Pray to replace the desire to have a sexual relationship with the longing for a healthy, satisfying, and God-honoring relationship with friends. Ask God to instill a need for a growing relationship with Him. Encourage the teen to rely on God's Word to shape his character. "How can a young man keep his way pure? By living according to your word" (Psalm 119:9).

Train your child against the slippery slope of compromise in moral, legal, or ethical issues. Coercion happens from external sources, usually peers, and compromise begins in the mind. Ready your child with the knowledge that sin likes company. Arguments and persuasion are techniques people use to get others to join in sinful activities.

Kids involved in substance abuse entice others to join them. It starts small: "Hey, if you want, I have some extra weed. You can give it a try. It's safe. You at least have to try getting high once in your life." Or "Marijuana? It's no big deal. It's even legal in a lot of states now. Even some doctors give it to their patients." The young person thinks, "Yeah, it's no big deal. I'll just try it once."

The persuasion then moves to a group activity, where kids bond with other kids who are involved with pot. "Jackson's parents are out of town. He's having a party. Everyone is going to be there.

Come." The teen reasons, "All the cool kids will be there. I can always leave if I want."

New friend connections are established, and the experience is pleasurable. In the child's mind, *it's all good.*

What the child needs is a way out. Show him how to pray for a temptation escape: "Lord, when I feel tempted, You promise to provide a way out of the situation. Help me to have eyes to see the open door." "No temptation has seized you except what is common to man. And God is faithful; he will not let you be tempted beyond what you can bear. But when you are tempted, he will also provide a way out so that you can stand up under it" (1 Corinthians 10:13). God provides a way out of any tempting situation, yet we often don't make use of the escape route He offers. We believe we can handle it ourselves, accepting the lie that it only takes will power. Instead, supernatural power is needed to engage in the temptation battle.

Pray for your child. Pray he gets caught if he has done wrong. Young adults are typically impulsive people, not thinking through the consequences of an action, slowly by degrees making small compromises that end up leading to trouble. There are a lot of lies that come at the beginning of a tempting circumstance. *No one will find out. Just try it; it's no big deal. Everyone does it. Come on, it's fun.*

Our families, both the Wildenbergs and Danielsons, have experienced situations where the slippery slope has been evident. One poor decision leads to the downhill slide of more bad choices and consequences. This is the time to train not blame or shame. Mistakes and poor choices are opportunities for kids to learn and for parents to instruct.

In my (Lori) home we have found timelines are a very effective means of turning a nasty circumstance into a teachable moment. A visual timeline demonstrates the slippery slope of compromise. Diagram the choices in a linear fashion, asking questions such as, "Where do you think things started to go badly?" followed by, "What could you have done differently? What will you do the next time?" Get the child thinking. Help him connect the dots from action to consequence, identifying how many opportunities he had to turn things around.

After having yielded to the actual temptation of drugs, alcohol, stealing, lying, sneaking out, same-sex attraction, premarital or casual sex, a connection in the brain has been established. Now it's easier to repeat. This pattern is why your child needs to know how to handle temptation and be aware of the precursors leading up to the sinful behavior. The "whatevers" from Philippians 4:8 will help your tween or teen renew his mind and retrain his brain. Whatever is true, noble, right, pure, lovely, admirable, excellent, or praiseworthy, think about and practice these. Replace evil with goodness to stop sin's progression.

Discussing your child's struggles brings them out of the shadows and into the light, eliminating the power of secrecy and shame. This type of conversation needs to be ongoing rather than a one-time event.

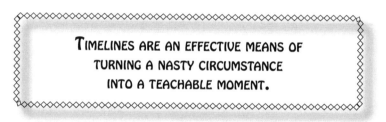

TIMELINES ARE AN EFFECTIVE MEANS OF
TURNING A NASTY CIRCUMSTANCE
INTO A TEACHABLE MOMENT.

IT'S MY LIFE

There are kids who refuse to recognize their behavior as sinful, or they simply don't care. A parent's best defense is to pray and allow the natural consequences to take over. This course of action is painful.

We need to seek professional help for ourselves if the child is unwilling to admit he needs help. A good prayer for a child who isn't able to see his sin is to pray that the activity or relationship leaves him empty and unsatisfied. This prayer works well with inappropriate relationships and substance abuse. Continue to love the tween or teen child unconditionally by regularly verbalizing your affection. Honestly and firmly tell him you don't agree with his choices or actions. Don't compromise beliefs; a consistent stance in conviction is critical.

TreeHouse, a faith-based organization that offers hope, guidance, and unconditional love to at-risk teens, recommends the following:

1. Control what you can, not what you can't. Parents cannot control the behavior but can control the consequences.

2. Have the right parenting goal. Help the teen learn from his mistakes and successes to become self-responsible.

3. Your influence or lack of influence comes from your relationship, not your rules.

4. Work at understanding the teen and why he chose a particular behavior.

5. Don't cover for your teen when he makes poor choices.[28]

Pray for wisdom and kindness before speaking with the kids about a poor choice they made. When considering what to say, keep the words to a minimum. Fewer words deliver a more powerful message, and we are less likely to regret what we have spoken. When we listen, without being on the defense or offense, we demonstrate we can deal with the issue and love the child.

Look for common ground as a starting place, seeking unity to restore the relationship. Pray that our kids have an open heart and a desire to stop the harmful behavior. Build other bridges so the disappointing and heart-breaking behavior isn't the only topic of conversation.

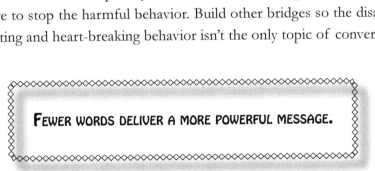

FEWER WORDS DELIVER A MORE POWERFUL MESSAGE.

SEIZE THE MOMENT

Kids are of the opinion that they are only young once so they must make the most of it. The issue of sex is a difficult one. Our kids are exposed not only to premarital sex but recreational hooking-up sex, experimental sex, group sex, friends with benefits sex, same-gender sex. If we want to get the message of purity across, we need to be well-equipped. The lines "Because I said so" or "Just say no" won't fly without reason and sound biblical truth.

It's a challenge for young people who live in the moment to understand sexual sin has long-lasting effects. Sex prior to or in the absence of marriage creates unique problems. Doug Herman, national speaker on purity and author of *Come Clean*, says, "... you're forced to believe one of two lies to avoid getting hurt. Either you can disconnect with your emotions to keep from feeling anything, or you can view sex as non-emotional, only physical entertainment. It's not possible to separate emotion from what you do with your body. You will feel something—someday."[29]

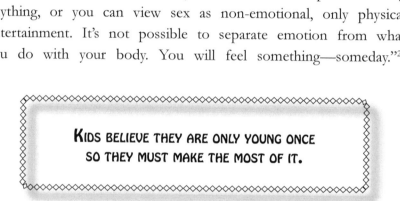

KIDS BELIEVE THEY ARE ONLY YOUNG ONCE SO THEY MUST MAKE THE MOST OF IT.

There are typically two types of guys when it comes to dating. The ones who want to conquer and the ones who want to protect. The boys interested in conquering want to win in the relationship. Winning often means conquering the girl's purity. This type of guy is all about immediate gratification; he's impatient, immature, selfish, and may be quick to anger. The second type of young man is more mature, able to demonstrate self-control, unselfishness, patience, and protection. He sees waiting as honorable and his date as valuable.

Typically, a boy will take the girl's lead but may continue to test the boundaries. How he responds to her "No" says a lot about his character. A true gentleman doesn't even try to push past the boundaries. This type of guy is a rare breed.

Another difficult scenario is the young man who wants to wait for marriage. He needs to be forthcoming with his date if she's leading him down a path that will tempt him. If the young woman is not able to respect his limits, then he needs to end the date and possibly the relationship. Researcher Jeannie Jasper Edwards has observed this phenomenon. "Now with equal rights, the instant access of technology and the popularity of hooking up, girls are just as likely to be the pursuers as the boys traditionally were. The girl being the aggressor is becoming the norm! A girl who values purity is the exception."[30]

For both boys and girls who value purity and commitment, it's always better to stay out of situations that could lead to sex. But if the young person does find himself or herself in a bad spot, fleeing like Joseph did in Genesis 39 is the way to go.

Make a pact with your child that you will come rescue him or her from any situation. Promise you will not ask questions but will come running. Allow him or her the freedom to tell you what happened or not. Let your young person know you will be there when he or she feels uncomfortable with a situation.

Purity is often something that is hoped for but often not achieved. Most parents hope their child will handle sexual temptation better than they did. Pray asking God if and when transparency is called for. When having a tough and tender conversation, be bold *if* God moves in this direction. It will be awkward and uncomfortable. Focus on the heart-breaking effects of the experience rather than specific details. The child may only listen and not share his personal experience. This is okay. The blessing will be what God does in the child through the honest and very personal communication. If a child has disappointed himself or herself by crossing that line, there is hope. Virginity can't return, but through recommitment, purity can be reestablished. The greatest result is peace because repentance is part of God's plan. The enemy whispers, "Oh well, you did it, so now what's the point?" Kids don't have to buy the lie. They can repent and recommit.

> **VIRGINITY CAN'T RETURN,
> BUT PURITY CAN BE REESTABLISHED.**

LOOSE LIPS

We sin with our bodies and we sin with our mouths. "Nothing good can come of gossip. Gossip—which includes passing along secrets and talking negatively about others—destroys relationships, ruins lives, and causes a host of emotional and psychological problems. Is it any wonder God so frequently told his people to control their tongues?" writes Marcia Ford and Lila Empson in *Checklist for Life for Teens*.[31] If we want our kids to be innocent of gossiping, we must be also. When we talk with our tween or teen about what gossip looks like, its harmful results, and techniques to avoid being a part of it, we train them to handle situations they may encounter. Aside from not passing it along, other ways to rise above gossip are to walk away from the conversation, change the subject, or make a direct statement regarding not gossiping. The Spanish proverb that says, "Whoever gossips to you will gossip about you," rings true. With all the social networking sites, cell phones, Twitter and others, gossip travels even faster than a wildfire. Let's teach our kids to extinguish gossip rather than fan it.

When we help our kids distinguish between gossip and getting help, they can better discern how to assist a friend who is involved in a harmful situation. *Telling to get someone out of trouble is a moral responsibility and is not gossiping.* Train the young person to ask himself, "Am I concerned for my friend's physical safety or emotional well-being? Who would be the best adult to help in this situation? (Parents? Police? Teacher?) Confiding in a friend is sometimes a cry for help.

Preteen and teen friendships are often fickle, and girls in particular use gossip as a means of jockeying for position in a social group. "The tongue is a small part of the body, but it makes great boasts.

166

Consider that a great forest is set on fire by a small spark. The tongue is also a fire" (James 3:5-6a). Gossip is a sin that hurts and humiliates. It's typically used to build one's self-esteem while tearing down another's.

What if your child is gossiping? Speak privately and build empathy by asking your child to put himself in the other child's place. Brainstorm ideas on how to fix the problem, including an apology and a request for forgiveness. Later discuss the results to keep the child accountable.

When our kids are the victims of gossip and they trust us enough to confide in, be available and listen. We want our kids to feel love, affirmation, and security. This situation is embarrassing for teens to admit, so we need to be sensitive and calm, asking for permission to assist. If he's agreeable, we can help the child figure out how to respond, although we can't promise not to be angry.

Advice that begins with ignoring the situation seems reasonable but often doesn't work at the middle school and high school level. Each day, each hour, other students are watching to see how the victim will respond. If the young person wants to deal with this on his own, we can assure him we are available to be a sounding board or a shoulder to lean on.

Rosalind Wiseman, author of *Queen Bees & Wannabes*, lists five possible options for the parent to recommend to the child. The child can confront the "Really Mean Girl" (RMG) or ask a teacher or counselor for help. The next three suggestions involve the parent calling the RMG's parents, talking with the teacher, or contacting an administrator.

If the child chooses the confrontation option, help him prepare by rehearsing a few short, direct statements with a clear and calm voice, steady eye contact, and good posture. The conversation includes three thoughts. First, the thing that's bothering him. Second, a request of what he does or doesn't want. Third, affirmation of the person and/ or the relationship.[32] For example, "I don't like what you said about me on Facebook. You have the power to remove it. I want it off, and you can do that." The confrontation should not be a challenge and should optimally be done privately in a neutral place. Unfortunately, there is no control over the victimizer's response, so pray for a soft heart.

When the teen or tween does ask for assistance and the chosen course of action is to speak with the other child's parents, assume they don't know what is happening. Then ask for their help. By seeking assistance we avoid accusing the other parent of poor parenting. The hope is to work together to resolve the problem. (To find information on cyberbullying, go to Chapter 11, Choose to Protect.) The harassment could escalate if it's handled with anger.

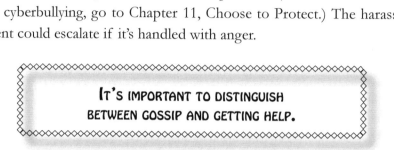

IT'S IMPORTANT TO DISTINGUISH
BETWEEN GOSSIP AND GETTING HELP.

THE WINNING TEAM

Any sin can be overcome with Jesus. He's fighting for us against the enemy. Jesus Christ is the ultimate victor. Satan has no real hold on God's children. Our kids will be tested in their faith by how they respond to temptation. The purpose of the testing is to take them to the next level of maturity. God allows this. Let's be prepared rather than surprised when it's revealed that our kids have been presented with temptation or succumbed to it. Jesus said to Peter, "Watch and pray so that you will not fall into temptation. The spirit is willing, but the body is weak" (Mark 14:38).

We can coach our children to look at the situation, recognize temptation and the enemy's efforts to distract, discourage, and derail. We can help them with strategies of prayer, avoidance, flight, or fight when temptation calls. We can pray for our kids to have clear eyes to see life through a heavenly perspective and choose goodness over evil.

LOVE NOTES ON GOODNESS

LORI WRITES: Recently, I was paging through a parenting book by another author. There was a picture of this writer's family in the book. The entire family looked as if they had never committed a sinful action or had a sin-laced thought. I felt defeated with my own sin nature and discouraged with my loved ones. My perception was inaccurate. Every family deals with sin. There have been times I have thought, "I have no business writing a parenting book." A friend of mine consoled me, "I don't want to hear from someone who never struggled with anything. That's not my life. I want to hear from someone who can relate and help me."

BECKY WRITES: I deeply desire to do things perfectly. Using the gifts God has given me combined with wanting to do things well is strength, but the dark side of this characteristic is perfectionism. Like work-a-holism, it hurts the people I love and it hurts me. My drive to be perfect can cause me to be frustrated and my children to feel inadequate. Sometimes good is good enough. Perfection comes from Jesus alone.

QUESTIONS

1. What tempts you?

2. What tempts your child?

3. Where do you compromise your morals or values? How can you change this?

PARENTING TIPS

1. Use the Replacement Technique when praying with and for your children.

2. Train kids to recognize their own area of weakness and vulnerability.

3. Be a Coach and help your child create a plan. Teach how to flee from, avoid, or stand up to tempting situations.

PRAYER

Father in Heaven,

You are holy, holy, holy. I am not. Bring to mind the things that tempt me and tempt my kids. Lord, I pray that when my children are engaged in a particular sin that it comes to light. I pray that the sin does not satisfy but leaves my children empty and unsatisfied. Move in their hearts. Replace the sin addiction with a spiritual craving for You. Renew my mind and those of whom I love.

Amen

WHILE WE WERE STILL SINNERS, CHRIST DIED FOR US.

Romans 5:8b

CHAPTER 10

CHOOSE TRUTH

LOVE REJOICES WITH THE TRUTH.

1 Corinthians 13:6b

I TELL YOU THE TRUTH

Have you ever wondered why, in John 18:38, Pontius Pilot walked away and didn't wait for the answer to his question, "What is truth?" I (Becky) have. His question was one of the most profound questions ever asked of Jesus. It's a thought philosophers of yesterday and today have debated. Truth today is viewed as a matter of perspective, perception, and personal experience. Yet we intuitively know and can distinguish right from wrong, good from evil. God gives us a desire to seek truth, yet our worldly notions cloud the heavenly perspective.

Twenty-seven times in the gospels Jesus begins His teaching with, "I tell you the truth." This phrase is a "sit up and take notice" statement. The teaching following this phrase is important. He told His followers the truth of how to live and love others. But we've manipulated and twisted Jesus' words to suit our notions. Through free will we are able to receive or reject what He has taught. The culture responds with, "What's true for you may not be true for me."

Arming our youth with truth, biblical truth, prepares them for the world. School, friends, and society challenge the notion of absolute truth. Lack of truth permeates our society.

In this chapter, Lori and I will discuss absolute truth, the power of eternal moments, intentional family time, worship, and how to teach the Word of God to our children.

A PARENT'S MOST IMPORTANT JOB

Kids today don't know biblical truth. And few parents are taking the time to teach the truth. "Many have estimated that between 69% and 94% of their young people are leaving the traditional church after high school…and very few are returning," states Josh McDowell in his book *Last Christian Generation*.[33] Our children's faith is floundering.

One sixteen-year-old girl knew the cultural differences between Christmas and Easter, Santa and the Easter Bunny, but she had no clue about our Savior's birth and resurrection. Hard to imagine but true. Another teenager asked, "What does Jesus have to do with Christmas?"

There is hope. Study after study shows the tremendous impact parents have on their children's faith. Research done at Fuller Institute by doctors Kara E. Powell and Chap Clark found kids are most influenced by and connected to parents when it comes to faith development. Graduating seniors highlighted five groups of influential people: youth group friends, other friends, youth leaders, parents, and other adults. Parents ranked first in the quality and quantity of faith support.[34]

Parents are number one in leading youth to Christ. This is an awesome responsibility and a great privilege. Yet some of us feel inadequate to teach the Word of God. If you are in this boat, know you are not only uniquely qualified but divinely chosen. It's a beautiful thing to learn alongside your child, trusting the Holy Spirit to be the teacher.

There are some tough kids, the ones who reject their family values. They refuse to attend church and appear to dismiss faith completely. In *The Myth of the Perfect Parent*, Leslie Leyland Fields cites a study done at the Center for the Developing Child at Harvard University and Birbeck University in London. "[Researchers] found that the child most likely to adopt his parents' values is not the mellow, compliant child, as one would expect, but the fussy, difficult child. The fussy child is genetically wired through the presence of DNA variants to be more sensitive and attuned to her parents and surroundings."[35]

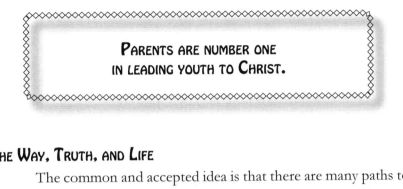

PARENTS ARE NUMBER ONE
IN LEADING YOUTH TO CHRIST.

The Way, Truth, and Life

The common and accepted idea is that there are many paths to heaven. Jesus answers that claim with, "I am the way and the truth and the life. No one comes to the Father except through me" (John 14:6). This verse *is* truth, the truth regarding the only way to heaven. Salvation is found in Christ alone. "...For there is no other name under heaven given to men by which we must be saved" (Acts 4:12b). Unfortunately, many in our open-minded culture find this truth too restrictive and intolerant. God makes it simple and fair, one way for all without any confusion. The Bible is God's revelation to His children containing all we need to know about the character of God and the way He desires us to live.

"As Christians we must understand that whatever opposes God's Word or departs from it in any way is a danger to the very cause of truth. Passivity toward known error is not an option for the Christian. Staunch intolerance of error is built into the very fabric of Scripture. And tolerance of known error is anything but a virtue. ... We can't tell the world, 'This is truth, but whatever you want to believe is fine, too.' It's not fine. Scripture commands us to be intolerant of any idea that denies the truth," states John McArthur.[36]

Absolute Truth

Wisdom and discernment keep us living in the truth as opposed to becoming "captive through hollow and deceptive philosophy, which depends on human tradition and the basic principles of this world rather than on Christ" (Colossians 2:8). We're warned to watch for deceptions throughout life.

There are right and wrongs, absolutes in the world. Train children to know the difference between subjective truth, opinion or preference, and objective truth, which is fact. Subjective statements place emphasis on a person's mood, attitude, experience, and opinion. Opinion and preference are not absolute truth. Consider the tug-o-war between the Green Bay Packers and the Minnesota Vikings; each group having the confidence that their team will prevail over the other is evidence of that opinion. (Lori and I were born and raised in Viking territory, so we are very familiar with this rivalry.) Cheese-heads love their team, rooting for them with gusto. With equal enthusiasm and loyalty, Vikings fans support the Vikes. This is preference. The teams' stats demonstrate, without emotion, which team is having the best year. That is fact.

Objective fact is observable and proven. Those things considered objective, such as mathematical equations, the Law of Gravity, and God, are examples of absolute truth. Math always has a correct answer, things will fall when dropped, and God is God. We all agree that two plus two equals four, but we may disagree on which team to cheer on—the Vikings or the Packers. Our kids need the tools to speak up and stand up for truth when they go to school.

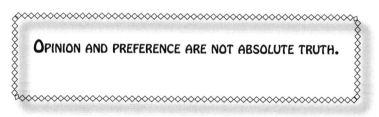

OPINION AND PREFERENCE ARE NOT ABSOLUTE TRUTH.

CHALLENGING TIMES

Our young people need the tools to filter through other religions and New Age thoughts of the day. They will see rejection of God's Word all around them. Oswald Chambers states the rejection phenomenon succinctly, "Men do not reject the Bible because it contradicts itself but because it contradicts them."[37]

Discernment is necessary for children of faith from preschool to college. A college student was given an assignment to support God's existence or to deny it. This could have been a hard assignment if the student was not grounded in his faith. Take the time to address questions as they arise to plant the seeds of faith as it relates to science and philosophy. Questions like, Where did God come from? Why do bad things happen if there's a God? What about the dinosaurs? How was the earth created? Does heaven (hell) exist?

The big bang and evolution theories resurface in college. Heaven and hell are pondered. The existence of God is questioned. These are opportunities for the parent to introduce a Christian worldview as children begin to ask us about the world. Questions are good. Questioning shows interest and a desire to learn. Academic challenges cause us to dig deeper. While raising your kids, teach them answers to these questions before they leave the nest. And train them to ask questions. One dad taught his tween-aged kids to ask, "How do you know that to be true?" when presented with theories like evolution or the big bang. He said this question came in handy when his kids became college students. Here are some facts to present to the teen in regard to popular questions:

- ♥ Nothing comes from nothing. (A big bang can't self-combust if there is no spark.)
- ♥ God is the uncreated creator. (You have to start somewhere.)
- ♥ We live in a fallen world. (That's why there is sickness, poverty, and natural disasters.)
- ♥ Dinosaurs, koalas, some historical events, and the western continents are not mentioned in Scripture. (The Bible doesn't cover everything. Its purpose is for God to make Himself known to man. It is interesting to note many scholars consider the behemoth, Job 40:15, and the leviathan, Job 41:1, to have been land-dwelling dinosaurs.)
- ♥ Order is never the result of chaos. (Big bang can't produce an orderly universe.)

- ♥ Bad things happen due to the gift of free will. (God didn't make us puppets.)
- ♥ We know good and bad because we are given a conscience. (In the theory of evolution a conscience wouldn't develop, only the notion of survival of the fittest.)
- ♥ If there's no hell, what's the point of living rightly and receiving God's love or justice? (If there's no eternity, we may as well live with reckless abandon and hopelessness.)

I (Lori) have found it beneficial to have responses or sound bites to typical "trick" questions. Hopefully, these statements will be helpful when talking with your kids. Training the young person how to stand up for his faith, articulate his beliefs, and how to discover answers to his own questions are important as well. One of the most helpful tools contained in most Bibles is the concordance. BibleGateway.com and the BibleAnswerMan.com are excellent resources, too.

GET SCHOOLED

"The big bang and the theory of evolution are a part of the science curriculum in our school district," one mom stated. "I was worried how this would be handled. I have to say I was pleasantly surprised. The teacher gave the definitions of both, stated they were theories not proven facts, and then moved to the next portion of the curriculum. There was no preaching or influencing. I was thankful my sophomore was in her class."

Be in the know regarding school curriculum. Attending conferences and back-to-school meetings helps parents to be informed. These meetings are opportunities to respectfully ask questions. A mom of a tween shared this story: "At conferences, I made a point of asking the teacher if he planned on using the Constitution, Declaration of Independence, Federalist Papers, and the Bill of Rights in their entirety. I asked specifically because the Mayflower Compact had been read to my tweens and the teacher left out all mention of God. Faith was the defining reason the Pilgrims came to the New World, 'Having undertaken for the Glory of God, and Advancement of the Christian Faith.'"[38] Propaganda is not only what is added but also what is left out.

My (Lori) eleven-year-old nephew keenly deduced his teacher supported one political candidate over another. I commended him on his critical thinking skills and his ability to understand persuasion and identify opinion. To increase discernment in children, talk about the power of influence, critical thinking, and objective and subjective truth. While watching TV shows, point out the subtle nature of the programs and commercials. Slants and bias are used to influence the viewer. Increase discernment by seizing the moment to develop critical thinking skills. Train your child to ponder, "Why is this material presented in this way? Does one person or group of people have something to gain? Is this opinion or fact?" Watch for opportunities to sort fact from fiction. Election years are excellent times to train the young person in critical thinking skills.

WATCH FOR OPPORTUNITIES TO SORT FACT FROM FICTION.

GET SMART

Charles Spurgeon wrote, "One of the best ways of convincing men of error is not so much to denounce the error as to proclaim the truth more clearly. If a stick is crooked, and you wish to prove that it is so, get a straight one, and quietly lay it down by its side, and when men look they will surely see the difference. The Word of God has a very keen edge about it."[39] When we know what we believe and why we believe it, we can then develop the skill to communicate those beliefs to others.

A high school freshman was given an assignment in her English class to write a paper and then give a persuasive talk on the chosen topic. The subject matter was to be hot social topics like prochoice, prolife, euthanasia, and capital punishment. This student chose prolife. After much research and writing she was ready to present and articulate her beliefs. The teacher, personally prochoice, was to be commended. She was a true educator. The point of the assignment was to encourage the students to logically present their personal stands on important issues. This teacher allowed for all kinds of dialog. She provided a safe environment for freedom of thought and speech. The teacher didn't try to shut down or override this student's persuasive speech with her own personal views. Following the talk, some students came up to the presenter and had changed their opinion on abortion.

A real education is one that moves students to a place where they're learning to think and problem solve for themselves. There are some classroom teachers that prevent this occurrence. These are places where the teacher chooses to indoctrinate rather than educate. The atmosphere is stifling and intimidating. The teacher's personal bias dictates the grades and assignments. Knowing the type of educational environment in which the child is immersed is helpful. It will vary from district to district, school to school, and classroom to classroom. When students are given assignments like the one above, it's good to know if the teacher is one who wants to educate or indoctrinate. Start by asking the child about the tone in the classroom. If it appears to be hostile or one of indoctrination, make an appointment with the teacher. Respectfully ask questions about the lesson's objective and discuss how your student is meeting that criterion. I have found it best to ask rather than accuse. If parent and instructor are not able to come to a meeting of the minds, the principal is the next stop.

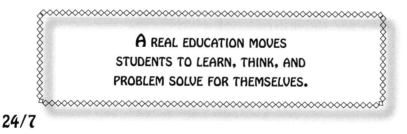

A REAL EDUCATION MOVES STUDENTS TO LEARN, THINK, AND PROBLEM SOLVE FOR THEMSELVES.

24/7

What are other ways to bring Scripture into everyday life? The two greatest commands are to love God and love others (Matthew

22:36-40). Be the Coach, talk about how a life for Christ is going to look different in the lunchroom, on the playground, the sports field, and in a high school science class. Sitting with or playing with the kid who is alone at lunch or on the playground is a way to show compassion. Playing by the rules and encouraging teammates to do their best shows determination and kindness. The ability to support creationism in biology class points to conviction and acceptance of God's Word. During the classroom discussions, teach children to acknowledge man's other scientific theories, but coach them to be able to defend God's truth respectfully. Confidence in God's truth will lead others to Christ.

Lori and I recommend talking about faith matters any day, anytime. Mealtime is especially well suited for this conversation. On Sunday, discuss the sermon during dinner. Share the events of the day with one another, both the highs and the lows. "What was the best part of your day? What was the hardest part?" When appropriate, weave faith applications into the conversations without getting preachy. High-powered, guilt-ridden words like "should," "ought," "need," "always," and "never" have the power to shut down or stir up a teen in no time flat. Sentences that start with, "That's not what the Bible says," or "Scripture doesn't support that," or "God would be so disappointed," may be true statements, but they are also conversation killers. The idea isn't to lecture, shame, guilt, or preach but to dialogue. One mother of two teens shared her family's dinner time question, "What did you do today that made God smile?" These are nonthreatening Chum-like ways to encourage deeper conversations rather than simply asking, "How was your day?"

Some families read a page in a devotional together. A mother of four and foster mom of many puts a daily verse on a white board near the back door for her kids to read. They see the verse both leaving and entering the home, similar to the doorframe thought in Deuteronomy 6:5-9. "Love the LORD your God with all your heart and with all your soul and with all your strength. These commandments that I give you today are to be on your hearts. Impress them on your children. Talk about them when you sit at home and when you walk along the road, when you lie down and when you get up. Tie them as symbols on your hands and bind them on your foreheads. Write them on the doorframes of your houses and on your gates."

Scott and I have found morning is the best time for Bible study in our family. The boys have similar schedules. Breakfast as a family has become a great time for the four of us to come together to read God's Word. We read a chapter or two in the Bible, discussing as we go.

Different family circumstances may prevent this time and venue from being successful in other homes. If your family is currently faith resistant, start small. Notice Deuteronomy 6 doesn't say, "Sit down and force feed Scripture." It does remind us to build faith into everyday activities. The setting doesn't have to be formal or structured. Informality and a lack of structure are okay and often just as effective. Regular conversations and daily actions are ways to live faith. Informal and impromptu lessons are eternal moments. "They are moments in time that we instill our own love of the Lord in our children. Eternal moments are the times we spend enriching our souls and minds or teaching spirituality to our children."[40] Find a time and venue that works for your family. Engage in spiritual spontaneous moments, too.

Incorporating prayer into the day impresses the importance of communication with God. Pray with and for your kids before they leave for school. A quick prayer for God to protect and provide are usually welcomed. Some teens or tweens are adverse to prayer. If so, pray for him on your own.

Many parents with older teens have expressed their "biggest regret" to me (Lori). They look back wishing they had prayed together as a family. If you happen to feel this way, too, don't worry. We have an omnipresent God who isn't constrained by the element of time. Go ahead and start now. Praying before eating is a nonthreatening way to begin but a big first step in introducing the family to prayer. Be flexible and willing to listen to God's Spirit for the best way for your family to embrace prayer and the Bible.

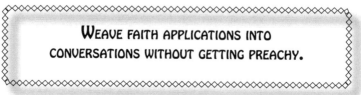

WEAVE FAITH APPLICATIONS INTO
CONVERSATIONS WITHOUT GETTING PREACHY.

WALKING IN TRUTH

My (Becky) favorite verse in regard to parenting is, "I have no greater joy than to hear that my children are walking in the truth" (3 John 1:4). What greater joy could there be for Christian parents than to see their children living out a faith-filled life following Jesus Christ as Lord and Savior?

Please don't be dismayed if you have a prodigal child—one who rejects God. Persist in prayer. Keep in mind God specifically chose to place that child in your home. God's purposes will prevail. It's possible the present situation looks bleak. Focus on the eternal rather than the temporal and have hope. In some families a sibling introduces a brother or sister to God. There are situations where the parent isn't as involved in a child's spiritual growth. The disciples are perfect examples. Think of Peter; he met Jesus because of his brother Andrew. James was brought to the Lord because of his brother John. Peers can be a positive influence as well. After Jesus told Philip to follow Him, Philip quickly found his buddy Nathanael and told him about Jesus (John 1:35-51). Pray that God will use the people in your prodigal child's life to show the way.

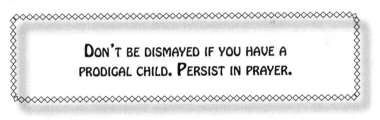

DON'T BE DISMAYED IF YOU HAVE A PRODIGAL CHILD. PERSIST IN PRAYER.

BE INTENTIONAL WITH FAMILY TIME

In teaching tweens and teens to rely on God and His precepts instead of society, we need to help them become critical thinkers to discern truth and live a Christ-like life. Here are some guidelines for families to use.

1. Know biblical truth by studying the Word of God.

2. Practice apologetics, facts of faith, to defend belief in Jesus Christ.

3. Be responsible in sharing the gospel in love and truth using respectful statements.

4. Know Scripture passages that define Jesus as the Way, the Truth, and the Life.

5. Recognize the difference between opinion and fact.

6. Follow God's will and design versus personal wants and desires.

Kirk Weaver is in the business of intentional and formal spiritual training in the home. He says, "If you haven't started intentional spiritual training in the home and your children are already teenagers, do not be discouraged. If you can get thirty lessons in the home before they leave, your children will remember the home as having had formal spiritual training."[41] He cautions parents of teens, "Providing deliberate home lessons isn't a guarantee that teens won't use drugs or have premarital sex. Our teens live in a culture filled with beliefs that contradict the Christian faith."[42]

By using Kirk's *Family Time Training* tool or another method of teaching God's Word, "teens will have a plumb line of right and wrong in making decisions."

"We desire to communicate our ethics, values, morals and faith to our kids. When we deliberately present these standards teens may still choose to do something wrong but they will know that they are doing something wrong. They are growing up in a culture with peers who do not even know pornography is wrong, recreational drug use is wrong and casual sex is wrong. They are going to school with teachers who do not have the same guidelines or faith values. When we obey God's commandments, which include parents teaching their children about the faith (Deuteronomy 6), good things happen." [43]

GOOD NEWS

The Bible is our daily bread and the communication tool God most often uses to guide His children. Talk to Him in prayer and allow

Him to speak to you through His Word. Study Bibles for teens are wonderful and include thought-provoking questions teens can dive into that reflect issues they deal with today. The Bible is a life-giving tool on which we can depend. "For the LORD gives wisdom; from his mouth come knowledge and understanding" (Proverbs 2:6). This wisdom comes from prayer and His Word, the absolute truth.

Godly parenting is leading children to absolute truth found only in Jesus Christ—truly a parent's most important job. Society will continue to preach open-ended tolerance and declare there are many paths to heaven. Be an encourager in your children's faith development. Provide biblical truth and pray with and for your children to build a solid foundation of faith. Our primary duty as parents is to lead a godly lifestyle using gentleness and respect. St. Francis of Assisi said, "Preach the gospel at all times, and if necessary, use words."

Love Notes on Truth

Lori writes: My greatest prayer is for each of my four children to have a dynamic faith. The way God is working with each one is as unique as they are. I'm trusting God's faithfulness and timing to grow and draw each child to himself.

Becky writes: The Word of God is the only solid ground I can offer my children. The legacy I choose to leave for them is one of faith, hope, and love. In their darkest moments, I pray they will trust in the only real Truth there is in this world.

Questions

1. When society declares there are many paths to heaven, how do you teach your kids Jesus is the only way?

2. What experiences has your child shared with you that can be used to dialogue about a Christian worldview?

3. How do you preach Christ to your family?

Parenting Tips

1. Plan a family devotional time for your family. Discuss, apply, and memorize verses.

2. As the Controller, teach the difference between objective and subjective truth.

3. Discuss what your kids are learning in school. As the Coach and Consultant, guide them through questions to aid in discernment.

4. Pray together as a family. Take turns leading the prayer at mealtime or bedtime.

Prayer

Lord Jesus,

You are truth, absolute truth, in a world of contradictions. Forgive me for not looking to You to guide me. Your truth provides solid ground and light for my path. Lord, assist me in being intentional in how I teach my children Your ways. Provide time and opportunities each day for me to share Your Word as truth. Help me teach my children to discern between objective and subjective truth. Let each one of my family members be a light of Your truth in the world. To You be the glory forever and ever.

Amen

AS THE RAIN AND THE SNOW COME DOWN FROM HEAVEN, AND DO NOT RETURN TO IT WITHOUT WATERING THE EARTH AND MAKING IT BUD AND FLOURISH, SO THAT IT YIELDS SEED FOR THE SOWER AND BREAD FOR THE EATER, SO IS MY WORD THAT GOES OUT FROM MY MOUTH: IT WILL NOT RETURN TO ME EMPTY, BUT WILL ACCOMPLISH WHAT I DESIRE AND ACHIEVE THE PURPOSE FOR WHICH I SENT IT.

Isaiah 55:10-11

SECTION SIX

LOVE IS AN ACTION

Chapter 11

Choose to Protect

Love always protects.

1 Corinthians 13:7a

The Parent Trap

Parents have a protective instinct. When making a quick stop while driving, I (Lori) still whip out my right arm to steady the passenger. (My new drivers have informed me this is an unsafe practice due to the airbag. *I, Becky, while riding shotgun, have also experienced Lori's "I'm saving your life" reaction!*) Safety concerns surface at all developmental ages, from a toddler holding hands to cross the street to a teen driver buckling up in the car. Legal issues and moral values become challenged in the tween and teen years.

We may want to hold on tighter, but in order for our young people to be successful, our parenting style needs to shift. Moving to a less hands-on position has been tough for Tom and me. One of my teens told my husband and me we love too much. It wasn't a compliment. This child felt smothered and wanted to break free.

"These overly strict boundaries can stunt the emotional and spiritual growth of teens, keeping them from the essential learning that comes with good and bad decision making. Young teens need to be given small, safe tastes of independence so that they learn how to apply their faith to the decisions they make. If all of their decisions

186

are made for them, that discernment 'muscle' will wither away. The opposite extreme seems even more common these days and is possibly even more destructive. I see this extreme in exasperated parents who say, 'I don't know how to say no to him. He seems to want complete independence, and all his friends can do whatever they want. I don't know where to draw the line, so I let him decide for himself,'" states Mark Oestreicher, author of *Understanding Your Young Teen*.[44] If you're too soft, over-emphasizing feelings (the exaggerated Chum), yet fail to teach obedience, your teens will disrespect you. If you're overly authoritarian and oppressive (the extreme Controller), they'll shut you out.

Becky and I will explore when to step in and when to step back, allowing kids enough freedom to grow within the proper constraints at home, school, and in their relationships.

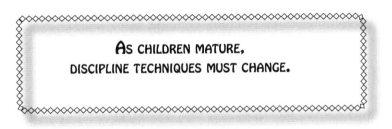

AS CHILDREN MATURE, DISCIPLINE TECHNIQUES MUST CHANGE.

ROAD WARRIOR

Getting a driver's license is a rite of passage. The teen moves from being driven to driving—exhilarating for the teen, terrifying for the parent. Unfortunately, car accidents and teens go together. Calling, "Be safe," as your child drives off isn't enough. Sadly, three of my (Lori) four children have experienced the death of a friend due to a car accident. My son and his college roommate were in a rollover accident in the mountains. The car was totaled, but thankfully both boys walked away unscathed.

Driving is serious business. Car accidents are the leading cause for death in fifteen- to nineteen-year-olds.[45] According to the Institute for Highway Safety, "In the United States, teenagers drive less than all but the oldest people, but their numbers of crashes and crash deaths are disproportionately high. In the United States, the fatal crash rate per mile driven for 16-19 year-olds is early 3 times the rate for drivers ages 20 and over. Risk is highest at ages 16-17. In fact, the fatal crash rate per mile driven is nearly twice as high for 16-17 year-olds as it is for 18-19 year-olds."[46]

Before relinquishing the keys, be clear and specific regarding family expectations. State consequences for broken rules then diligently enforce them. Basic car rules are wear a seat belt, don't use cell phones, follow the laws of the road, be a courteous and defensive driver, avoid tailgating, choose waiting if it's between that and rushing, and keep emotions in check. A natural consequence for not abiding by the rules could be loss of driving privileges for a period of time or driving only to designated locations.

Your child must have a clear understanding of these rules before you trust him to drive or allow him to ride with a friend. Engage your child's brain. Ask, "Who do feel safe riding with? What would you do if the driver has been drinking? What would you do if your friend was driving recklessly?" Driving is directly linked to responsibility; it is a privilege not a right.

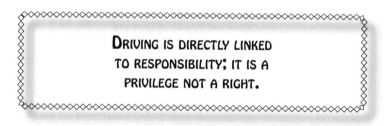

DRIVING IS DIRECTLY LINKED TO RESPONSIBILITY; IT IS A PRIVILEGE NOT A RIGHT.

MEDIA MADNESS

The information superhighway is another venue where safety is a concern. In a desire to keep the child safe on the Internet, we talk with him about what and what not to say on the social networks. The child thinks, "Mom and Dad don't get it." Maybe we don't.

Guidance regarding safety is important, but understand that these networks are social and self-promotional. Kids *want* to display personal pictures or comments on the Internet, getting a kick out of the attention generated. In the age of reality TV nothing is sacred or private. The unintended messages may not be what the young person had in mind. Give your tween or teen a basic guideline: "If you would feel uncomfortable having your grandmother see your words or pictures, don't put it out in cyberspace."

Most sites are not evil in and of themselves, but the potential for evil use is high. Doing our best to stay updated and informed is a start. The concerns are obvious: the display of inappropriate photos and exposure to those pictures, crude language, and cyberbullying. But consider the less obvious issues. The subtle problem these social sites feed is the stirring of envy or discontent. Seeing things others are doing and not being included, the feeling of not having a fulfilling life, not getting attention (likes, views) as compared to someone else. These places can be a breeding ground for insecurity. If your preteen or teen struggles with self-worth, these sites can make that feeling worse.

Applications can be outdated quickly. It is almost impossible to keep up. The best way to stay abreast of what's new in social media is to be tuned into your child and his conversations with peers. Ask him about the new apps available on the web and what he thinks about them.

The best and most proactive way to approach technology is to train our young people to discern the positive and negative uses for each site. Have the child verbalize the upside and downside to each app before downloading it.

Here's a basic rundown of some of the more popular media applications. Most of these spots have a required age of thirteen or older.

Facebook: A site where people post (or write) updates or photos. You can ask someone to be your friend or accept friend requests. There is an option for blocking and other privacy settings.

Instagram: A free app for a Mac or a Smartphone. Followers (must be approved) are able to see photos with captions added. Individual Instagram photos can be privately sent to one other person. (There is potential for inappropriate use with this feature.)

Twitter: Short text messages of 140 characters or less. Anyone can choose to follow another. There is no accepting or requesting followers. There is the option to block.

Vine: Similar to Instagram but rather than pictures, short six-second videos make up this app.

SnapChat: A smart phone application. People can SnapChat anyone on their phone contact list who also has the app. The photo can be set to be viewed for one to ten seconds. Then it disappears, unless a screen shot is taken. The person who sent the SnapChat is alerted if a screenshot is taken. (You can imagine how this application can be misused.)

The list goes on and continues to grow: ASK.fm (linked to some recent cyberbullying and suicides), Kik, Whisper, Tinder, and an especially disturbing online dating site called Plenty of Fish (POF).

Becky told me about an assembly her son attended at his high school. An administrator spoke, telling the students about a young man who was very successful in college. Right after graduation he was offered a job. Shortly after the young man accepted, the offer was withdrawn. The personnel department had done its research and discovered questionable pictures on a social media site. They felt the young man's actions did not line up with the company's philosophy. He lost the job before he even started.

Becky said this story made quite an impression on her son. I'm sure the rest of the students were affected as well. Rather than talking to your young person about reputation, ask what image he wants to project. Reputation is based on another's opinion rather than truth. Image is based on your opinion of yourself. We have more control over image than reputation.

> ASK YOUR CHILD, "WHAT IMAGE DO YOU WANT TO PROJECT?"

CANDID CAMERA

Unfortunately, tweens are now exposed in an up-close and personal way to the antics of older kids. Becky and I believe this to be a serious problem. Years ago there was a natural separation between middle school and high school, high school and college, but no longer. Social networks are exposing younger and younger kids to the activities of unwise older teens. Older teens are often highly influential in a preteen's life. The online conversation is often crass and offensive. Drinking and sex can be the main themes. Every action documented with a photo. All leave an impression on the viewer.

Pictures and videos can be taken on many gadgets. Two common practices in dating or even casual interacting are "sexting" and sexual "Skyping." Take time to discuss this degrading behavior. (By the way, if caught by law enforcement, the "sexter" will be listed as a sex offender—a potentially life-long label.)

In order to limit phone access, Scott and I (Becky) have the charging station for all cell phones in our bedroom. Phones are turned in for the night. We know the locking password to see what's on the phone: text messages and photos. If the password changes and we cannot unlock the cell phone, it isn't returned. As my mom always says, "He who pays the fiddler calls the tunes."

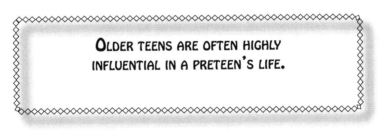

OLDER TEENS ARE OFTEN HIGHLY INFLUENTIAL IN A PRETEEN'S LIFE.

CYBERSPACE

Our kids can be affected by what they see online, and they can be affected by what directly happens to them online. Electronic aggression occurs in our kids' world. Cyberbullies are real-life bullies in virtual form.

The social bully, like the mean girls talked about in the goodness chapter, differs from the cyber ones. Cyberbullying is typically anonymous, sometimes done in a group but often perpetrated by one person. Electronic bullying is insidious and its messages spread like wildfire. Physically removing a child (like switching schools) may not solve the problem. Sadly, the bullying can take place anytime and anywhere. The victim is harassed, embarrassed, and sometimes even threatened. The mode these bullies use changes as quickly as our technology advances: text messages, chat rooms, and social media can all be used as weapons.

The statistics vary according the study and the definition of bullying. Anywhere from 16 to 50 percent of high school kids experience (or participate in) some form of Internet aggression. Lewd language, insults, and intimidation are the bully's tactics. It seems there are a variety of motivations for a bully to come after a victim: revenge, jealousy, attention, boredom, control, and even fun.

Kids who are bullied are typically Caucasian high school girls. The effects may be seen in truancy, substance abuse, poor grades, health issues, and low self-esteem. If it's suspected a preteen or teen is being bullied, Googling the child's name may help confirm a parent's suspicion.

Here are some things a parent can do to support his child and prevent or stop cyberbullying: change the young person's cell number and email address, adjust social sites to private and block the offender (if known), encourage the child to ignore and to not respond with anger (this only increases attacks), make copies and keep evidence of the messages, note frequency and intensity of threats, and provide hope to the child that this is temporary. If more drastic steps are needed, go to the parent of the bully and enlist his help (this may backfire, but it is worth the risk), get some software monitoring (Spector Soft is one type), contact the bully's ISP and report the offenses (if terms are violated, the Internet may be shut down for the cyberbully and his family), go to the school officials for support, talk with the police, or bring in legal actions. There have been kids who have committed suicide, known as bully-cide, due to this type of harassment. Cyber-aggression is serious.

MEDIA EXPOSURE

Set media limits to support your family values. Ratings are only part of the equation. When setting family guidelines for media, be clear about family standards for Internet usage, smart phone apps, and audio-visual material. Discuss with the kids what other children can and cannot bring into your home. "Parents have been lulled into lalla land by ratings. The most dangerous movies on the market are the PG13. They are targeting the youngest of the young adults with very positive views of homosexuality, abortion, and glorified sex. The issue is not the rating but the content and teaching discernment," states Chuck Stecker, president of A Chosen Generation.[47] There's no way to screen everything, but here are a few ideas that can be implemented for any type of media:

1. Limit screen time. Keep the computer and other Internet devices in a common area. Check the computer history. Join your child's social network(s) and "friend" him (of course he can block things he doesn't want you to see.) Or require he gives you his password if you allow him to set up a social network account.

2. Set the standard for appropriate material. Discuss family values when watching a show together. Be clear about the type of media other children can bring into the home. Provide the child the words to use to say no to unacceptable entertainment. Movie reviews can be thoroughly checked at www.pluggedin. com.

3. Listen to his music. The lyrics can be found at www.lyrics.com.

4. Determine if the child is developmentally ready for a cell phone. Look over your cell phone bill for additional charges. Learn texting language; help can be found at www.lingo2word. com.

When enforcing family guidelines, it is better for the child rather than the parent to communicate family media expectations to friends. If he's unable to speak up, the parent will need to take the initiative. This means being aware of what is being viewed and serious enough to enforce the rule. The child will most likely feel embarrassment when the parent puts a stop to the inappropriate entertainment. Give the tween or teen a heads-up that this will be the case.

This scenario has occurred in my (Lori) home. I sat down with my child and her friend while they were watching a movie the friend brought to our home. The material didn't fall within our viewing guidelines. An uncomfortable silence filled the family room. The young people waited it out. I hoped they'd turn off the movie. They didn't.

"This makes me feel uncomfortable."

No response.

"What do you think about this show?"

"It's not a big deal, Mom." Big sigh.

I verbalized what we were watching. The girls laughed and admitted it was a bit out there but didn't turn it off.

I took up the gauntlet, "This material is inappropriate. Find another show."

Now my kids do the monitoring to avoid embarrassment. Don't be afraid to take a stand. It's your home, your TV, your rules.

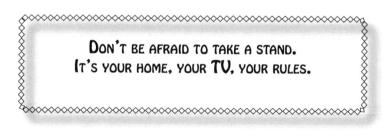

**DON'T BE AFRAID TO TAKE A STAND.
IT'S YOUR HOME, YOUR TV, YOUR RULES.**

WHO ARE YOU?

It's worth taking the time to get to know your child's friends and their parents. When picking up or dropping off children, go to the door and introduce yourself. The opportunity to meet the parents provides a point of reference for future communication. It's nice to get to know one another.

I (Becky) received a phone call from a mother whose son was a new friend of my teen. Her boy had been invited to our home for dinner and a movie. She was checking to see if Scott and I were going to be home. She also asked about the movie rating and what beverages were going to be served. I was not offended. I was so glad she inquired, and I told her. Many parents are afraid or hesitate to ask questions, but most don't mind being asked. Our kids are worth a little parental momentary discomfort.

Teachers can provide insight friendships as well. Teacher Natalie Larson recommends having strong communication with your child's teachers, especially in middle school. "Teachers are a good contact if you have social/peer concerns."[48]

Okay, so what do you do if a child chooses to be with a wilder crowd? A positive solution is to be the home where the kids hang out. Collecting and possessing landline, cell numbers, and home addresses of friends is critical. Cell phones make it easy for kids to say they're one place when they are in another. Parents can be fooled, and the kids know it. Know where they are. Know who they are with. If there is a party, contact the parents to see if they will be supervising the gathering.

I (Lori) recall a conversation with a mom who claimed the kids who came to her home following a school dance were so good. She went on to exclaim she'd be glad to host them again. I asked her why she thought they were so good. She stated the kids were so quiet she was even able to go to bed and sleep. Wait. What? By asking some questions I realized my definition of good and her definition of good were completely different. I made a mental note that her home was one with little to no supervision.

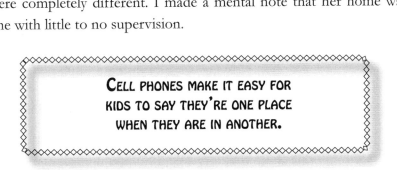

CELL PHONES MAKE IT EASY FOR KIDS TO SAY THEY'RE ONE PLACE WHEN THEY ARE IN ANOTHER.

Bottoms Up

While on Facebook, a mother of a teenage boy discovered a party had taken place at her home when she was out of town. With humor, grace, and truth she commented on the pictures taken in her home. She noted she was out of town when those photos were taken. Her son's friends responded with a single word, "Busted," and her next response was, "Let's talk." She kept the relationship and respect in tact while dealing with the issue.

Alcohol has become an easily accessible drug of choice for today's youth. One mother of teen boys shared a tactic she uses; she turns the alcohol bottles in her home upside down and marks them, then turns them upright again. She periodically checks to see if any alcohol is missing. Occasionally she drinks out of her sons' water bottles to test the contents.

Kids clandestinely drink at the most unlikely times and in the most unlikely places. Even religious activities could be places where young people sneak a swig. In an effort to keep teens from drinking on one youth retreat, the counselors searched the teens' baggage before loading it on the bus. Parent care packages were to be deposited in bins for delivery at camp later in the week. To get around the system, kids packaged individual size liquor bottles in large envelopes addressed to themselves and placed them in the parent package bins. During camp, the liquor was delivered to the kids via a parent care package. Where there's a will, there's a way!

A party where alcohol is supplied by parents is a growing and alarming trend. Some parents believe they're keeping the underage children safe by hosting a party and collecting car keys. Others are of this opinion: "Kids will drink anyway, so it's better to give them an opportunity to see how much liquor they can responsibly handle." And there are other parents who are opposed to these ideas. (Just so you know, your authors are in this camp.) If you hold the philosophy that supervised underage drinking is okay, consider the following: Drinking is currently illegal for people under twenty-one. Those who supply and host parties leave themselves open to potential legal issues.

196

By choosing not to follow the law, you give the subtle message of being above the law. The more experience and the younger a person is when experimenting with alcohol the more likely he is to become an alcoholic.

If you still choose to host a party and provide alcoholic drinks, be honest with and respectful to the parents of the children attending and give full party disclosure. In doing so, the other parents will then have the opportunity to allow their child to attend or opt out.

In a study done at The National Center on Addiction and Substance Abuse, a correlation was found between family dinnertime and the reduction of high-risk behavior, including alcohol use. Joseph A. Califano, Jr. states, "There are no silver bullets; unfortunately, the tragedy of a child's substance abuse can strike any family. But one factor that does more to reduce teens' substance abuse risk than almost any other is parental engagement, and one of the simplest and most effective ways for parents to be engaged in teens' lives is by having frequent family dinners."[49] Eating together, talking, knowing your teens' friends and their parents, and paying attention are all positive things parents can do to while navigating the teen years.

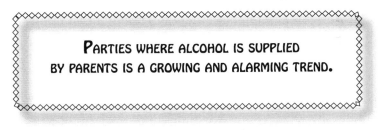

PARTIES WHERE ALCOHOL IS SUPPLIED
BY PARENTS IS A GROWING AND ALARMING TREND.

THE DATING GAME

The world says, "Kids will drink anyway. Kids are going to have sex anyway." The world has a defeatist attitude. The cultural behavior bar is low. We don't have to buy this.

As tears flowed, one mom confided in me (Lori) she had discovered her tenth-grade daughter was having sex. She had gone into her daughter's bedroom to talk and saw her clutching her teddy bear while sleeping. The mom was struck by the irony of this scene.

Her daughter was still a little girl, yet she was dabbling in grown-up behavior. This mom, although broken-hearted, handled things well. They had a loving and honest talk.

While sitting on her daughter's bed rubbing her back she said, "I want you to know I love you. I love you no matter what. I know you and Kegan are having sex. We need to talk about this. I am ready to listen." The girl acknowledged she had some unmet needs and agreed to go to Christian counseling. Both mom and daughter worked together to deal with the situation without added guilt or shame.

Talk with your kids about where your family stands on sexual activity. Ask them what they see in their teen world. What goes on at school, outside of school? How do they feel about what other students are doing? Tread lightly. Too many questions feel invasive. When we stay in control of our emotions, we keep the conversation going.

When I have had conversations about the teen culture, I've learned (the hard way) to listen more than talk. I also know if I ask too much the conversation shuts down. I've realized that it is best to have this type of dialogue while I'm working in the kitchen. I guess it feels less intense, more casual if I'm cooking while we are talking. I've also learned it is better not to voice an opinion about another young person after my child has just confided in me. Rather than saying, "I can't believe she's involved in that!" I've learned a calm "Oh, I'm sorry to hear that. How do you feel about that?" keeps the conversation going.

Approach the topic of sex in a positive way, affirming physical intimacy as a gift from God to be used in marriage. High school and the early years of college are high-risk times. Many Christian kids have sex because they don't want to hurt feelings or be considered immature by saying no to sex. Sex has become normalized and generalized to "do whatever makes you happy whenever you want." Unfortunately, the happiness of the moment leads to long-term unhappiness or relational difficulties.

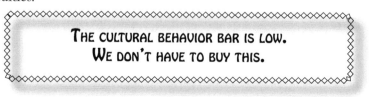

THE CULTURAL BEHAVIOR BAR IS LOW.
WE DON'T HAVE TO BUY THIS.

The Next Level

Let's take our role of giving wise counsel to the next level and coach our kids how to handle difficult and tempting situations. Arm both boys and girls with responses they can use and believe are true. If a date says, "You would if you loved me." Train your child to respond with, "If you loved me, you wouldn't ask."

Whatever the persuasion, the motivation is to convince the other person to have sex. The discussion focuses on the person interested in purity to change her or his mind. It's all about the persuader wanting his or her way. If the date isn't able to honor the "No," it's time to leave.

It's easier to refuse when hormones and emotions aren't raging. In a seminar I (Lori) attended, a powerful illustration was given. The speaker instructed a young male teen to run full force and then stop at the finish line. He ran, tried to put on the brakes, and went right past the finish line. He couldn't stop. His illustration showed how it is just before a sexual encounter. Slowing down before the line is important. Spell out situations for both daughters and sons. Help them see how a situation may make it difficult to say no. Doug Herman says, "The line you should never cross is the tan line."[50] Parents can help their teens and tweens by enforcing two rules: no one of the opposite sex in the bedrooms, and no one of the opposite sex in your home or another house when a parent isn't home.

Rules may not guarantee teens will follow them, but a stated rule sends a clear message. Aside from setting limits we can take action, *No Fear Actions*. Implementing these takes an element of courage.

With *No Fear Actions* don't be afraid to:

1. State your expectations. Tell your child's date the family curfew. Tell your son or daughter to honor the other family's curfew if it's earlier.

199

2. Walk in on your child and the date; do this often, bearing food. The gift of food makes the situation less awkward even if kids know what you're up to.

3. Tell them to keep their feet on the floor and sit up.

4. Say no to a get-together at another's home if there will be little to no supervision.

Red Flag

Aside from avoiding tempting situations be on the lookout for unhealthy relationships. When friends and family disapprove of the person the teen is dating, it is a big red flag. Discuss relationships that have abuse potential. Identify characteristics like control regarding time and relationships, possessiveness, jealousy, frequent and angry outbursts, intimidation, inconsistent behavior bouncing from charming and loving to demeaning and disrespectful.

"I wish I had listened to my daughter right from the start. I should have asked some questions after she told me she didn't like her brother's girlfriend. I just assumed she was a little jealous and brushed it off. As it turns out, she had good reason not to like this girl." Apparently the girlfriend was highly controlling and the young man was very passive. The mom said this relationship alienated the boy's friends and, "Basically ruined his senior year."

If a relationship has been hurtful and unhealthy, emotional and physical distance from that person is important, smart, and encouraged in Scripture. Proverbs 22:3 says, "A prudent man sees danger and takes refuge, but the simple keep going and suffer for it." Give your young person the words, "I feel controlled when you are upset that I am with my friends. I need more space."

Kids will experience some problematic relationships. When children understand healthy-unhealthy, they have the ability to make wise relational decisions. Ask, "How does this person bring out the best in you? How do you bring out her best?" This teaches relationship reflection and evaluation.

TEACH RELATIONSHIP REFLECTION AND EVALUATION.

SHERLOCK

If a parent suspects the child is involved in an abusive relationship or risky behavior, it's time to seek more information. Complete privacy is a myth for a minor. If there's reasonable cause, parents have the right to snoop. The tween or teen will be angry and say, "You had no right to go through my stuff." Don't let the search be the issue. Parents, legal guardians, and homeowners have both the right and responsibility to do so.

Don't betray your child's trust if you're just curious. Investigate when there are warning signs like a significant drop in grades, changes in behavior and mood, poor friend choices, skipping school, withdrawal from the family, excessive secrecy, defiance, inability to concentrate and make decisions, dramatic changes in appearance, too much or too little sleep.

A mom of a high school senior discovered on Twitter that her son was skipping school to smoke pot. She shared the information with her husband. They chose a time to talk with their son when the siblings were not around. They were able to remain calm because they had practiced what they were going to say and how they were going to say it. They also had a plan in place because they had time to do some research on marijuana and on rehab facilities. They were able to get some help because their son was under eighteen. If he had been eighteen, he would have needed to check himself into the facility.

God will reveal the problem. At the proper time, with knowledge and evidence, with the proper words and the right heart talk with your child. Plan out what you will say and how you will say it. Wait for a private moment, be kind and calm when speaking, let your child know how much you love him and that you are committed to walking with him through this. Discussing the situation honestly and determining the next steps provides some relief for the teen and parent.

"Be as shrewd as snakes and as innocent as doves" (Matthew 10:16b). Good kids can make poor choices.

STEP BACK

Ownership is important as is parental support. When a child owns his success and failures, he develops responsibility Where is the line between healthy interest and hovering?

My daughter and I (Lori) attended a college orientation. The speaker, a university advisor, shared how some parents are over-the-top involved with their students' academic experience and careers. Employers have told her how some parents of new hires or interns get involved in the job process, from asking questions about benefits to telling them how to interact with their son or daughter. According to the speaker, some parents act as their student's alarm clock while others do their student's homework. As a result some graduates leave college with high expectations of their employers.

Young adults are accustomed to being bailed out of difficult circumstances by their parents. They're often protected from adversarial situations rather than learning what it takes to fight through them. Due to the parents' shield, they are ill-equipped to handle the future realities and conflict. Being patient and allowing the child to persevere and wrestle with a social or academic situation takes guts but can cultivate self-worth and confidence. When it's time to figuratively step back, the best thing to do is to literally kneel down and pray.

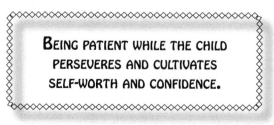

BEING PATIENT WHILE THE CHILD PERSEVERES AND CULTIVATES SELF-WORTH AND CONFIDENCE.

In His Grip

In our society, growing up means moving from dependence to independence. Young adults do need to be able to manage their finances, plan a meal, cook, pay the bills, do laundry, all without Mom and Dad. Nevertheless, there is more to life than shifting from parental reliance to self-reliance. As a culture we value independence so much we forget to train our kids how to be dependent on God.

Successful maturation is moving from dependence on parents to dependence on God. By loosening our grip and releasing them to the One who will never let go, we demonstrate our belief that our kids belong to the ultimate protector.

My (Lori) daughter had a potentially fatal snowboard accident. She ruptured her spleen and lost approximately one gallon of blood. An ambulance transported her from the mountains to a level-one trauma center in Denver for emergency surgery. Before she went into surgery, she went into shock and passed out. I spoke to her. God gave me just the right words, "God is with you."

Following surgery I asked her if she had heard me. "Yes, you said, 'God is with you.'" God supernaturally intervened in her unconscious state so she could hear and comprehend. During her time in the surgical ICU, Isaiah 41:10 was read over the PA system. "So do not fear, for I am with you; do not be dismayed, for I am your God. I will strengthen you and help you; I will uphold you with my righteous right hand." God is with my daughter. He is with me. He is with you and yours. He will never let go.

Being proactive in our efforts to protect our kids will eliminate some potential problems. Our children need guidelines and strategies to use in potentially tempting circumstances. They also need room for error. And we parents should avoid rescuing. We must step back as our children develop their skills and character, yet stay connected. Allow your kids the opportunity to grow from dependence on you to dependence on God.

Love Notes on Protection

Lori writes: The issues are so big in the teen years. There are days I want to throw in the towel, other days I want to come out swinging. No matter how I feel, my kids need me to pray for them, guide them, and step in or step back according to the specific situation. I continually pray for God to grant me wisdom.

Becky writes: My teenage boys know to have the details of their plans determined before making the pitch to me. I expect answers to my questions regarding their outings. If all the bases are covered, my sons are much more likely to get permission. Their goal is to hear, "Sounds great. Have fun!"

Questions

1. How well do you know your young person's friends and families?

2. What are your family guidelines regarding media content?

3. Where have you needed to step back and allow your child to step up?

Parenting Tips

1. Enforce basic driving rules.

2. Establish boundaries for dating.

3. Be engaged in your child's life.

Prayer

Father, my protector,
Thank You that You protect me. Thank You for watching over me. Thank You for watching over my family. Please keep my children safe in Your loving arms. Protect them

and move them out of harm's way. Speak to each child when he has stepped out of Your plan for his protection. Thank You for covering each member of my family in the shadow of Your presence.

Amen

...MAY YOUR LOVE AND FAITHFULNESS ALWAYS PROTECT ME.

Psalm 40:11b

CHAPTER 12

CHOOSE TO TRUST

LOVE ALWAYS TRUSTS.

1 Corinthians 13:7b

TRUST ME

"You don't trust me," a typical teen tactic to manipulate Mom and Dad. The same approach we most likely used as kids is now being used by our offspring. When you hear, "You don't trust me," Becky and I recommend responding with, "I'll trust you unless you give me a reason not to trust you. Tell me your plan." Trust is developed through respect and relationship. It's the secret ingredient in the parenting shift as a child matures. Trust loosens the parental protective grip. Privilege is gained and responsibility increases when trust grows. In 1 John 5:3 it says if you love God, you will obey Him. Obedience demonstrates love and respect. Sharing lives and honest communication are the bonding forces in relationships. The more agreeable, loving, transparent, and forthcoming the child, the more trust increases. Full disclosure leads to more freedom. Love trusts until lies enter the relationship. When trust is broken, it is difficult to reclaim. We love our children and desire to trust them. True love isn't blind; it has eyes wide open. Blind trust is unwise and reckless.

Let's delve into the topics of keeping promises, telling lies, experiencing anxiety, and having doubts. We'll present family trust accounts as a way of rebuilding trust and how to respond when children go through a faith crisis. Patterns of truthfulness, openness, fulfilled obligations, and integrity build trust in the family. We'll take an honest look at our children and ourselves. Trust is built gradually but can be destroyed in a moment. When we can trust our kids in the small things, we can trust them in bigger matters. "Whoever can be trusted with very little can also be trusted with much, and whoever is dishonest with very little will also be dishonest with much" (Luke 16:10). "Love always trusts" is the outcome of established trustworthy relationships. Ultimately, trusting in God builds faith.

FULL DISCLOSURE LEADS TO MORE FREEDOM.

EMPTY WORDS, HOLLOW PROMISES

To build a trustworthy relationship between parent and young person sincerity and accountability are two critical components. Tweens and teens can see right through empty words and hollow promises. It takes parental courage and honor to do and say the right thing.

Be a promise keeper and stay accountable for words and actions to other family members. Show children how to reach for the attribute of honesty by being honest yourself. In demonstrating honesty children will begin to value and emulate that virtue. Values and morals are best learned through observation. If honesty is valued in your home, be honest. When at the checkout lane and the cashier incorrectly rings up an item, correct the mistake.

Look at these two different situations and think about the message each conveys:

"The cashier forgot to ring up that bottle of shampoo! Guess it's my lucky day."

Or "The cashier forgot to ring up that bottle of shampoo. Even though it's not really convenient, I need to go back and pay for it."

At Bible study, one mom told me she had a situation like this occur. She said her teen daughter tried to give her a free pass, "Mom, don't worry about it. It's only ten bucks. The store won't even miss it."

The mom was tempted to just let it go but then decided she needed to live what she had been teaching her kids.

"I'm heading back to the store. My integrity is worth more than ten dollars."

What the daughter witnessed that day was priceless! Kids pay close attention to and evaluate how Mom and Dad handle situations. Accountability and honesty with others will increase the child's trust in his parents.

GET A CLUE

We can't fool ourselves into thinking that teen and tween lies won't be an issue simply because we demonstrate, discuss, and expect honesty. Modeling and discussing are important pieces of prevention but are not foolproof. Think back to your own years as a teen. Maybe you were always truthful. Many of us weren't. Good questions to ask teens include, Are the parents going to be home? Who will be attending the party? Who are you riding with tonight and how many will be in the car? What movie are you going to see and does the content meet our family guidelines?

Determining if all the facts have been disclosed is challenging. Favorite phrases can muddy the details. "Everybody is going," or "Everybody has it." The first question parents need to ask is, "Who is everybody?" Most often, not everybody is going or has the coveted item. Sorting out the truth and then the reasons why the teen wants to take part starts a dialog as to the pros and cons of the situation. Discussions are learning opportunities, yet they have the potential to place parents in the uncomfortable position of appearing to judge others.

Like you, we've heard, "Everybody is…," from our teens. Asking, "Who?" narrows the field. A mom of a sixteen-year-old relayed this account:

Her teen wanted to attend a high school athletic event. She expressed her desire to cheer the team on with her friends. Thankfully, the mom asked where the game was to be held. She had assumed it was a home game.

"It's an away game."

"Where?"

The game was to be played in a community at least forty-five minutes away. The forecast was for inclement weather, so the driving conditions wouldn't be good. The conversation continued this way.

"No, it's too far and the roads won't be safe."

"Everybody's going'"

"Who's going?"

The teen rattled off the names of children of parents that the mom was surprised gave their stamp of approval given the driving details. She decided to call one of the mothers. It was quickly apparent the other mom hadn't realized it was an away game either. With the new details presented she came to the same conclusion. New drivers, bad weather, far distance; the answer was an easy, "No."

This mom discovered the importance of talking through and asking questions rather than assuming details. She learned not to be afraid to follow up by contacting other parents.

Admittedly, there've been times Tom and I have been guilty of being Clueless or Checked Out parents. Life is busy. We don't always connect. We want to trust. Being tired, over-worked, inconvenienced, or distracted is a part of living in a family. It takes extra effort to stay in touch. Sometimes smart people can be the Clueless or the Checked Out parents.

Poor listening skills on the part of the parent can be the cause of confusion and misunderstanding. We had one situation play out in our home that turned ugly; one of us had forgotten our teen had communicated his plans for the evening. Distraction and preoccupation prevented us from being tuned in. The other parent wanted to know where the child was and the distracted parent was "checked out." Our assumption was our son neglected to fill us in rather than considering that he had told us but we were not paying attention to his words.

When our son returned home, he was between a rock and a hard place. If he insisted on his innocence, he looked argumentative and disrespectful; if he stayed silent, justice wasn't served and the truth remained unknown. Unfortunately, we misread his response, assumed his guilt, and punished him. Two years later he brought up the incident. We'd almost forgotten the experience, but he hadn't. We asked for forgiveness. A word of caution before punishing: make certain you have the facts straight.

Being naive and blindly trusting are also potential pitfalls. Both may become opportunities seized by the child. Thinking, "My young person would never_____ (fill in the blank)" could backfire. Parents typically believe they have a good kid. Unfortunately, no one has a perfect one.

Cheater!

How do we raise an honest kid? And what do we do if he ends up committing a dishonest act like cheating? Awareness and prevention are two key strategies when it comes to honesty training.

Be in tune with what's going on in the life of the child, note the friends he hangs with and the culture that surrounds him. Knowing which stressors are trigger points for dishonesty helps parents determine how to better coach each child. A busy schedule and a lack of necessary provisions are potential catalysts to cheating.

Children need some guidance to manage their homework and activity schedule. When every moment is filled with school, a heavy course load (AP classes), activities, family responsibilities, and friend time, the pressure on the teen mounts. The teen years are stressful. Here are some ways a parent can help alleviate some stress: help the child in choosing classes and activities, provide a workspace, have school supplies on hand, and listen to his concerns.

When a child is under pressure, the Consultant may ask, "How can I help you?" or the Coach may encourage by saying, "You are doing great juggling all your responsibilities. I'm noticing you could use some extra time. Skip doing the dishes and go ahead and get going on your work." If there is little time for the middle or high school child to do homework, the possibility of cheating increases.

Students may not define cheating the same way an adult would. Depending on the study, 50 to 90 percent of teens have cheated on an exam or plagiarized. One poll claimed that 75 to 98 percent of college kids cheat.[51]

Cell phones, the Internet, and the cut and paste option on the computer make cheating easier. No longer are kids writing answers on their hands. They are clandestinely texting answers, receiving answers, and checking photographed notes on their phones. Some kids don't consider this activity wrong.

Here are some things that parents can do to reduce the likelihood of cheating:

1. Define cheating.

2. Talk about character, values, and morals and how integrity is more important than any test score.

3. Ask, "What happens if someone is caught cheating? Do you know of times when a student has cheated?" (With our teens, keeping the conversation less personal makes them more willing to talk.) This provides the window into the child's world.

4. Encourage the teen to do his best rather than apply pressure to get the best grade. (The students most likely to cheat are the ones with the higher grade point averages.)

Most educational institutions attempt to prevent cheating from occurring. Some even ask for parental cooperation. Becky received a mass email from the principal of her son's middle school asking parents to please help teachers and administrators in reducing cheating on tests. Parents were asked to encourage teens to leave cell phones and other electronic devices at home.

One of the biggest deterrents to cheating is the risk of being caught. If the child's school has strict guidelines and severe consequences for cheating, there is less cheating in the school.

If the teen does cheat, it's too bad, but it isn't the end of the world. It's an opportunity for the parent to show unconditional love and to work with the child to rectify the situation. The teen's admission of guilt and willingness to accept the consequences are indicators of the child's heart. Remorse for the act rather than regret for being caught lets the parent know how much heart work and character training need to be done. Pray your child learns from his mistakes.

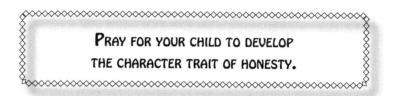

PRAY FOR YOUR CHILD TO DEVELOP THE CHARACTER TRAIT OF HONESTY.

PANTS ON FIRE

Less time increases the cheating phenomenon, but too much free time increases opportunities for kids to engage in inappropriate activities. Teens can be schemers, and schemers rely on lies for the cover-up. Unlimited unsupervised free time can lead to trouble.

Being a liar is hard work. A great memory is needed for all the various fabrications and to whom they've been told. Telling the truth is much easier, less confusing, and certainly more appreciated. Lies have a way of coming into the light.

"My son wanted to meet a friend at the movies. As I was driving him to meet his pal, he was especially quiet, looking down at his cell and texting the entire ride. My mom antenna was up. Something was amiss. I dropped him off in the parking lot and the friend was there waiting. They walked up to the theater door and I pretended to drive off. I waited and watched. The two boys, thinking I was gone, started walking away from the theater. They had no intention of seeing a movie. I pulled up next to them, had my boy to get back in the car. The other child needed to find his own way home. I figured he could work it out with his own parents."

What this mom experienced was her child telling a lie of commission. The movie was a made-up story. It falls into the category of an avoidance lie. Lies of avoidance are efforts to keep oneself out of trouble. These lies come in two forms: commission and omission. Commission is the bold-faced lie. Lies of omission conveniently leave out the truth. Lies of omission are more difficult to address because there's less information to deal with, which is of course by design. When a child purposely leaves out details to make an activity less objectionable to the parent, it's a lie of omission. An example of this could be a teen making plans to spend the night at a friend's but conveniently leaving out the fact that the host's parents will not be home. Later the parent discovers the other parents were out of town that night. This is a lie of omission.

This sort of lie is even illustrated in Scripture. Abram (Abraham) used this half-truth technique in Genesis chapter 12. Rather than trusting the LORD, he lied to Pharaoh about his relationship to his wife Sarai (Sarah). He claimed Sarai was his sister, which was a partial truth since they were related to one another. He did this out of fear of being murdered rather than speaking the truth in faith and trusting God with the outcome. A half-truth adds up to a lie.

JUST THE FACTS

We hurt others and ourselves when we lie or misrepresent the truth. God commands us, "You shall not give false testimony against your neighbor" (Deuteronomy 5:20). Our parental job is to get the facts, address the situation, discover the reason for the lie, and discuss how the lie has exacerbated the problem. It's very possible the youth will lash out and get angry after the lie is exposed. Keep the conversation calm and focused. The child's emotion is a last-ditch attempt to blame his lying on someone else. Don't get caught up in the whirlwind of emotion. Following the lie being discovered, restitution and punishment need to be put into place. Trust needs to be reestablished and rebuilt. The way in which to do that is with a "Family Trust Account."

FAMILY TRUST ACCOUNTS

Trust binds families together. It is a necessary attribute in family life. Hold your tween or teen accountable if he proves himself untrustworthy. Plan ahead what the consequences will be for inappropriate conduct. Scott and I have found that when we have a situation in which the boys have misbehaved, we need to talk and pray privately before discussing the ramifications of the behavior. Parenting is easier when the two of us are on the same page. For single-parent families, strategies can include taking time away from the situation to pray and talking to a trusted friend. Being in control helps parents respond wisely.

A helpful tool in teaching the concept of trust is a Family Trust Account. This account is characterized by fulfilled responsibilities and hoped-for privileges. Some kids mistakenly believe privileges are rights. Privileges and freedom for tweens and teens are earned. The more privileges and freedom given, the bigger the responsibility the child carries.

For teens (and tweens) to understand what privileges are, it may be helpful to list them on a piece of paper. A later curfew, going to the movies without parental supervision, staying home alone for a few hours, using the car to visit a friend are a few. Every time the child shows he can be responsible in those situations trust is deposited in the trust account.

This account can be literal or figurative. Some families have an actual jar that contains pieces of paper with specific deposit information: Came home on time. Drove car to and from friends without incident. Stayed home alone successfully.

A withdrawal is made when trust is broken: Missed curfew. Half hour late and no phone call. When a withdrawal happens, trust needs to be earned back before the privileges return. Each family will handle how long it takes to do that differently.

In my (Lori) home we actually wrote up specific ways to earn trust back. It was written like a contract. Once the contract terms were fulfilled, the revoked privileges were reinstated.

Building trust by being responsible and obedient are likened to making deposits in the account. More deposits equal greater freedom. Other ways children can to add to the account are having a close and respectful relationship with Mom and Dad, demonstrating love for family members, pitching in around the house, carrying through with responsibilities, fully disclosing plans, and opening up about relationships. The child's formula for building parental trust and thereby increasing his freedoms looks like this:

RESPECT + RELATIONSHIP = TRUST

Discomfort begins to stir in a parent when the child becomes secretive, withdrawn, highly private, and retreats from the family. When trust is depleted, a withdrawal is made from the account. Less freedom is allowed. For example, a missed curfew results in a withdrawal from the account. Trust has been abused and the teen's freedom is diminished. When this happens, retraining needs to be the first response. Discuss why the curfew is in effect. Talk about how trust is lost when curfew is broken. Review expectations of obedience and what lost trust looks like.

Try to make the punishment fit the crime. If the child is late, he owes you time. If the child has lied about where he's been, car privileges are decreased or revoked. You may even need to follow up with calling landlines to make certain your teen is where he said he'd be. A mom whose teen son had repeatedly broken trust has a list of home phone numbers and parent cell phone numbers for all of her teen's close friends. If he is not home on time, she begins to make the phone calls.

Losing freedom is the worst consequence. Provide concrete things the child can do to build trust, a way to measure success. If car privileges have been taken advantage of, have the child keep a mileage log for a period of time. If the child isn't where he said he'd be, a natural consequence could be having the child check in via a landline. If he's repeatedly late, he can come home a little earlier than the previous curfew without complaint or argument. Put a reasonable time limit on the training. If it's a first offense, start small. You can always go bigger.

When parents have been deceived, there's a tendency to go ballistic. Hurt feelings and anger at being tricked add fuel to the fire. In the heat of the moment if you've declared, "You're grounded for life," you've dropped an atom bomb when a firecracker will do. Retract your statement. Say, "I'm angry with you for deceiving me. Do you want to build trust back into our relationship?" Notice the responsibility is left to the child. He will say yes because he doesn't want to know what life will look like without it. Together come up with a plan of action. Use the ideas suggested above or come up with your own. Find a tangible way to measure those actions. All these consequences are for the child not the parent.

After the plan has been made the child needs to stick to it. No arguing, bargaining, or asking to change the course midstream. If this begins to occur, restate the plan with the expectations to be carried through. For example, if an earlier curfew is the action necessary to aid in building trust, the child cannot call during an evening out to beg and plead to stay out past the decided upon time.

Finally, set a conference date to discuss how things are going. This is the time for renegotiation or adjustment. While conferring, the parent and child may agree the trust account is now full so the plan can come to an end. If it appears more work needs to be done, continue with the plan. Once you've declared the trust account is back in balance, return privileges.

Another side of trust is reminding children that they have a responsibility to the family as a whole. Whether out and about in the community, at a game, church or school activity, kids need to remember they represent their family. My husband, Scott, and I tell our boys to remember who they are as a member of the Danielson family. We expect polite, respectful behavior.

More importantly, we remind them as followers of Jesus, their actions speak louder than their words with respect to their Christian witness. "Remember your name and to Whom you belong" is our family tagline. Remember your name! Remind your teens to remember who they are as well.

When the child shows love and consideration to family members and follows family guidelines, trust is established. Increased trust increases privileges; increased privileges increases freedom; increased freedom increases responsibilities.

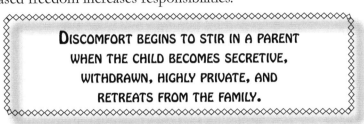

DISCOMFORT BEGINS TO STIR IN A PARENT
WHEN THE CHILD BECOMES SECRETIVE,
WITHDRAWN, HIGHLY PRIVATE, AND
RETREATS FROM THE FAMILY.

THE INCONVENIENT TRUTH

Most people consider themselves honest and would say they value honesty. Inconvenience and discomfort are honesty indicators. If we're serious about being honest and demonstrating integrity, it will cost something. Doing the right thing is rarely convenient.

A college student experienced a situation where his honesty was costly. He had accidently spilled water on his notebook computer. He brought it back to the store.

"If you don't know why your computer keyboard isn't functioning, I can replace or repair it. But if your keyboard doesn't work because you spilled on it, the warranty isn't valid," the clerk prompted.

The temptation to lie was looming. He would have to dig into his savings to buy a new computer.

"I did spill on it," he confessed.

"Have it your way," the baffled clerk responded as she handed back the laptop.

This young man valued his integrity more than the cost of a new computer. Honesty is more valuable than a good deal.

DOING THE RIGHT THING IS RARELY CONVENIENT.

Trust God

Trust is woven into the fabric of our lives. Think about it. We trust the bus driver with the lives of our children. We trust the mechanic who fixes the brakes on the car. We trust our spouse to be faithful. Do we trust God? Do we believe He can be trusted with our lives and the lives of our loved ones?

"One of the most difficult things I've done is turning my child over to God," the mother of a college kid said. "I told my daughter I gave her to God and how difficult it was for me. It made an impression on her. Once I stepped back, stopped trying to fix things, and trusted God, my daughter seemed to have a better sense of personal responsibility."

This was not an easy process for this mom. It did not happen overnight. Every day for almost two years she sat at her desk holding a photo of her daughter in her hands. Before checking her morning emails she would pray, "Lord, I release my precious daughter to You. Take care of her. Watch over her. Draw her to You and away from the things that are displeasing to You. Give me peace and strength while waiting for her to change. Give me the ability to trust You in this process."

She's watching her daughter begin to blossom when previously her spiritual growth was stagnant. Since the mother has moved out of the way the young woman is starting to understand her faith walk is personal, between her and the Lord. This action has also resulted in a more vibrant mother-daughter relationship.

God is trustworthy and so is His Word. He wants us to trust Him with all our hearts. "Trust in the LORD with all your heart and lean not on your own understanding; in all your ways acknowledge him, and he will make your paths straight" (Proverbs 3:5-6). The Bible is loaded with the blessings we will receive if we trust in Him and His plan. The blessings include unfailing love (Psalm 32:10), never being put to shame (1 Peter 2:6), help (Psalm 28:7), steadfast heart (Psalm 112:7), salvation and hope (Psalm 119:41-43) just to name a few!

We have been called to parent our kids in truth and grace, teaching them to trust the Father and be trustworthy themselves. *Love always trusts* doesn't mean blind trust between humans. Rather it is trusting in a faithful God in the midst of difficult circumstances. "Those who trust in the LORD are like Mount Zion, which cannot be shaken but endures forever" (Psalm 125:1).

> **GOD WANTS US TO TRUST HIM WITH ALL OUR HEARTS.**

LOVE NOTES ON TRUST

LORI WRITES: There are times when telling the truth is difficult for kids. Frankly, it can also be hard to hear. But reality can always be dealt with. When our kids are transparent, Tom and I are willing to loosen the parental controls. If we uncover a lie, those ties tighten. God has been so faithful to answer our parental prayer to reveal truth. We may not know everything (like my parents didn't know everything), but God shows us what we need to know. And we trust Him with the rest.

BECKY WRITES: My Bible study teacher, mentor, and friend Bev Conaris says, "Go to the throne not to the phone." This phrase encourages me to trust God over man when I need direction. The Lord is my first line of defense: more trustworthy, always available, and able to do far more than I could ever imagine.

QUESTIONS

1. When has your child told a lie of omission?

2. How have you rebuilt trust when your tween or teen has lied? How would a Family Trust Account be beneficial?

3. Where do you need to loosen the reigns and allow your child more freedom plus responsibility?

Parenting Tips

1. Pray your child gets caught when dishonest.
2. Remind your children to remember their name and to whom they belong.
3. When more trust is demonstrated, more freedom is given.

Prayer

Heavenly Father,

You are trustworthy at all times, faithful and loyal. Please forgive me when I distrust Your plans for me or the ones I love. Help me to be worthy of trust. Assist me in teaching my children lessons in trust. Make me discerning so I may gently guide my children into Your truth. I pray that when my children sin, they will be caught and ready to repent. I pray my family lives daily looking through lenses of Biblical truth until You come again in glory.

In the trustworthy name of Jesus Christ I pray.

Amen

Surely God is my salvation; I will trust and not be afraid. The LORD, the LORD himself, is my strength and my song; he has become my salvation.

Isaiah 12:2

Section Seven

Love Is a Commitment

Chapter 13

Choose to Hope

Love always hopes.

1 Corinthians 13:7c

Great Expectations

A mom of a senior in high school had just learned she was going to be a grandmother. She expected to be planning her daughter's graduation not her grandchild's birth. So where is the hope in this dilemma?

The mother and daughter made an adoption plan for the baby. Soon after the adoption plan was set, a customer came into the popular coffee shop where the newly pregnant teen was working. After the female customer placed her order she spoke to the cashier. She began describing her heartache over a failed adoption.

"I don't know why I'm sharing this with you. I'm sorry."

"I know why. God brought you here. I'm having a baby."

Hope and a latte were served that day. No matter how bleak or unexpected the situation, have hope because with God all things are possible.

Many parents of teens go through trying times, expressing surprise or disbelief in their circumstances. "I can't believe we are dealing with this." "I never did this stuff when I was a kid." "How

222

could this be happening? This is not what I've taught my kids," are statements Lori and I hear from parents in our classes. (We have spoken these sentiments as well.)

We all have great expectations as we move into parenthood, dreams and hopes for our kids' lives and futures—some realized others shattered. Along with our kids we deal with discouragement and disappointment. In life we all come face to face with death. In these times God calls us to put our hope in Him and not luck or superstition. Rather than sitting in despair, remember who God is and that He has His children's best interests at heart. Trust that disappointment may very well be a divine appointment.

In this chapter, we will discover that when suffering produces hope, a paradigm shift occurs, moving us from defeat to expectation. First God teaches us to trust Him so we can have true hope and be ready to respond in hope when circumstances appear to dictate otherwise. Hope isn't wishful thinking. Our greatest hope is the result of trusting in a sovereign God who loves us more than we can imagine. Hope does not disappoint. Hope isn't paralyzed while carrying the burden. Hope is an action that moves forward. Love hopes.

THE HAND OF HOPE

It's hard to be hopeful when you feel isolated. Hopelessness arrives in turbulent times. Suffering, worry, and anguish are our companions. Tossing and turning fill the nighttime hours. Preoccupation and obsession belong to the waking hours.

Our faithful Father has made us relational. We are to share each other's burdens rather than suffer in silence. When we suffer, we can reach out to others to gain support; conversely, when we see someone hurting, we can reach out to provide support.

The people who have come alongside me (Becky) in those tough times have been gifts from God. The first day of my dad's cancer treatment, a number of my "prayer warrior" friends came over to pray with me. When I spoke with my dad later that day to check on his progress, I told him about the prayers on his behalf. "That's how I made it through the day," he replied. When my dad succumbed to the cancer six years later, my tenderhearted girlfriends stepped in on the day of the funeral. They kept watch over our home and prepared and served a hot meal for the entire extended family. I was asked later that day, "Your friends did this for you?" Yes, my sweet sisters in Christ, who loved me through a very difficult time in my life, helped me persevere and gave me hope in the darkness. What a great witness for my boys to observe, seeing the community of believers lending a helping hand or shoulder on which to cry.

FAITHFUL FAMILIES

The support provided within the family makes the individual members interdependent. That interdependence is strengthened when God is invited to into the home. Commitment to God, spouse, and children draws the family together. Lori and I encourage parents to cherish their marriage. When the spousal relationship is nurtured, the family unit is stronger. Stability in the marital relationship encourages the children's feelings of security and safety. When these basic needs are met, a hope-filled atmosphere permeates the home.

Even with a hope-filled home, tweens and teens may worry about parents splitting up. When they observe disagreements, apathy, or uncaring behaviors between their parents, the level of concern rises. Kids are exposed to divorce at an early age. Most tweens and teens have at least a few friends with divorced parents. They worry, "Are my parents next?"

When a young person observes his parents spending time together, laughing with each other, and enjoying one another's company, he is less likely to be concerned when "discussions" occur. When Mom and Dad spend intentional time together, the marital bond is strengthened, modeling a healthy marital relationship.

Couple solidarity is shown in small things like holding hands, going for a walk, and running errands together. Words like *we* and *us* are subtle indicators parents are a united front. One couple assigns the kitchen clean-up tasks after dinner to their teens while they relax, have a cup of coffee, and talk. A scheduled date night or an occasional weekend away is a great booster for the marriage. Some couples enjoy going on a marriage retreat to rejuvenate the relationship.

Scott and I planned a ski trip and the boys really wanted to go with us, especially our younger son. He was expressing his dismay in being left behind to his older brother. His big brother responded with, "Don't you understand? Mom and Dad need to spend time together." He was right. Moms and dads need to make time for one another, to date and to have fun.

Parents who want to create a strong family will have these five observable components in their marriage: **G**od-focused, **L**aughter, **U**nified, **E**njoy time with each other, **D**isplay affection. The relationship will be G.L.U.E.D. Make a commitment to be a faith-filled family with God at the center. Get G.L.U.E.D.

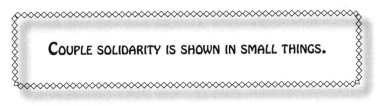

COUPLE SOLIDARITY IS SHOWN IN SMALL THINGS.

PRAYER AND PLANNING

Praying for family members and their concerns is one of the best ways to cement relationships and provide hope. When I've asked Lori for parenting advice, her wise counsel ends in prayer for my family. Prayer is hope in action. Anxiety and worry get in the way of trusting our good God.

Anxiety and worry are present in all families. The apprehension builds when waiting for the diagnosis, watching the stock market rise and fall, wondering if you'll get the job. The tension comes to a head when the answers are delayed or the outcome isn't the one desired. Kids have similar experiences: worrying if they made the team, got the part, or if they'll be invited to the party. In the waiting, hopefully and preemptively praise God, letting go of the anxiety. We can pray for strength to trust Him with whatever the result. The psalmist writes, "...do not fret—it leads only to evil" (Psalm 37:8b).

How often in our worry do we quiet our hearts and silently wait to hear the still small voice of our Father guiding and comforting us? If you're like me (Becky), you may be too busy talking at God to listen to Him. Psalm 4:4b states, "…when you are on your beds, search your hearts and be silent." Being still before God is a spiritual discipline, one with big dividends. Laying our concerns before God, knowing who He is, provides security. Being anxious shows a lack of trust, forgetting God is sovereign and good.

Michelle Terwilliger of Prayer Ventures is a prayer warrior. She teaches parents the power of prayer and provides excellent guidelines to follow when praying for children. Her ongoing request is for God's authority and the anointing of the Holy Spirit over all aspects of the lives of her children. She prays for her kids daily using the Six Ps.

1. Purpose to know God's purpose

2. Passion to know God's Word

3. Protection from illness, injury, crime, abuse, accidents

4. Peers, godly friends

5. Partner, future godly spouse

6. Purity in thought, mind, and body[52]

This is a terrific pattern for prayer. The alliteration makes it easy to recall. If you have never prayed like this, don't despair, simply start now. Even if your children are rounding the bend to young adulthood it isn't too late. Prayer is powerful and not bound by time.

Prayer diffuses worry resulting in a hopeful attitude. Our children can observe this tactic and apply the prayer practice to their own concerns. Praying before an exam, audition, or speech can help calm fear and worry. If the situation can be fixed, teach kids to ask God for the strength to fix it, then fix it. If the dilemma can't be fixed, give it to God and wait.

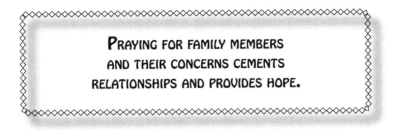

FAST FORWARD FUTURE PRAYERS

Growing up in a family prepares our children to eventually have a family. One of the greatest shifts a parent may need to make in regard to family dynamics is with a new son-in-law or daughter-in-law. We can be proactive in praying for a godly young woman or man to be raised to love the Lord, to be pure, and to have a Christian worldview. Pray that these future mates are learning daily the treasure of Jesus as Lord and the Bible as a lifelong guide.

Have you noticed that many young people choose to live together instead of or prior to marriage? Rhonda Nordin, author of *After the Baby: Making Sense of Marriage After Childbirth*, offers this valuable information: "Marital commitment provides the 'stick-to-it-tive-ness' needed to hold couples together. Lack of commitment is cited in 66% of divorces. It's no surprise, given the state of marriage and divorce, many couples fear commitment and choose instead to cohabitate (live together outside of marriage). The goal: To 'test drive' the relationship. If they get along, they'll marry. If not, they'll go their separate ways. Rates of cohabitation have increased 1400% in the last few decades alone. Couples who have lived together prior to marriage are twice as likely to divorce. Most cohabitating couples don't make it down the aisle at all. Only one in five couples that live together before marriage end up marrying. When cohabitating couples break up prior to marriage, it becomes a strong predictor of future failed relationships.

"The fundamental nature of cohabitation differs from that of marriage. A successful union is built on interdependence which typically doesn't occur when living together outside of marriage.

Interdependence becomes harder to foster later if the couple does marry. Cohabitation is also known to change an individual's view of marriage, making marriage less likely the longer the couple cohabitates.

"Negative qualities often develop in the relationship in spite of compatibility. This noncommittal arrangement creates an environment that sometimes hurts the union rather than allowing it to thrive. Studies show that cohabitation tends to be less satisfying than marriage. Women especially experience lower levels of happiness, less sexual exclusiveness, less sexual satisfaction, poorer relationships with parents and friends, and lots of uncertainty about the relationship. This leads to stress, depression, increased illnesses, and more frequent conflict; all distracting to the relationship and often lead couples to break up rather than make wedding plans."[53]

Share this research with your young adult before he's in a serious relationship. If he's already in a relationship and toying with the idea of playing house before becoming a spouse, he needs wise guidance and counsel from you, his parent.

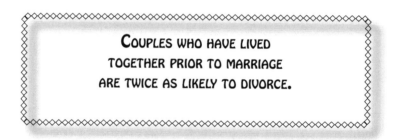

COUPLES WHO HAVE LIVED TOGETHER PRIOR TO MARRIAGE ARE TWICE AS LIKELY TO DIVORCE.

SHAKY GROUND

Hoping in anything other than God is like standing on shaky ground. Imagine the absurdity of clutching a four-leaf clover during a violent earthquake and wishing for good luck. Many choose to put their trust in rabbits' feet, crystals, and other charms, but Scripture says, "God's solid foundation stands firm" (2 Timothy 2:19a). Superstition is rampant. Friday the thirteenth, breaking a mirror, and stepping on a crack are not only silly but show a lack of trust in God. With God, there's no room for hocus-pocus.

How do you respond when you are blessed and someone comments on your good luck? Coincidence is God-incidence. "Every good and perfect gift is from above, coming down from the Father of the heavenly lights, who does not change like shifting shadows" (James 1:17). All things other than God are shifting shadows, without power and sure to disappoint. In reality, everything we put our hope in (family members included) other than God is an idol.

We often place our hope in people instead of God. Or we may include God, but He's not at the top of the list. We hope for our children to get into a good school, for our spouse to get a better job, or the doctor's treatment plan to eliminate the disease.

Tarot cards, horoscopes, and channeling spirits are all detestable to God (Deuteronomy 18:10-12). Slumber parties are popular ways for kids to spend time together. Arm your children with information about the occult and activities that appear harmless but are actually playing with fire. Kids need the tools to avoid getting involved in tantalizing predicaments such as levitation, Ouija boards, and séances. Role play, or "What if...," with kids to help them practice saying, "No thanks."

When one of my (Lori) daughters was twelve, she went to a slumber party where the girls were playing with a Ouija board. The previous week in Sunday school the leaders had talked about a similar situation and what to do if the kids found themselves in that predicament. My daughter, along with another girl, was able to speak up and say she was uncomfortable with that activity. All the girls decided they wanted everyone to feel okay and abandoned the game for another.

Joni Eareckson Tada contrasts Christianity to other religions and schools of thought. "No other religion, no other philosophy promises new bodies, hearts, and minds. Only in the Gospel of Christ do hurting people find such incredible hope."[54] Rather than crossing our fingers and closing our eyes, let's fold our hands and bow our heads.

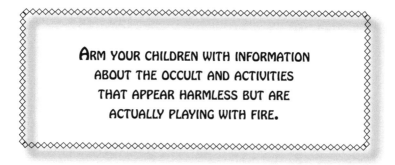

DOUBTING THOMAS

Superstitious actions happen when we are in a place of uncertainty or doubt. It's our nature to want proof, to witness with our own eyes. If Thomas, one of Jesus' disciples, could doubt, so can we and so can our children. Thomas accompanied Jesus for three years. Twice he passed out bread and fish multiplied by Jesus to feed thousands. Thomas witnessed Jesus raise Lazarus from the dead. He observed countless healing miracles and listened to Jesus' teachings. Yet when his comrades spoke of seeing Jesus after his crucifixion, Thomas didn't believe; he was in crisis. Thomas wanted proof, to see Jesus with his own eyes. A faith crisis isn't uncommon and may even be a necessary part of spiritual growth. Crisis is one of the three influences on individual faith development. Meeting Jesus in a critical time produces trust and increases faith.

THREE INFLUENCES ON INDIVIDUAL FAITH DEVELOPMENT AND THE RESULTS

1. **DEVELOPMENTAL EXPERIENCE:** family modeling and influence; child's experiences combined with his personality.
   RESULT: Faith caught.

2. **FORMAL LEARNING:** intentional, deliberate instruction at home, church, and mission field.
   RESULT: Faith taught.

3. **FAITH CRISIS:** individual's own experience, wrestles with faith. **RESULT:** Faith owned.

Trust God when the child is in stage three; this is where the rubber meets the road. Everyone will experience a crisis at one time or another. The degrees, length of time, and experience will vary. This time is really hard on a believing mom and dad. It helps to know that a difficult time in a child's life can be the catalyst that brings the tween or teen child closer to the Lord. As crazy as it sounds, parents can rejoice when the child is wrestling with God. This means he cares enough to consider and doubt what he'll ultimately call his own. These struggles are opportunities for growth, so pray and continue to gently lead and model. Once Thomas did see Jesus, his first response was to proclaim, "My Lord and my God!" (John 20:28).

Even when the young person struggles with faith, God is still there. God is faithful. Jesus didn't leave Thomas alone in his unbelief, Jesus met him face to face. He will do the same for our doubting Thomases, too!

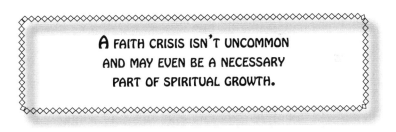

A FAITH CRISIS ISN'T UNCOMMON AND MAY EVEN BE A NECESSARY PART OF SPIRITUAL GROWTH.

FOLLOW ME

The disciples modeled faith and loyalty in Jesus Christ. They followed Him, knew Him, and trusted Him. When others deserted Jesus, He asked the twelve, "You do not want to leave too, do you?" Peter's response was beautiful. "Lord, to whom shall we go? You have the words of eternal life. We have come to believe and to know that you are the Holy One of God" (John 6:66-69). Christ's question is one each of us and our children will need to answer. Pray your children will be able to answer like Peter.

Jesus is the essence of hope for Christians. "We have this hope as an anchor for the soul, firm and secure" (Hebrews 6:19a). Hope in life eternal through the death and resurrection of Jesus Christ became real for me in the intensive care unit not long ago.

My (Becky) dad battled cancer for six years. The pastor came to pray with my family. As we circled his bed, we all joined hands, including my dad who had not responded to us since the previous day. His hand was warm and soft. As the pastor concluded his prayer, my dad's hand pulled away from mine and rose as if in worship. This was definitely out of the ordinary as he was not demonstrative in church. Yet he held his thin arms high, I believe worshipping his Savior who would soon lead him home. Later that afternoon, my dad began to talk to his mother, who had passed away many years ago. How gracious of God to send a beautiful message of hope and comfort to my family on the most difficult day we had ever faced.

My dad went to his heavenly home shortly after that, leaving his ailing body for a life in paradise with Jesus. Hope was tangible for me on that day. The words of Nehemiah filled me with peace beyond measure, "Do not grieve, for the joy of the LORD is your strength" (Nehemiah 8:10b). I miss my dad every day, but I know I will see him again. I know he's no longer suffering. I know my Redeemer lives and has prepared a place for those who believe and trust in Him (John 14:3).

Pure Hope

Trusting in God leads to hope in daily and eternal life. Knowing God's Word, trusting Him, and being obedient prepares our kids to do the same.

My son and I (Becky) were working together in the yard. He was furiously raking. His emotions were running high. We had just received the news that one of his good friends had died on a hiking trip in the mountains.

"Why, Mom? He was only fourteen! Why would God take him now?"

"I don't know. Your dad and I are broken-hearted too. I cannot imagine the pain his parents and siblings are feeling right now." I responded with a tight hug. My heart ached for my son as well. "I'm so sorry."

As we raked, he and I discussed how Jesus had prepared a place for his friend. In an attempt to speak truth and give comfort I told him, "God's plan is perfect, even when we question and doubt. Someday you'll be reunited with your friend. I promise."

A few hours later, as we were putting the yard tools away, he looked at me and said, "Mom, how many Christian guys get to meet their Savior on a mountain?"

Sweaty and dirty from working in the yard, my eyes met his and I said, "You're right, not everyone meets Jesus on a mountaintop." My aching heart was given a small respite in his hopeful tone. Hope is looking for the blessings in every situation, especially the difficult ones. Hope keeps us moving forward even in our pain.

My son still misses his friend, but he has hope and faith in the promises of God. He knows heaven is real and God's love is true. I don't know all the answers, but God does. Paul wrote of this hope for all believers in Jesus Christ in a letter to Timothy. "...we have put our hope in the living God, who is the Savior of all men, and especially of those who believe" (1 Timothy 4:10b).

FIRST 22 THEN 23

Ultimate trust and joyful hope is found in the 23rd psalm. "The LORD is my shepherd" (Psalm 23:1a) is a common passage read at funerals and memorial services. The chapter ends with, "I will dwell in the house of the LORD forever" (Psalm 23:6b). Some of the verbs used to describe God's intervention in these verses are "leads," "restores," "guides," "comforts," "prepares," and "anoints." Looking back, we can see what God has done for us in the midst of suffering. In the middle of the trials we may be blinded due to pain, but God is with us and very near during the hard times. He promises to never leave nor forsake us.

Tina Cotton, a Bible study teacher, said, "You can't have Psalm 23 without Psalm 22." Read Psalm 22. It's a psalm filled with anguish and suffering. David begins the prayer with, "Why are you so far from saving me?" (Psalm 22:1b). Asking why in the pain, he cries out in loneliness, fear, and distress. Emotions we share.

Hope is born as we walk through the valley of the shadow of death. Philip Yancey wrote, "Faith means believing in advance what only makes sense in reverse."[55]

Hope doesn't disappoint us. Even though we will have trouble in this world Christ encourages us to take heart! He has overcome the world (John 16:33).

Live with the knowledge that God will always be with us, even in the valleys, filling us with His peace. God is the true essence of love and hope. The outcome may not be what we desire, but God is always faithful. Love is hope-filled.

LOVE NOTES ON HOPE

LORI WRITES: Tom and I used to lead a small group of engaged couples as they prepared for marriage. Years later we ran into one of the women who attended our group. She and her husband had endured some tough times. She said, "The biggest take-away from the engagement sessions was, no one knows what the future holds. Commitment to the marriage and trusting in God are the two sure things that provide hope and keep a family together." Now this same truth is one we communicate to our kids as they enter their young adult years.

BECKY WRITES: I'm all over the Boy Scout motto, "Be prepared," as it relates to raising kids. If my boys know the Bible and the character of God, they will know if they are living in the truth or not. This brings me hope.

QUESTIONS

1. What can you do when anxiety peaks?

2. If not in God, in what or whom do you place your hope?

3. What tools have you given your child to address superstitious thoughts and activities?

PARENTING TIPS

1. Pray for your child's future mate.
2. Replace superstition with the solid ground of biblical truth.
3. Have hope and trust God when your teen is wrestling with his faith.

PRAYER

Father,
Hope in You and in Your plan is my anchor in the storm. Give me eyes to look past the hardships and to see You. Help me remember You and Your promises for me and for my family during difficult times. Give me the ability to demonstrate and communicate hopefulness to my loved ones. Your ways are not mine. I don't always understand, but I do know Your ways are best.
Amen

BE JOYFUL IN HOPE, PATIENT IN AFFLICTION, FAITHFUL IN PRAYER.

Romans 12:12

Chapter 14

Choose Tenacity

Love always perseveres.

1 Corinthians 13:7d

Synchronism

"He didn't make the team." With tears, a mom of a thirteen-year-old was telling me (Lori) how her youngest son, with a passion for baseball, was cut from the team during tryouts. *Ohhhh, I know.* Disappointing times are painful for kids and parents. Parenting is a visceral experience, isn't it? A mom's heart is one that is in synch with her child's heart, feeling every ache and each joyful leap. A dad's experience is usually a little less intimate. His vision is broader, an all-encompassing perspective. I have a theory that this is why kids look to mom for encouragement and dad for direction during the trials. Moms have the pulse and dads the perspective, yet both hurt when their children hurt.

Parents often say, "I just want my kids to be happy," but focusing on happiness leads to small thinking, poor decision-making, and weak praying. "God, please, let my child get the part in the play, make the team, be accepted into the university...." Those are goal-oriented and happy-motivated prayers. We all pray them. I prayed like crazy for my son to make the Columbine varsity hockey team. It was the desire of his heart. God gave him his heart's desire. The Lord

236

delights in giving His children good gifts. Yet my prayer for my son needed to go beyond just the accomplishment, "God, train my son to persevere when the practices get difficult." That takes the happiness prayer up a notch.

A thirteen-year-old girl tried out for a part in a middle school play. She really wanted that role. It seemed the mom wanted this as much as the child. She didn't get the part. Both the daughter and mom were upset. To make matters a little worse, the girl's best friend got the part. At this point the prayer may be, "Father, train my daughter to deal with disappointment. Let this experience be one where she learns how to be gracious in the midst of disappointment." Those are powerful, strong prayers focused on character development rather than only happiness due to an achieved goal.

The young man in the baseball story above moved on from baseball to tennis. New team, new sport, and having a ball. Maybe, just maybe, when rejection happens, God has another blessing waiting for the child just around the corner.

Life is made up of trials and triumphs. Along with you, Becky and I want our kids to persevere in difficult circumstances. Our Corinthians passage speaks of hope just prior to perseverance. Hope provides energy and forward focus for tenacious perseverance. John 16:33 states, "In this world you will have trouble." We want to know *why*, but we may never know the answer. What we do know is everyone experiences hardship and it won't be wasted. God uses trials to draw us closer and make us stronger.

No matter how long or short, suffering stinks. The approach we take will depend on the type of suffering experienced. God promises, "And we know that in all things God works for the good of those who love him, who have been called according to his purpose" (Romans 8:28). Since everyone suffers we need to consider how we will experience it, *with* or *without* God. Romans 8:28 is a conditional promise. All things will work to the good for *those who love God*; conversely, for the person who doesn't know or love God all things will not necessarily work toward that end.

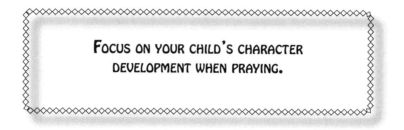

CORRECTIVE SUFFERING

Corrective or punitive suffering is the direct result of experiencing natural consequences due to sin or yielding to temptation. Hopefully we gain wisdom and redemption through this type of suffering.

A mother confided that her fifteen-year-old daughter was caught shoplifting. The store filed a complaint with the police. The young teen went to court, faced a trial, and was sentenced to community service. She suffered the natural consequences of stealing. Her parents didn't attempt to get her out of the shoplifting charge. Suffering natural consequences for poor choices could also look like a child receiving an F on a report card due to ditching class or not doing assignments. Another mom told me she knew her high school junior was working to keep up his grades not because he cared about academics but because he valued athletic participation. He exerted more academic effort when he realized his place on the school football team could be in jeopardy. Both of these parents handled their child's situation well. Each parent could have attempted to bail out the child yet resisted the urge and allowed the child to figure out how to handle the predicament.

If lessons aren't learned and the wrong actions continue, the still small voice is drowned out. When punitive suffering is the result of a deliberate bad choice, it's important for the child to experience the consequence rather than be rescued. Will it be uncomfortable? Yes. Will he remember? I'm pretty sure he will. Better to learn these lessons while living at home rather than out in the world. The world's consequences are even greater. Be thankful for opportunities for kids to experience corrective suffering.

Common Life

Some suffering is innocent and unmerited. Living in a fallen world is the cause. Natural disasters, some financial problems, many health issues, or another person's poor choices cause us to suffer. The question often asked is, "Why me, Lord?" Rather ask other questions such as, Who can I touch during this time? What can I learn? Where is God's glory in this? When have I seen God during this trial? and How can I respond to this struggle in a way that honors God? Becky and I have personally found it helpful to ask God questions beginning with who, what, when, where, and how, saving why for later. Pondering these questions during innocent suffering is where peace is found. God may or may not choose to reveal the *why*.

Redemptive suffering can be the result of either punitive or innocent suffering. The sufferer may be refined or the suffering may benefit another. Peter is a picture of redemptive suffering. He suffered when Jesus was arrested (not Peter's fault), and he suffered when he denied Jesus (Peter's fault). With his denial, Peter experienced great sorrow, yet because of Peter's suffering his pride and self-reliance were dealt with, his character developed, his faith increased, and he learned to rely on the Lord rather than himself. Peter was the one Jesus called to be the leader in building His church. Redemptive suffering is for God's glory and our good.

Suffering is closely related to sanctification and character growth. It is the process of refinement and a necessary prerequisite to demonstrating God's glory. William Penn said, "No pain, no palm; no thorns, no throne; no gall, no glory; no cross, no crown."[56]

Cosmic Causes

Not all suffering is meted out as a consequence for wrongdoing. Sometimes it's cosmic. In the book of Job, Satan attacked Job, a blameless and upright man. The plan of our adversary, the devil, is to destroy mind, body, and spirit. His goal is to keep us from fulfilling God's purpose for our lives. He wants to ruin our family, character, and job. The father of lies wants to replace our peace with fear, happiness with depression, contentment with discontent, generosity with stinginess, patience with impatience, kindness with harshness, humility with pride, gentleness with cruelty, goodness with evil, and love with indifference. Peter tells believers, "Be self-controlled and alert. Your enemy the devil prowls around like a roaring lion looking for someone to devour. Resist him, standing firm in the faith, because you know that your brothers throughout the world are undergoing the same kind of sufferings" (1 Peter 5:8-9). The enemy attacks all believers; he considers God's children a threat. We are a threat because "the one who is in you is greater than the one who is in the world" (1 John 4:4b).

Charles Stanley defines a satanic attack this way: "A satanic attack is a deliberate, willful, intentional, and well-designed act intended to bring harm to a person in any way—physical, mental, economic, relational or spiritual."[57] Stanley goes on to list the enemy's four objectives.

1. Satan seeks to draw us away from God. That's his ultimate goal.

2. Satan seeks to thwart us in God's purpose and plan for our lives. He seeks to get us off track and out of the will of God for our lives.

3. Satan seeks to deny God the glory, honor, and praise due Him as we live godly lives of faith and trust in Him.

4. Satan seeks to destroy us—literally and eternally.[58]

But Satan is on a leash. Suffering is limited to a period of time. The adversary cannot snatch us out of God's grip; he cannot separate us from God's love or protection. He cannot keep us from receiving God's blessing. He can destroy the quality of our lives, stir up trouble, and use others to undermine our reputation and cause misunderstandings. His plan is to make us less effective witnesses for Jesus.

240

God and Satan are not equal. God is omnipotent, while Satan is not. God is omniscient, Satan is not. God is omnipresent, Satan isn't. God is infinite, Satan not. Who is Satan? He is a defeated foe (Revelation 20:10). So when we or our kids are under attack, we can call on the power of Jesus and respond to the trouble in a way that honors God.

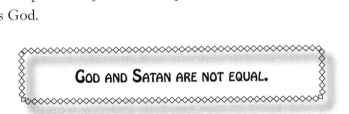

GOD AND SATAN ARE NOT EQUAL.

GROWING PAINS

To be honest, wouldn't you pick comfort over suffering for character development? Character development stretches us and is painful work. Just as God disciplines to develop those He loves (Hebrews 12:4-13), we must discipline our children. As parents it is a God-given responsibility to correct and train our kids. If family relationships are honest, loving, and loyal, its members will not only receive and give praise but also experience correction and confrontation within the context of those relationships.

Helen Keller stated, "Character cannot be developed in ease and quiet. Only through experience of trial and suffering can the soul be strengthened, vision cleared, ambition inspired, and success achieved."[59]

Character growth, encouraging our kids to become the persons God created them to be, is part of the parental job description.

A mother of a nineteen-year-old girl shared the story of her daughter's rebellious years. Prior to being a young adult, this girl was a compliant kid who loved the Lord. Mom and daughter had been very close. When this child went off to college, she got involved with a young man, started drinking, skipping classes, and ended up living with her boyfriend. The mother was heart-broken—so devastated by her daughter's behavior that she became physically ill. She didn't have the strength or desire to even get out of bed. Her daughter severed the relationship with her mom and dad.

"She refuses to see us. Not only are we not welcome, we are not even certain where she lives."

The girl didn't want to hear what her parents had to say regarding her lifestyle. She chose to put up a big barrier between herself and her parents. The heart-broken mother began to withdraw from other relationships until God intervened and gave her hope to go on.

The Lord used the husband and younger daughter to reengage the woman. She decided she needed to stop looking at her present circumstance and instead look ahead with hope. She was able to function once her focus was off the child and back on God. She still carried the pain, but she was able to move forward. Two years passed. The daughter and boyfriend broke up and the young woman had no money and no job. God used this difficult time to draw the family back together. The entire family reconciled. The daughter moved back home. The parents welcomed her with open arms. From a heavenly perspective this young adult learned a lot about unhealthy relationships, poor behavior, and faith. The parents learned to look to the Creator rather than focus on the storm. Troubled times, although terrible to endure, become opportunities for building character and developing trust.

TROUBLED TIMES BECOME OPPORTUNITIES
FOR BUILDING CHARACTER.

STEP BY STEP

There are typical phases kids go through when experiencing grief, loss, or separation. Of course individuals will vary according to time spent in each phase and may repeat certain stages: denial, anger, bargaining, depression, acceptance, or detachment. Other manifestations for grief may include a lack of self-concern, difficulty making decisions, memory loss, and confusion.

By allowing our child to take the lead in his grieving, we encourage him not to push past or deny the grief. Grief may take longer than expected. It will zap energy and show itself in all facets of life. If anger is the vehicle, remember the outburst is about the pain not the person to whom it is directed. Children may lament future, current, and symbolic events. Certain dates, events, and anniversaries can trigger tears. When my (Lori) son's good friend died, he grieved about how much fun they would have had together on an inline hockey team.

It is possible unresolved conflicts may resurface. This reappearance often happens when death is the result of suicide. A college woman struggled with unresolved issues with a friend after he took his own life. Having open communication with her mom helped her through this tough time. Others who are grieving need to verbalize their feelings while some may only want to verbalize a few thoughts. Different personalities respond differently. Ask permission to pray with or for him. When the time is right, with great sensitivity, discuss what plan of action to take in the midst of the difficulty.

There are a few warning signs that a child's grief has turned to despair or detachment. Watch for substance abuse, changes in relationships, abuse of money or credit, and compromised values. If any of these occur, an intervention and professional assistance are highly encouraged.

When my (Lori) daughter was in the surgical trauma ICU, one of her best friends was overwhelmed with concern. She couldn't concentrate. She was grieving. Her mother allowed her to miss school so she could come to the hospital. This mom listened to her child's heart and could see the bigger issue. Her daughter needed to know her friend was going to be okay. Her mom was wisely flexible in the situation. (Oh, and by the way, my daughter did recover. Praise God.)

LET THE CHILD TAKE THE LEAD IN HIS GRIEVING.

Support System

We are to grieve with those who grieve. Scott and I had pastoral support when death entered our sons' world. Our pastor took the time to sit down with our boys and help them process the loss by listening to their recollections of good times and discussing the disease that took their grandpa home.

Ministers, family friends, and counselors can provide additional ears to listen and shoulders on which to cry. God moves the body of Christ to compassion during these difficult times. It's a gift when others want to give our children support and encouragement.

Identity Crisis

Another area in which tenacity and tenderness are helpful is in assisting our children define their place in the family. God places babies in specific homes. He chooses forever families for orphans. Our Heavenly Father created the family unit and continues to be in the business of putting moms, dads, and kids together. My (Lori) family has been knit together through adoption and biological means. What a blessing!

When adoption is part of a family, there are questions the adoptee may ask, questions such as these: What's my medical history? Do I have any biological siblings? What happened to make my birth mom choose an adoption plan? Why would she give me up? Do I look like my biological parents? Are they still alive? There are typical times that these thoughts arise. The questions seem to be accompanied by a variety of emotions and intensities. Critical times revolve around events and life stages, such as making a family tree in school, pre-puberty, puberty, late teens, filling out health history forms, young adulthood, and becoming a parent.

Over the years my eldest daughter has asked various questions regarding her birth family. Tom and I have done our best to answer her. There have been some hard times for me as a mom because I cherish my role and don't want to share the "mom" spot. This is something I need to get over. It is more important for me to assist my child in coming to terms with her feelings regarding her adoption rather than throw my issue into the mix. She has confessed that she has a hole in her heart regarding her biological parents. No matter how much I love my child I can't fill the void adoption created, no human being can. Only our Heavenly Father is able to fill that space. What I can do is provide an atmosphere of security and openness when questions arise. Parents determine when, what, and how much is appropriate to share. Always be honest. Avoid saying, "I know your biological mother must have loved you so much to give you up so you could have a better life." This implies the more the child is loved the more he is at risk of being abandoned. Instead say, "Your biological mom must have been in some sort of difficult circumstance to make this choice. And we are so blessed you are ours."

Continue to love and support the adopted child without feeling anxious or threatened when curiosity is piqued. Adoption is a choice for everyone except the adoptee. Adoption could cause angst, innocent suffering. "Why wasn't I wanted?" combined with "No one asked me." For the adopted child the most basic of human needs are in question, "Where do I belong?" and "Am I loveable?" As the child matures, continue to communicate unconditional love and family unity. It's possible challenging behaviors will surface. Adopted kids want to know we love them no matter what and may push the limits to test our love and commitment, pulling out all the stops when not getting their way. They may go for the jugular with comments like, "I wish you hadn't adopted me," or "I'm not really part of this family," or the final blow, "You're not my real parents." When these things are uttered, know the child is hurting and lashing out. The upside is he feels safe and secure enough to spew those hurtful comments. It's helpful to the adoptee when we reaffirm the relationship with comments like, "I know you're angry. I love you, and you still may not go out past your curfew." The adopted child needs love and security, and we can provide that by being the authority figure who loves unconditionally.

Look to God's Word. God used Joseph as Jesus' adoptive father. God calls us His adopted children, heirs to the Kingdom, co-heirs with Christ. Adopted kids and families have a special place in God's

245

heart. "Religion that God our Father accepts as pure and faultless is this: to look after orphans and widows in their distress and to keep oneself from being polluted by the world" (James 1:27). Adoption is a beautiful thing. "In love he predestined us to be adopted as his sons through Jesus Christ" (Ephesians 1:4b-5a).

ADOPTED KIDS WANT TO KNOW
YOU LOVE THEM NO MATTER WHAT.

SHOW OFF!

Paul boasts in his sufferings. He had been through a lot. In 2 Corinthians 11:16-33, Paul lists the things he's endured. Here are a few: frequently imprisoned, severely flogged, exposed to death many times, whipped and beaten, stoned, shipwrecked three times, in danger in many circumstances with many people, cold and naked. Yet he'd boast only of his weakness. Why? Because he knew in his own weakness, God would be strong.

Here is my (Lori) list from an eighteen-month span. It doesn't compare to Paul's, but I'm not competing with him. Here are the main events: January—my dad died; February—I was in a ski accident and injured my knee, a couple days later my middle daughter separated bones in her foot while going over the hurdles in track; March— knee surgery for me and foot surgery for my daughter; June—our family's big dog was bitten by a rattlesnake; August—my daughter and I each had to have a second surgery; November—same daughter in a snow board accident got a   concussion; December—our little dog died, my son and his roommate were in a rollover car accident; January— youngest daughter involved in a near fatal snowboard incident, then, only hours after our youngest came home from a week in the ICU, the middle daughter cut her hand and needed to go to urgent care for stitches; March—son had irregular heartbeats.

Three of our four kids took ambulance rides to the hospital

within six weeks of one another. Yet each incident is a boast because God's glory has shone through.

My dad in his weakened state reached heavenward just before his soul left his body. My daughter and I recovered together, giving us extra time together before she went off to college. The big dog survived the snakebite due to our son's quick thinking. Our daughter recovered from her concussion. Our son and his roommate were unscathed from the rollover accident. Our little dog lived a year longer than we expected. Our middle daughter, prone to fainting, didn't when she cut her hand and was able to laugh at the unbelievable chain of events. Our son's heart issues weren't life-threatening.

God let us know He was with us when our youngest daughter had her life-threatening snowboard accident. At the scene of the accident He gave her friends the presence of mind to get help. He was with her in the Colorado medical clinic when she was treated by a Dr. Smiley, originally from our hometown in Minnesota and fellow high school alum. God was in the details when He sent two ambulances, both arriving at the same time. One truck had the more skilled paramedics, other better equipment. The paramedics jumped on board the better-equipped ambulance. She received the best care with the best equipment.

The driver told me, "I'll get her down the hill, but it's gonna be messy. I just came back from Denver. The traffic is really bad headed down the mountain."

God gave me peace. "I know you will. I'm praying."

He cleared the road as if He was parting the Red Sea. Dumbfounded, the driver exclaimed, "No traffic! I can't believe it."

My husband following ten minutes behind was in bumper-to-bumper traffic.

God answered my husband's plea, "Let me know you have her," with a bumper sticker on the car in front of him, "Shalom."

God gave me supernatural peace when a nurse said, "We'll do the best we can. These things don't always turn out as we hope."

God gave us comfort and support though our pastor and friends who came to pray. (One friend was in the middle of having her hair highlighted when she got the message. She whipped out the foils saying to the stylist, "I have to go!") God brought the saints to pray.

God was present while we prayed at my child's bedside.

God gave us encouragement when the male nurse assigned to our daughter said, "I want you to know I'm a believer, too. Here's how to pray next." The Lord handpicked her medical personnel.

God showed off when He gave me the gift of a very dear friend, from out of state, who "just happened" to be in Denver to provide additional comfort at the hospital.

Point out God's presence. Teach your kids to hear and see God in Scripture, in a friend's love, and in an inexplicable sense of peace. When we suffer, the Lord is near.

TEACH YOUR KIDS TO HEAR AND SEE GOD.

POUND IT

When meat is tenderized, it's pounded. That's the way it is with people, too. We're most tender after experiencing suffering. "… Now for a little while you may have had to suffer grief in all kinds of trials. These have come so that your faith—of greater worth than gold, which perishes even though refined by fire—may be proved genuine and may result in praise, glory and honor when Jesus is revealed" (1 Peter 1:6b-7). Nothing is more valuable than the development of our faith.

Suffering yields compassion. Adversity produces faith. Persevere with purpose. Empathy, spiritual endurance, and trust are direct results of spiritual tenderizing. In the trials wait with expectancy and tenacity knowing God has a firm grip on you!

LOVE NOTES ON TENACITY

LORI WRITES: For the readers who are in a season of suffering, my heart aches for you. Please remember God is near and your suffering will last for a season—not forever. May the peace of Christ comfort you.

BECKY WRITES: There is usually a calamity of some sort on the days I teach God's Word. Sick children, missing schoolwork, or terrible weather are a few examples. When I step out for God, I expect an enemy attack. Rather than cringe and quit, with a determined smile, I pray and press on. Why? Because if I'm facing opposition, I know I'm on the right track.

QUESTIONS

1. What type of struggles or suffering have you experienced: innocent, punitive? What have you learned?

2. What struggles is your child going through? How can you support him?

3. Where have you seen God's loving compassion during your suffering or your child's?

PARENTING TIPS

1. Provide a stable environment and a flexible schedule when your child is grieving.

2. Pray with your child regarding small and big struggles.

3. Allow God's work to be done in your child's corrective suffering.

Father,

You know suffering more intimately than I. Thank You that You understand my anger and my grief. Thank You that You are the God of all compassion. I pray that the compassion I've received from You I show to those who may be suffering. Help me to keep my eyes focused on You. Bless me, in your perfect timing, with the knowledge of Your purpose in the struggle. Help me to be more like Jesus when in the midst of his greatest suffering, he showed love and concern for others.

Amen

WE ARE HARD PRESSED ON EVERY SIDE, BUT NOT CRUSHED; PERPLEXED, BUT NOT IN DESPAIR; PERSECUTED, BUT NOT ABANDONED; STRUCK DOWN, BUT NOT DESTROYED.

2 Corinthians 4:8-9

SECTION EIGHT

LOVE IS ULTIMATE STRENGTH

CHOOSE TO FLOURISH

CONCLUSION

CHOOSE TO FLOURISH

LOVE NEVER FAILS.

1 Corinthians 13:8

BLOOMING LOVE

Picture a flourishing garden, bursting forth with life, variety, and color. I'm not much of a gardener so I'm describing Becky's garden. She spends hours getting her soil ready for spring. She delights in tending and weeding the land during the growing season. It takes lots of love, time, and hard work to create a beautiful garden. A garden is like raising a child. Parents sometimes need to get a little dirty, scraped up, and sweaty to reap good fruit in their children.

"I love you," the most tender and yet strongest words ever spoken. Throughout 1 Corinthians 13 Paul carefully lays out what excellent love looks like. This is the type of love that provides the specific soil in which a child can blossom.

Insert your name in the **Love** passage: _____*is patient. I am kind. I don't envy or boast. I am not proud. I am not rude, self-seeking, or easily angered. I don't keep a record of wrongs or delight in evil. I rejoice with the truth. I always protect, trust, hope, and persevere.* Convicting, huh? There is a name that fits perfectly–Jesus. The more we become like Christ the more we'll be able to love like Him. With God's help, we can love abundantly and unconditionally just like Jesus. In *The 1 Corinthians 13 Parent: Raising*

Big Kids with Supernatural Love, we've discovered how to fix our eyes on Jesus rather than the circumstances at hand. Putting Paul's description of love into practice, with God's help, transforms our families.

Loving like this and expecting nothing in return can *only* be done with divine intervention. It is a matter of will over emotion, a deliberate, intentional, cognitive choice. Together we've walked through fifteen ways to respond with love in our families. We've seen kindness and patience as a decision. Contentment and humility are internal loving attitudes while respect and unselfishness are outward-focused. Self-control is seen in peace-filled and forgiving interactions. Love has a heavenly perspective when goodness and truth are sought. Love is an action as we protect our children and trust God with the details. Love as a commitment is lived out in hope and perseverance. Loving like this is sacrificial, and the result is ultimate strength.

Without love there is no connection or relationship, no life. Truth spoken to our children without love is brutality. Yet love without truth is hypocrisy. We need both love and truth while raising our children. Love has everything to do with life.

TAILORED FIT

In the previous chapters we've looked at tailoring our parenting style according to our children's development. The approach used when our kids were toddlers won't fit the teen years. Parenting is fluid, moving back and forth from Controller to Coach and Chum to Consultant. When looking at the Parenting Style Chart (see the introduction), review the approach you most often use. If you tend to be more rules- and structure-oriented, like the Controller, include grace and mercy in your approach. If you're more relational in your parenting, like the Chum, watch for opportunities to apply truth and justice through natural consequences. Balance your Controller and Chum responses. Parenting is creative and flowing not a static formula. As we all know, each day provides new challenges. Helping children navigate through life by cultivating an environment of unconditional love combined with limits will move a child from being irresponsible to accountable.

We have different goals at different times while our children continue to grow and change. Having the awareness of the best parental response given the child's personality, age, and circumstance then applying it is wisdom. When the focus is justice, we use punishment. When the goal is training, we discipline (teach). Always start with training. Think about what you want the child to do or learn before you decide what happens next. Use punishment as a last resort.

A mother of a young teen boy described a typical scene, "The agreement was to complete the homework assignment and get the musical instrument practice done before joining the guys to play basketball. Then the call came from the friends.

'Let's go.' His buddies were ready to head out to the court.

'Okay!' My son was ready to drop everything and join them. His homework wasn't completed. I held my ground and refused to allow him to leave before everything was finished. As you can imagine, this refusal didn't go over well. He expressed his displeasure. It would have been a lot easier to cave in and allow the homework to be completed later. Internally, I wrestled with this for a moment then concluded the loving decision was to enforce the agreement and teach my teen the valuable lesson of being a man of his word."

This is a perfect picture of looking at a long-term goal and knowing what is valued in a family. In this family integrity was worth the fight. As situations arise determine what's worth fighting for in your home. The battles come at a cost. In the case above the cost was twofold: a struggle between parent and child and the boy missing the start of the game. The collateral damage was short-term. The lesson the young man learned was one of honoring his word. Each family will have moments when the situation calls for grace or truth, mercy or justice. Pray that God grants wisdom in determining which way to go.

Another outcome for the story above could be the parent choosing to allow the child to leave the homework for later. This wouldn't have been a wrong choice, just a different one. The scenario could look like this:

The agreement was to complete the homework assignment and get the musical instrument practice done before joining the guys to play basketball. Then the call came from the friends.

"Let's go." His buddies were ready to head out to the court.

"Okay!" My son was ready to drop everything and join them. His homework wasn't completed. "Mom, can I go?"

"You've consistently shown responsibility regarding your homework. If I agree to let you leave now, tell me your plan for getting your work done and your instrument practice completed."

Same scene, different emphasis. The first example stresses the importance of following through with a commitment, while the other gives a reward for being responsible by allowing for some flexibility. You are perfectly suited to parent your child. You know your child. Determine your course by knowing what character trait needs reinforcing.

Positive reinforcement and honest encouragement is biblical. As parents we are called to encourage and not embitter or exasperate our children (Colossians 3:21 and Ephesians 6:4). Every child is going to make mistakes. Parents make mistakes, too. I (Becky) sat on my son's bed one night after a really difficult day. His ideas of teenage freedom and decision-making were very different than mine. I asked him to be patient with me because parenting a teenager was new to me. I was learning the ropes while he was attempting to assert his independence. It takes time for children to mature and for parents to adjust, effectively shifting parenting styles according to the child's emerging developmental stages. Hefty doses of patience, resolve, and intentionality are necessary in the growing and changing family.

PURSUERS OF LOVE

Pursuing love is a hopeful thing, something parents do daily. We hope for the best as we look toward the future. We have high hopes for our families and the things God will do in the midst of our children's struggles, sufferings, and victories. Raising kids to walk away from society's misdirected and temporal love and turn to God and His love is a daily commitment. Encouragement is found in Philippians 4:13, "I can do everything through him who gives me strength." Leading by example in regard to living godly love is very effective.

When we regularly live out love, we'll reinforce the belief that love is not just a feeling, it's an action. "This is how we know what love is: Jesus Christ laid down his life for us. …let us not love with words or tongue but with actions and in truth" (1 John 3:16a, 18). True Love laid down His life for you and for me. Love never fails.

A Legacy of Love

Children are a gift from God. They are a reward from the Most High, a heritage (Psalm 127:3-5). Our legacy and most valuable gift we leave with our children is faith. Nothing else even begins to compare. "Bring them up in the training and instruction of the Lord" (Ephesians 6:4b). In God's perfect timing, when He captures our children's hearts, loyalty and allegiance to Him will follow.

By bringing Jesus into our daily life, we can teach our young people right from wrong and explain the reasons behind moral conduct. With sincere love, let's find opportunities to discuss the "why" or reasons for faith. If we haven't yet begun, we can start now.

Let's lovingly articulate the hope found in Christ Jesus. "Be strong and take heart, all you who hope in the LORD" (Psalm 31:24). We can pray God gives our kids a hunger to know Him.

Remember the ABCs:

A-Ask Jesus to forgive your sins.

B-Believe in your heart God raised Jesus from the dead.

C-Confess with your mouth that Jesus is Lord.

"If you confess with your mouth, 'Jesus is Lord,' and believe in your heart that God raised him from the dead, you will be saved. For it is with your heart that you believe and are justified, and it is with your mouth that you profess your faith and are saved" (Romans 10:9-10). Jesus Christ is the legacy of love God graciously gives.

God tells us in Exodus 20:6 that those who show Him love and keep His commands will be blessed to a thousand generations.

God grabs one heart and whole generations are affected. Love never divides; love multiplies. Christ-filled families are blessed in present and in future times.

Our (Becky) family has had the gift of generational faith. My teenage son hugged me as we stood in my grandmother's nursing home room. At 101 years old she was called home. It really doesn't matter how old the ones you love are, it still hurts to say goodbye for now. His words made me smile: "You need to remember, Mom, Grandma Kit Kat is having a much better day than we are." Yes, eternal life, what's better than that? Continue the family legacy or be the first generation to step out in faith. Generations that follow will be impacted by what we do in our homes today. Real love thrives and flourishes!

CONCLUDING PRAYER

Heavenly Father,
Your son was the ultimate gift of love. You love me unconditionally. Thank You. Refocus me so I am able to love my spouse and children sacrificially and unconditionally. Help me to love with patience and kindness, remembering to be content, respectful, and unselfish. Give me peace in my circumstances and a forgiving spirit. Give my children the desire to seek goodness and truth. I ask for Your loving hand of protection on my kids and spouse. I pray I'm able to trust in Your sovereignty when circumstances are dire. The longing of my heart is to leave a legacy of faith for my children. Give me hope and strength. While developing my children's character I pray You grow mine, too. Give my children the will to pursue You with all their heart, mind, and soul. Please draw them to Yourself. When they look for love, I pray they find You, the source of true love.
In Jesus' name,
Amen

...FAITH, HOPE AND LOVE. BUT THE
GREATEST OF THESE IS LOVE.

1 Corinthians 13:13b-c

LOVE IS...

PATIENT, TOLERATING REPEATED ERRORS

KIND, SPEAKING WITH GENTLENESS AND ACTING WITH SELF-CONTROL

CONTENT, SUSTAINING SATISFACTION

HUMBLE, HONORING OTHERS

RESPECTFUL, APPRECIATING OTHERS

UNSELFISH, PUTTING OTHERS FIRST

PEACE, REMAINING CALM IN THE STORM

FORGIVENESS, DEMONSTRATING HUMILITY

GOOD, SEEKING GOD'S BEST

TRUTH, BELIEVING GOD'S WORD

PROTECTION, PROVIDING SECURITY

TRUST, ACTING WITH INTEGRITY

HOPEFUL, EXPECTING THE BEST

TENACIOUS, SHOWING STEADFAST DETERMINATION

MATURITY, CULTIVATING A FLOURISHING CHARACTER

LOVE IS...GOD.

P.S. From Lori and Becky,

We are hopeful our prayer has been answered, that God will use His Word and our experiences to encourage and equip you as you raise your tweens and teens. It has been our privilege to be on the parenting journey with you. If we can be of further assistance you can contact us by visiting our websites. You can find us at www.1Corinthians13Parenting.com or connect with us individually. You can find Lori at www.loriwildenberg.com or Becky at www.beckydanielson.com. May the Lord bless you as you parent your children His way.

With faith, hope, and love,

L & B

His Way

Now I understand, beyond any doubt
That wherever we go, whatever we do
Always we are about our Father's business
Amen

******

-Rockman[60]

Follow the way of love...

1 Corinthians 14:1a

ENDNOTES

INTRODUCTION

1. For reasons of uniformity and simplicity, we have chosen the universally accepted masculine pronoun to represent the child. The feminine pronoun is used only when a topic is mainly geared toward the female.

CHAPTER ONE

2. Mary Heathman, "The Purpose of Attraction" (lecture, Where Grace Abounds. Denver, Colorado, June 24, 2010). Mary Heathman is the founder of Where Grace Abounds Ministry aiding people with sexual and relational conflicts. She speaks of her reaction to life in a fallen world.

CHAPTER TWO

3. Merrill F. Unger, R. K. Harrison, Howard Frederic Vos, Cyril J. Barber and Merrill Frederick Unger, *The New Unger's Bible Dictionary* (Chicago: Moody Press, 1988), 738. Kindness is defined.

4. Mother Teresa, *Promises and Prayers for Women* (Grand Rapids: Family Christian Stores, 2007), 93. Mother Teresa's wise words conclude the chapter.

CHAPTER THREE

5. Pastor Larry Renoe, "The Seven Deadly Sins: Envy" (sermon, WaterStone Community Church, Littleton, Colorado, September 9, 2001). Pastor Larry Renoe is the teaching pastor at WaterStone Community Church. His thoughts on envy resulting in competition or spite are helpful in the context of parenting.

6. Taken from The Quotable Lewis by C. S. Lewis. Copyright © 1990 by Wayne Martindale and Jerry Root. Used by permission of Tyndale House Publishers, Inc. All rights reserved.

7. Joyce Meyer, *100 Ways to Simplify Your Life* (New York: Faith Words, 2007), 3. Joyce Meyer comments on being content with what one has been given.

CHAPTER FOUR

8. Victoria Clayton, "Is Cosmetic Surgery a Good Gift for Grads?" Children's Health on MSNBC, last modified May 11, 2007, accessed May 13, 2010, http://www.msnbc.msn.com/id/17932515/ns/ health-childrens_health/t/way-go-grad-heres-check-new-nose/#. Tt_YkmBuH-Z. The questionable trend in cosmetic surgery is outlined by Victoria Clayton.

9. Kelli Muehlbauer and Laurie Muehlbauer, email message to author, January 12, 2011. The experience highlights the benefits of missions work for the child and the family.

CHAPTER FIVE

10. Reprinted by permission. *Checklist for Life for Teens*, Lila Empson, ed., Copyright ©2002 GRQ Ink, Inc., Thomas Nelson Publishers, Inc., Nashville, Tennessee. All rights reserved.

11. Kevin Leman, *Have a New Kid by Friday: How to Change Your Child's Attitude, Behavior & Character in 5 Days* (Grand Rapid: Revell, 2008), 178-179. The "bread and water" treatment is defined as a means by which teens are taught to be respectful.

12. *ibid.* Kevin Leman provides a specific response for parents to use when discussing respectful behavior with a teen.

13. Jacqueline Stenson, "When Teens Grind, Schools Freak," Children's Health on MSNBC, last modified February 16, 2010, accessed May 13, 2010, http://www.msnbc.msn.com/id/353394/ns/health-childrens_health/t/when-teens-grind-schools-freak/#.Tt_TTmBuH-Y. Practical suggestions are provided for parents in how to address the current high school dancing trend.

14. Reprinted by permission. *Checklist for Life for Teens*, Lila Empson, ed., Copyright ©2002 GRQ Ink, Inc, Thomas Nelson Publishers, Inc., Nashville, Tennessee. All rights reserved.

CHAPTER SIX

15. Jeff Johnson (director of Mile High Ministries), email message to author, July 10, 2010. In his years of experience working with the homeless, Jeff Johnson provides valuable insight on how to recognize the humanity of the less fortunate.

16. Kirk Weaver (executive director of Family Time Training), email message to author, June 6, 2010. Money management tools are provided by Kirk Weaver to assist in training children to be wise in financial matters.

CHAPTER SEVEN

17. Frederick Buechner, Daily Christian Quote, April 10, 2005, accessed May 27, 2010, http://dailychristianquote.com/dcqbuechner.html. Frederick Buechner's quote sets the stage for this chapter, highlighting the negative and self-destructive aspects of anger.

18. Dr. Scott Wenig (professor of applied theology, Denver Seminary), email message to author, July 30, 2010. Thoughtful questions are provided in dealing with anger linked to social injustice.

CHAPTER EIGHT

19. Corrie ten Boom, *Promises and Prayers for Women* (Grand Rapids: Family Christian Stores, 2007), 57. The declaration of forgiveness being an act of will is valuable insight.

20. Taken from *The Purpose Driven Life* by Richard Warren. Copyright ©2002 by Richard Warren. Used by permission of Zondervan. www.zondervan.com

21. *ibid.*

22. *ibid.*

23. Robin Chaddock's "Soul Snacks," accessed June 2, 2010, http://www.robinchaddock.com. Robin Chaddock shares her thoughts on forgiveness on her blog, Soul Snacks. (Site discontinued.)

24. Taken from *Boundaries: When to Say Yes, When to Say No to Take Control of Your Life* by Henry Cloud and John Sims Townsend, Copyright © 1992 by Henry Cloud and John Sims Townsend. Used by permission of Zondervan. www.zondervan.com

25. Mary Heathman, "The Purpose of Attraction" (lecture, Where Grace Abounds, Denver, Colorado, June 24, 2010). Confession is a necessary means by which the sinner requests forgiveness from God. Mary Heathman shares her practice in praying Psalm 51:1-4.

CHAPTER NINE

26. Cecil Murphey, *Invading the Privacy of God: Rush into God's Presence, Revitalize Your Prayer Life, Put an End to Devotional Boredom* (Ann Arbor: Vine, 1997), 135. The distinction between want and need is defined by Cecil Murphy.

27. Lori Wildenberg, *But Lord I Was Happy Shallow: Lessons Learned in the Deep Places* compiled by Marita Littauer (Grand Rapids: Kregel Publications, 2004), 198-99. Temptation for the forbidden arises from two sources, one's weaknesses and outside sources.

28. TreeHouse, "Dear TreeHouse: Tips for Parents in Crisis," *The Connection*, April/May 2010, 6. TreeHouse offers tips for families in crisis situations.

29. Taken from *Come Clean: It's a Pure Revolution, It's about Sex, It's about Your Future, It's about What You Deserve* by Doug Herman. Copyright © 2004 by Doug Herman. Used by permission of Tyndale House Publishers, Inc. All rights reserved.

30. Jeannie Jasper Edwards, email message to author, January 15, 2010. Research regarding dating trends is helpful in determining how to best arm the teen for social interactions.

31. Reprinted by permission. *Checklist for Life for Teens*, Lila Empson, ed., Copyright ©2002 GRQ Ink, Inc., Thomas Nelson Publishers, Inc., Nashville, Tennessee. All rights reserved.

32. Rosalind Wiseman, *Queen Bees & Wannabes: Helping Your Daughter Survive Cliques, Gossip, Boyfriends, and Other Realities of Adolescence* (New York: Crown, 2002), 138. Practical advice for dealing with issues in relation to bullying are described by Rosalind Wiseman, author and speaker.

CHAPTER TEN

33. Josh McDowell and David H. Bellis, *The Last Christian Generation* (Holiday: Green Key Books, 2006), 13-15. The authors reference the startling statistics regarding how many teens are leaving the church.

34. Taken from *Sticky Faith: Everyday Ideas to Build Lasting Faith in Your Kids* by Dr. Kara E. Powell and Dr. Chap Clark (author). Copyright ©2011 by Dr. Kara E. Powell and Dr. Chap Clark. Used by permission of Zondervan. www.zondervan.com

35. Leslie L. Fields, "The Myth of the Perfect Parent," *Christianity Today*, January 8, 2010, http://www.christianitytoday.com/ct/2010/January/12.22html. Difficult children are more readily drawn to the values of their parents.

36. John McArthur, "Error Intolerant," *Pulpit Magazine*, June 1, 2010, http://www.sfpulpit.com/2008/05/19/error-intolerant/ JohnMcArthur points to the truth found in the Bible as the measuring rod for all truth claims. Christians are to be intolerant of opposition to Scripture.

37. Oswald Chambers, *Breakfast for the Soul*, compiled Judith Couchman (Tulsa: Honor Books, 1998), 33. "Men do not reject the Bible because it contradicts itself but because it contradicts them."

38. "Mayflower Compact," The Pilgrim Society, last modified May 18, 2005, accessed June 2, 2010. http://www.pilgrimhall.org/compact.htm. The advancement of Christianity was the driving force for the Pilgrim settlement in the New World. This fact is often left out of history lessons.

39. Charles Hadden Spurgeon, *Breakfast for the Soul*, compiled by Judith Couchman (Tulsa: Honor Books: 1998), 38-39. Error is most readily identified when compared to the truth found in God's Word.

40. Lori Wildenberg and Becky Danielson, *Empowered Parents: Putting Faith First* (Gainesville: Synergy Publishers, 2003), 135. Eternal moments are defined for the reader.

41. Kirk Weaver (executive director of Family Time Training), email message to author, June 6, 2010. Kirk Weaver encourages parents to start lessons of faith with their children at any age, even as teenagers.

42. *ibid.* The authors recommend Kirk Weaver's Family Time Training.

43. *ibid.* When parents obey God's command to teach their children faith and values, a standard for life exists for the child.

CHAPTER ELEVEN

44. Mark Oestreicher, "Drawing the Line: How to Establish New Boundaries for Your Young Teen," *Christian Parenting Today,* Summer 2003, 25. Drawing clear boundaries for teens and providing opportunities for decision-making assists children in becoming independent.

45. The Children's Hospital of Philadelphia Research Institute, last modified April 2, 2013, accessed June 20, 2014, http://www. teendriversource.org/stats/support_teens#stat1.

46. Insurance Institute for Highway Safety. 2013. [Unpublished analysis of 2008 data from the U.S. Department of Transportation's National Household Travel Survey, General Estimates System, and Fatality Analysis Reporting System]. Arlington, Virginia, accessed June 20, 2014. http://www.iihs.org/iihs/topics/t/teenagers/fatalityfacts/teenagers.

47. The Reverend Chuck Stecker (president and founder of A Chosen Generation), email message to author, March 31, 2011. Parents are urged to be wary of movie ratings.

48. Natalie Larson, email message to author, April 12, 2010. As a teacher, Natalie Larson recommends open communication with teachers.

49. Joseph A. Califano, Jr., "The Importance of Family Dinners IV," The National Center on Addiction and Substance Abuse at Columbia University, September 2007, accessed May 16, 2010, http://www. casacolumbia.org/templates/Publications_Reports.aspx#r8.The tremendous benefits of family dinners are provided for the reader.

50. Taken from *Come Clean: It's a Pure Revolution, It's about Sex, It's about Your Future, It's about What You Deserve* by Doug Herman. Copyright © 2004 by Doug Herman. Used by permission of Tyndale House Publishers, Inc. All rights reserved.

CHAPTER TWELVE

51. June 29, 2011, accessed June 22, 2014, http://education-portal.com/ articles/75_to_98_Percent_of_College_Students_Have_Cheated.html.

CHAPTER THIRTEEN

52. Michelle Terwilliger, "The Power of a Mother's Prayer" (lecture, Christ Presbyterian Church, Edina, Minnesota, April 4, 2010). Michelle Terwilliger of Prayer Ventures lays out her "Six Ps" prayer model and emphasizes the power of prayer.

53. Rhonda Nordin, email message to author, June 15, 2010. Rhonda Nordin is the author of *After the Baby: Making Sense of Marriage After Childbirth* as well as an educator and speaker. She addresses the detriments of cohabitation.

54. Joni Eareckson Tada, *Promises and Prayers for Women* (Grand Rapids: Family Christian Stores, 2007), 85. Only the gospel of Jesus Christ can offer hope for the hurting.

55. Taken from *Disappointment with God: Three Questions No One Asks Aloud* by Philip Yancey. Copyright © 1988 by Philip Yancey. Used by permission of Zondervan. www.zondervan.com

CHAPTER FOURTEEN

56. William Penn, "William Penn Quotes," Proverbia, 2009, accessed June 17, 2010, http://en.proverbia.net/citasautor.asp?autor=15634. "No pain, no palm; no thorns, no throne; no gall, no glory; no cross, no crown."

57. Used by permission. *When the Enemy Strikes: The Keys to Winning Your Spiritual Battles*, Charles F. Stanley, 2004, Thomas Nelson. Nashville, Tennessee. All rights reserved.

58. Used by permission. *When the Enemy Strikes: The Keys to Winning Your Spiritual Battles*, Charles F. Stanley, 2004, Thomas Nelson, Nashville, Tennessee. All rights reserved.

59. Helen Keller, *Promises and Prayers for Women* (Grand Rapids: Family Christian Stores, 2007), 33. Character development happens through the trials in life.

CONCLUSION

60. Dr. Robert Appel, *His Way*, Edina, Minnesota. Rockman is Lori's dad. His poetry is a loving tribute to Jesus, his Lord and Savior.

INDEX

ABOUT THE AUTHORS

LORI WILDENBERG

Lori Wildenberg intimately knows the chaos and complexity of life with tweens and teens. At one point, she had four teens ranging from thirteen to nineteen! Lori is passionate about coming alongside parents to encourage, empower, strengthen, and support them. She communicates effectively with transparency, warmth, and gentle humor. Her straight-forward, realistic approach engages her audience and assists moms and dads in their quest to parent well. Lori has more than twenty-five years' experience working with parents and kids in both secular and faith-based settings. She is a licensed parent and family educator who meets parents where they are and helps them get to where they want to go. Lori openly shares her personal and professional experience using a "been there done that approach." Her parenting philosophy is focused on developing a child's heart and character; this sets her apart from many other parenting voices out there. Lori and her ministry partner, Becky Danielson, are founders of 1 Corinthians 13 Parenting. Together they have authored three faith-based parenting books, including the first 1 Corinthians 13 Parent book, Raising Little Kids with Big Love. Lori is also a mentor mom with The M.O.M. Initiative and writes curriculum for and trains teachers at the Professional Learning Board.

The Wildenbergs live in the foothills of the Rocky Mountains. A perfect day in Lori's world is hiking with her husband, Tom, four kids, and labradoodle.

Lori is available for speaking, parent consulting, and teacher in-service training.

Contact her at www.loriwildenberg.com or
www.1Corinthians13Parenting.com.

269

BECKY DANIELSON, M.ED.

Becky Danielson's favorite title is Mom. She and her husband, Scott, have two active and fun-loving teenage boys. She is a licensed Parent and Family educator and co-founder of 1 Corinthians 13 Parenting with her ministry partner, Lori Wildenberg. Above all she is a follower of Jesus Christ.

Becky has spent a lot of time in school as a learner, teacher, and volunteer. After attending Gustavus Adlophus College for her Bachelor's degree (K-6 Education, Early Childhood Education), she received her Master's degree from St. Mary's University, and a license in Parent and Family Education from Crown College. Before becoming a stay-at-home-mom, she taught kindergarten and first grade. The birth of her two boys changed her life and career completely. Sharing God's Word to equip and encourage families has become Becky's passion. The parents she works with, either in a large group setting or one-on-one mentoring, find her warm, honest, and supportive. Her ideas and parenting tips are practical, encouraging, and applicable. Becky candidly shares her life as a Christian wife, mom, and educator. Along with co-authoring the 1 Corinthians 13 Parent books, Becky contributes to Hooray for Family, a print and online magazine, The Pearl Girls, and Faith Village.

When she's not writing or meeting with moms and dads, Becky can be found in her kitchen garden, reading, or on an adventure with her Danielson men!

Connect with Becky at www.beckydanielson.com or www.1Corinthians13Parenting.com.

READERS RESPONSES TO
RAISING BIG KIDS WITH SUPERNATURAL LOVE

The truth in *Raising Big Kids with Supernatural Love* and the godly intent of the authors truly did empower some strong choices that my husband and I have had in coaching our diverse brood. Having read the book just before guiding my daughter through a major life decision made me way less controlling (which is also exhausting) and tons more trusting and expectant of her learning and growing and seeing God guide her in the process. Aside from a number of practical applications that we implemented right away, there is an overall change of spirit (or heart) in my approach to parenting given the book's content and tone. It is supernatural and transcends the specifics of the content. God is like that and Lori and Becky's commitment to build this up from the Word and from absolute truth just shines through. What also shines through is a positive regard for kids, families, and their audience. Hard to describe. "Anointed without being pious" occurs to me as accurate.

Jeannie mother of 2 teens and 1 young adult Morrison, CO

So many of us parents of teens go through the same challenges in raising our children, it is helpful to see that others have the same struggles and to see how other parents have handled them. Many great ideas, which I actually had the chance to put into practice while I was reading the book. I loved how you used the theme from Scripture, 1 Corinthians 13 and applied it to Christian parenting.

Karen mother of four teens, Miami, FL

Raising Big Kids with Supernatural Love is fantastic. Full of wonderful suggestions and thoughts. Loved the way the authors incorporated biblical wisdom in addressing cultural trends.

Carol B. Olsen, mother of three, grandmother of 8, Minneapolis, MN, author of *America's Forgotten Heritage*

Made in the USA
San Bernardino, CA
13 January 2015